JUDAISM'S LIFE-CHANGING IDEAS
A WEEKLY READING OF THE JEWISH BIBLE

OUPRESS   MAGGID

Other works by the author

Rabbi Jonathan Sacks

JUDAISM'S LIFE-CHANGING IDEAS

A Weekly Reading of the Jewish Bible

The Phillips Family Edition

Maggid Books & OU Press

Judaism's Life-Changing Ideas
A Weekly Reading of the Jewish Bible
First Edition, 2020

Maggid Books
An imprint of Koren Publishers Jerusalem Ltd.

POB 8531, New Milford, CT 06776-8531, USA
& POB 4044, Jerusalem 9104001, Israel
www.maggidbooks.com

Cover Photo © Courtesy of Kreina Haviv /
Ahavart.com, Judaica Concept Store

The publication of this book was made possible
through the generous support of *The Jewish Book Trust UK.*

ISBN 978-1-59264-552-7, *hardcover*

Printed and bound in the United States

*The Phillips family are delighted
to support the work of Rabbi Sacks.*

London, September 2020, תשרי תשפ״א

Contents

Foreword

The Secret of Our Staying Power

Bari Weiss*

I sit here typing these words down the street from a school for young Israelites in Pittsburgh. Or, as we now call them, Jews.

There are no schools for Amalekites or Moabites on planet Earth. The Roman Empire that destroyed the Temple in Jerusalem is long gone. And yet here, speaking in the language of King David, there are Jews.

"Why does no one find it remarkable that in most world cities today there are Jews but not one single Hittite, even though the Hittites had a great flourishing civilization while the Jews nearby were a weak and obscure people? When one meets a Jew in New York or New Orleans or Paris or Melbourne, it is remarkable that no one considers the event

---

* Bari Weiss is an op-ed editor and writer at the *New York Times*. She was previously senior editor at *Tablet* magazine and book review editor at the *Wall Street Journal*. Ms. Weiss's first book, *How to Fight Anti-Semitism*, won a 2019 National Jewish Book Award.

remarkable," noted the late Southern American Catholic writer Walker Percy. "What are they doing here?"

By every rule of history we should have disappeared long ago, a civilization only capable of being recalled, like those others, on Wikipedia. But we are here, in all those places Percy named and more. It seems to me that our very existence is an earthly miracle more astonishing than the parting of the Red Sea.

What are we doing here? Not just here, against all odds, but here still asking the eternal questions that gave us the name Yisrael in the first place?

I don't know the answer. I am no scholar, unlike the brilliant author of this volume. I am just a simple Jew.

But it doesn't take a genius to see that the secret is not our superhuman physical strength. Nor is it our ability to organize, or to wield political power. No, I believe the secret of our staying power is the subject of this volume: our ideas.

As Rabbi Jonathan Sacks shows in these soul-nourishing essays, those ideas – one God, freedom, Shabbat, the dignity of difference, the preciousness of human life – have not just sustained our desert-born tribe. They have also transformed the world.

These days, there is understandable cynicism about that very notion. But if I didn't believe that ideas have the power to change the world I would be in the wrong business, as a writer and editor of opinion columns. Indeed, one of the ideas that changed the way I live my own life was uttered by Rabbi Sacks, and its insight hit me right in the heart of a newsroom.

That idea? Non-Jews respect Jews who respect Judaism.

I bore witness to the wisdom of that lesson when I was a young editor at the *Wall Street Journal* editorial page. It was a heady place to work and I was eager to fit in.

So when the good people from Chabad showed up bearing *sufganiyot* at Hanukkah time, I was less than thrilled.

Why did my fellow Jews need to show up in their beards and black hats with boxes of high-caloric food with weird names in front of all of my staid, salad-eating colleagues? Chabad does amazing work. But did they really have to do it here, at my fancy newspaper job?

The shame hit me when I saw the reaction of my non-Jewish colleagues. Everyone loved them. The treats, sure, but more so the warmth and curiosity of the Chabadniks who would become my friends.

It's not just that non-Jews respect Jews who respect Judaism. That experience, and countless others that followed, taught me the unspoken part of Rabbi Sacks's teaching: Jews who respect Judaism respect themselves.

It was a reminder to me at the precise moment I needed it that my Jewishness is never, ever an obstacle to connection to people who are different from me. Just the opposite. The truth of that is perhaps the most powerful demonstration of the greatest of all Jewish ideas: That everyone is created in the image of God.

Since that day, I have made it a point in my own life to try to live by their example – and the example set by Rabbi Jonathan Sacks, who knows that ideas are not ancient ruins or mere ornaments, but lamps that light the way. And that it is the people who live by them that give them their glow.

Introduction

The Transformative
Power of Ideas

W hat is Judaism? A religion? A faith? A way of life? A set of beliefs? A collection of commands? A culture? A civilisation? It is all these, but it is emphatically something more.

It is a way of thinking, a constellation of ideas: a way of understanding the world and our place within it. Judaism contains life-changing ideas.

Too few people think about faith in these terms. We know the Torah contains 613 commands. We know that Judaism has beliefs. Maimonides formulated them as the thirteen principles of Jewish faith. But these are not all that Judaism is, nor are they what is most distinctive about it.

Judaism was and remains a dazzlingly original way of thinking about life. Take one of my favourite examples: the American Declaration of Independence (1776) and its most important sentence: "We hold these truths to be self-evident, that all men are created equal, that they are endowed by their Creator with certain unalienable Rights, that among these are Life, Liberty and the pursuit of Happiness." This is arguably the most important sentence in the history of modern politics. It was what Abraham Lincoln was referring to in the opening of the Gettysburg Address when he said: "Four score and seven years ago our fathers brought forth on this continent, a new nation, conceived in Liberty, and dedicated to the proposition that all men are created equal."

The irony of this sentence, as I have often noted, is that "these truths" are very far indeed from being "self-evident." They would have sounded absurd to Plato and Aristotle, both of whom believed that not all men are created equal and therefore they do not have equal rights. They were only self-evident to someone brought up in a culture that had deeply internalised the Hebrew Bible and the revolutionary idea set out in its first chapter, that we are each, regardless of colour, culture, class, or creed, in the image and likeness of God. This was one of Judaism's world-changing ideas.

We also see from this example that you can have an idea, formulate it in words, and declare it to the world, but you may still struggle to internalise it and you may have to fight to make it real. Thomas Jefferson, who drafted the Declaration of Independence, was a slave owner. Evidently he did not include black people or slaves in his phrase "all men." Eighty-seven years later, when Lincoln delivered the Gettysburg Address, America was fighting a civil war over just this issue.

However long it takes, though, ideas change the world. Some do so by leading to inventions. Think of some of the great ideas of recent times: the computer, the internet, search engines, social networking software, and smartphones. They all had to be thought before they could be made. As we say (talking about Shabbat and Creation): *Sof maaseh, bemahshava tehila*, which roughly means, first there needs to be the thought; only then can the idea be turned into reality by the deed. Shabbat itself, incidentally, is another one of Judaism's world-changing ideas.

But sometimes ideas change the world because they change us. It's these ideas I want to explore through the weekly *parasha*.

IDEAS THAT CHANGED MY LIFE

My own life has been changed by ideas, not always exclusively Jewish ones but ideas nonetheless. Here are three examples.

More than twenty years ago I started an organisation, Jewish Continuity, whose aim was to transform the Jewish community by intensifying education at all levels and ages. It was successful, but it proved to be intensely controversial. The lay leader of the organisation, Dr Michael Sinclair, was an extraordinary man who poured his money, energy, and time into the project, and was always thinking outside the box. At the height of the controversy I invited him to meet the rabbis of our community, so that they could express some of their concerns. The meeting did not go well. The rabbis were very candid but throughout it all, Dr Sinclair stayed beatifically calm. When the session was over I walked with him to his car, and apologised for the way he had been treated. He smiled at me, told me not to worry, and said, "This is a character-forming experience."

For me, at that moment, the impact of his response was electrifying, and it changed my life. Here was a man who had voluntarily given so much to our community, and all he had received in return was criticism. It reminded me of the famous remark, "No good deed goes unpunished." Throughout it all, though, he had remained serene because he had been able to step back from the immediacy of the moment and reframe it as an ordeal he had to go through to reach his destination, one that would ultimately make him stronger. Ever since, whenever I faced controversy or crisis, I said to myself, "That was a character-forming experience." And because I thought it, it was.

The second example: Like all too many people nowadays I have problems sleeping. I suffer from insomnia. I once mentioned this to my teacher, Rabbi Nachum Rabinovitch, of blessed memory. His immediate response was: Could I teach him how to have insomnia? He would love, he told me, to be able not to sleep, and quoted to me the rabbinic dictum, "Moonlight was made only for the purpose of study" (Eiruvin 65a). What I saw as an affliction, he saw as an opportunity. By sleeping less, I could study more. It did not stop me suffering from sleeplessness (though I found it helped me relate better to the line from Psalms, "The guardian of Israel neither slumbers nor sleeps"), but it did allow me to reframe it. I was able better to use the sleepless hours.

For me, the most personally transformative of all beliefs has been the idea of *hashgaḥa peratit*, divine providence. Whenever something unexpected has happened in my life, I have always asked, "What is Heaven trying to tell me? How does it want me to respond? Given that this has happened, how shall I turn this moment into a blessing?" I learned this through my early encounters with Chabad and with the Lubavitcher Rebbe. I learned it a second time, from a different starting point, through my study of the work of Viktor Frankl, the man who survived Auschwitz and turned his experiences there into a new form of psychotherapy based on what he called "man's search for meaning." His view was that we should never ask, "What do I want from life?" but always, "What does life want from me?" It was with surprise and delight that I discovered that the Rebbe was himself an admirer of Viktor Frankl's work. The result of that strong belief in providence, or as I sometimes put it, *living-as-listening*, has been to flood my life with meaning. For me, nothing just happens. It always comes with a call to respond in a particular kind of way.

Ideas change lives.

JEWISH IDEAS

Jews contributed to the world some of its most transformative ideas. It's worth listening to the testimony of non-Jewish writers on this subject. The Catholic historian Paul Johnson wrote: "To the Jews we owe the idea of equality before the law, both divine and human; of the sanctity of life and the dignity of the human person; of the individual conscience and so of personal redemption; of the collective conscience and so of social responsibility; of peace as an abstract ideal and love as the foundation of justice, and many other items which constitute the basic moral furniture of the human mind."[2]

Another Catholic historian, Thomas Cahill, wrote: "The Jews gave us the Outside and the Inside – our outlook and our inner life. We can hardly get up in the morning or cross the street without being Jewish. We dream Jewish dreams and hope Jewish hopes. Most of our best words, in fact – new, adventure, surprise; unique, individual, person, vocation; time, history, future; freedom, progress, spirit; faith, hope, justice – are the gifts of the Jews."[3]

---

2. *A History of the Jews* (New York: Harper Perennial, 1987), 585.
3. *The Gifts of the Jews: How a Tribe of Desert Nomads Changed the Way Everyone Thinks and Feels* (New York: Talese/Anchor Books, 1998), 240–41.

The late William Rees-Mogg, also a Catholic, once wrote, "One of the gifts of Jewish culture to Christianity is that it has taught Christians to think like Jews," adding, "Any modern man who has not learned to think as though he were a Jew can hardly be said to have learned to think at all."[4]

By far the most fascinating judgment, though, comes from one of Judaism's sharpest critics, Friedrich Nietzsche:

> Consider Jewish scholars in this light: All of them have a high regard for logic, that is for compelling agreement by force of reasons; they know with that they are bound to win, even where they encounter race and class prejudices.... Incidentally, Europe owes the Jews no small thanks for making people think more logically and for establishing cleanlier intellectual habits – nobody more so than the Germans, who are a lamentably *déraisonnable* race who to this day are still in need of having their "heads washed" first. Wherever Jews have won influence they have taught men to make finer distinctions, more rigorous inferences, and to write in a more luminous and cleanly fashion; their task was ever to bring a people "to listen to *raison*."[5]

This is a remarkable tribute from what in British politics they call "the leader of the Opposition."

One might think that the ideas Judaism introduced into the world have become part of the common intellectual heritage of humankind, at least of the West, and that they are by now, as Jefferson said, "self-evident." Yet this is not the case. Some of them have been lost over time; others the West never fully understood. That is what I hope to explore in these studies, for two reasons.

The first was suggested by Nietzsche himself. He wanted the West to abandon the Judaeo-Christian ethic in favour of what he called "the will to power." This was a disastrous mistake. There is nothing original

4. *The Reigning Error: The Crisis of World Inflation* (London: Hamilton, 1974), 11.
5. Friedrich Nietzsche, *The Gay Science*, translated with commentary by Walter Kaufmann (New York: Vintage, 1974), 291.

xxi

in the will to power. It has existed since the days of Cain, and its price is perennial bloodshed. But Nietzsche was right in one respect: the great alternative is Judaism. The choice humankind faces in every age is between the idea of power and the power of ideas. Judaism has always believed in the power of ideas, and it remains the only non-violent way to change the world.

The second is neither political nor philosophical but personal. Some ideas really are life-changing. In each chapter I will try to introduce you to one from the *parasha*. If we change the way we think, we can change the way we feel, which changes the way we act, which changes the person we become. Ideas change lives, and great ideas help us to courage, to happiness, and to lives filled with blessing.

It is not always easy to write books in the midst of the pressures of public life, which means that I have always been dependent on my office team. I have been especially blessed by my present team of Joanna Benarroch, Dan Sacker, and Debby Ifield, for whom I thank the Almighty daily. They are a joy to work with, and without their calm efficiency and devotion beyond the call of duty I doubt whether I could have written this book or any of the others these past few years.

In one of the most beautiful of Psalms, King David wrote: "Who can discern their own errors? Forgive my unperceived faults." It is always easy to get things wrong, and I have to thank two people in particular for pointing out mistakes in this as in other works: David Frei, registrar of the London Beth Din, and Professor Leslie Wagner. I am hugely in their debt. David has a range of knowledge that is simply breathtaking, and Leslie can spot faulty logic at a hundred yards. No one could ask for better or gentler friends.

My thanks as always to my publisher, Matthew Miller, and the team at Maggid Books for their wonderful enthusiasm and professionalism. It's a privilege working with them.

I am indebted to Bari Weiss for her engaging, uplifting, and generous foreword. I had the honour of hosting Bari at my home earlier this year for a Facebook Live conversation about her own insightful book on anti-Semitism. That book, together with her inspiring writing in the *New York Times* and elsewhere, is a *Kiddush Hashem*, and has shown the power of living a Judaism that is truly engaged with the world. I have no doubt she will continue to be a source of pride for all of us for many years to come.

I save my deepest thanks for my wife Elaine, and our children, Joshua, Dina, and Gila, and their respective families. They have taught me more about life than I have taught them. As I write in this introduction, the choice with which humankind is faced in every age is between the idea of power and the power of ideas. Judaism through the millennia has been a living embodiment of the power of ideas to sustain a people and be a transformative force wherever those ideas penetrated the world. I have taken great pride in seeing how my children have translated Judaism's ideas into their own lives, careers, and families with courage and imagination, each in their own way, and each in a way that I find inspiring. May Hashem give them and us the strength to be motivated by the pursuit of ideas, and thereby be a blessing to the Jewish people and the world.

Genesis
בראשית

Bereshit

The Faith of God

I n stately prose the Torah in its opening chapter describes the unfolding of the universe, the effortless creation of a single creative Force. Repeatedly we read, "And God said, Let there be … and there was … and God saw that it was good" – until we come to the creation of humankind. Suddenly the whole tone of the narrative changes:

> And God said, "Let us make man in our image, according to our likeness, and let them rule over the fish of the sea, and over the birds of heaven, and over the cattle, and over all the earth, and over every moving thing that moves upon the earth." So God created man in His image, in the image of God He created him, male and female He created them. (Gen. 1:26–27)

The problems are obvious. First, why the preface, "Let us make …"? In no other case does God verbally reflect on what He is about to create before He creates it. Second, who is the "us"? At that time there was no "us." There was only God.

There are many answers, but here I want to focus only on one given by the Talmud. It is quite extraordinary. The "us" refers to the angels with whom God consulted. He did so because He was faced with a fateful dilemma. By creating Homo sapiens, God was making the one being other than Himself capable of destroying life on earth. Read Jared Diamond's *Guns, Germs and Steel* or *Collapse*[1] and you will discover how destructive humans have been wherever they have set foot, creating environmental damage and human devastation on a massive scale. We are still doing so. This is how the Talmud (Sanhedrin 38b) describes what happened before God created humankind:

> When the Holy One, blessed be He, came to create man, He created a group of ministering angels and asked them, "Do you agree that we should make man in our image?" They replied, "Sovereign of the Universe, what will be his deeds?" God showed them the history of mankind. The angels replied (Ps. 8:5), "What is man that You are mindful of him?" [in other words, let man not be created]. God destroyed the angels. He created a second group, and asked them the same question, and they gave the same answer. God destroyed them. He created a third group of angels, and they replied, "Sovereign of the Universe, the first and second group of angels told You not to create man, and it did not avail them. You did not listen. What then can we say but this: The universe is Yours. Do with it as You wish."

Then God created man.

> When it came to the generation of the Flood, and then to the generation of the builders of Babel, the angels said to God, "Were not the first angels right? See how great is the corruption of mankind."

> Then God replied (Is. 46:4), "Even to old age I will not change, and even to grey hair, I will still be patient."

---

1. Jared Diamond, *Guns, Germs and Steel* (New York: W. W. Norton and Co., 1997); *Collapse: How Societies Choose to Fail or Succeed* (New York: Viking Press, 2004).

This goes to the core of the dilemma even God could not escape. Were He not to create humanity there would be no one in the universe capable of understanding that he or she was created and that God exists. Only with the birth of humanity did the universe become self-conscious. Without us, it would be as if God had created billions of robots mindlessly doing what they been programmed to do for all eternity. So, even though by creating humans God was putting the entire future of creation at risk, God proceeded to create humankind.

This is radical theology indeed. The Talmud is telling us is that the existence of humankind can only be explained by the fact that God had faith in man. As the *Sifrei* explains the phrase in Moses' song, "the God of faith" (Deut. 32:4) – this means, "the God who had faith in the universe and created it."[2] The real religious mystery, according to Judaism, is not our faith in God. It is God's faith in us.

This is the extraordinary idea that shines through the entire Tanakh. God invests His hopes for the universe in this strange, refractory, cantankerous, ungrateful, and sometimes degenerate creature called Homo sapiens, part dust of the earth, part breath of God, whose behaviour disappoints and sometimes appals Him. Yet He never gives up.

He tries with Adam, Noah, Abraham, Isaac, Jacob, Moses, Joshua, a string of judges and kings. He tries with women also, and here succeeds much better. They are more faithful, less violent, less obsessed with power. But He refuses to give up on men. He has His most passionate relationship with the prophets. They understand Him and become bearers of His word. Yet most of the prophets end up as disappointed with people as is God.

The real subject of the Torah is not our faith in God, which is often faltering, but His unfailing faith in us. The Torah is not man's book of God. It is God's book of man. He spends a mere thirty-four verses describing His own creation of the universe, but more than five hundred verses describing the Israelites' creation of a tiny, temporary, portable building called the *Mishkan*, the Sanctuary. God never stops believing in us, loving us, and hoping for the best from us. There are moments when He almost despairs. Our *parasha* says so:

---

2. *Sifrei, Haazinu* 325.

> The Lord saw how great the wickedness of the human race had become on the earth, and that every inclination of the thoughts of the human heart was only evil all the time. The Lord regretted that He had made human beings on the earth, and He was grieved to His very core. (Gen. 6:5–6)

But Noah, good, innocent, upright, consoles Him. For the sake of one good man God was prepared to begin again.

Of course, all of this is a matter of faith – as is all belief in the thoughts and feelings of persons other than myself. Do I really know whether those closest to me – my marriage partner, my children, my companions, my friends – love me or have faith in me, or is that just wishful thinking on my part? Atheists sometimes think that belief in God is irrational while belief in other people is rational. That is simply not so. The proof is the failure of the man who, at the dawn of the Enlightenment, sought to put philosophy on a rational basis: Rene Descartes. Descartes famously said, *Cogito ergo sum*, "I think, therefore I am." All he was sure of was his own existence. For anything else – the existence of physical objects, let alone other minds – even he had to invoke God.

I for one do not have enough faith to be an atheist.[3] To be an atheist you have to have faith, either in humankind as a whole, or in yourself. How anyone can have faith in humankind after the Holocaust defies all reason. The single most calculated, sustained crime of man against man happened not in some benighted third-world country, but in the heart of a Europe that had given birth to Kant and Hegel, Bach

---

3. Of course an atheist might say – Sigmund Freud came close to saying this – that faith is simply a comforting illusion. That really is not so. It is far more demanding to believe that God summons us to responsibility, that He asks us to fight for justice, equality, and human dignity, and that He holds us accountable for what we do, than to believe that there is no meaning to human existence other than ones we invent for ourselves, no ultimate truth, no absolute moral standards, and no one to whom we will have to give an account of our lives. Fifty years of reflection on this issue have led me to conclude that it is atheism that is, morally and existentially, the easy option – and I say this having known and studied with some of the greatest atheists of our time. That is not to say that I am critical of atheists. To the contrary, in a secular age, it is the default option. That is why now, more than at any other time in the past two thousand years, it takes courage to have and live by religious faith.

and Beethoven, Goethe and Schiller. Civilisation utterly failed to civilise. Humanism did not make men humane.

When I first stood at Auschwitz-Birkenau the question that haunted me was not "Where was God?" God was in the command "You shall not murder." God was in the words "You shall not oppress the stranger." God was saying to humanity, "Your brother's blood is crying to Me from the ground." God did not stop the first humans eating forbidden fruit. He did not stop Cain from committing murder. He did not stop the Egyptians enslaving the Israelites. God does not save us from ourselves. That, according to the Talmud, is why creating man was such a risk that the angels advised against it. The question that haunts me after the Holocaust, as it does today in this new age of chaos, is "Where is man?"

As for believing only in yourself, that is hubris. Every serious thinker since the dawn of history has known that this ends in nemesis.

There are only two serious possibilities to be entertained by serious minds. Either the one put forward by the Torah that we are here because a Force greater than the universe wanted us to be, or the alternative: that the universe exists because of a random fluctuation in the quantum field, and we are here because of a mindless sequence of genetic mutations blindly sifted by natural selection. Either there is or there is not meaning to the human condition. The first possibility yields Isaiah; the second, Sophocles, Aeschylus, and Greek tragedy. The Greece of antiquity died. The Israel of Abraham and Moses still lives.

I respect those who choose Greek tragedy over Jewish hope. But those who choose Judaism have made space in their minds for the most life-changing idea of all: Whether or not we have faith in God, God has faith in us.

There may be times in our lives – certainly there have been in mine – when the sun disappears and we enter the cloud of black despair. King David knew these feelings well. They are the theme of several psalms. People can be brutal to one another. There are some who, having suffered pain themselves, find relief in inflicting it on others. You can lose faith in humanity, or in yourself, or both. At such times, the knowledge that God has faith in us is transformative, redemptive. As David said: "Even were my father or mother to forsake me, the Lord would still receive me" (Ps. 27:10).

We may lose heart; God never will. We may despair; God will give us hope. God believes in us even if we don't believe in ourselves. We may sin and disappoint and come short again and again, but God never ceases to forgive us when we fail, and lift us when we fall.

Have faith in God's faith in us and you will find the path from darkness to light.

Life-Changing Idea #1

God believes in us even if we don't always believe in ourselves. Remember this, and you will find the path from darkness to light.

Noaḥ

The Trace of God

The story of the first eight chapters of Genesis is tragic but simple: creation, followed by de-creation, followed by re-creation. God creates order. Humans then destroy that order to the point where "the world was filled with violence," and "all flesh had corrupted its way on earth" (Gen. 6:11–12). God brings a flood that wipes away all life, until – with the exception of Noah, his family, and other animals – the earth has returned to the state it was in at the beginning of the Torah, when "the earth was waste and void, darkness was over the surface of the deep, and the spirit of God was hovering over the waters" (ibid. 1:2).

Vowing never again to destroy all life – though not guaranteeing that humanity might not do so of its own accord – God begins again, this time with Noah in place of Adam, father of a new start to the human story. Genesis 9 is therefore parallel to Genesis 1. But there are two significant differences.

In both there is a keyword, repeated seven times, but it is a different word. In Genesis 1 the word is *tov*, "good." In Genesis 9, the word is *brit*, "covenant." That is the first difference.

The second is that they both state that God made the human person in His image, but they do so in markedly different ways. In Genesis 1 we read:

> And God said, "Let us make man in our image, according to our likeness, and let them rule over the fish of the sea, and over the birds of heaven, and over the cattle, and over all the earth, and over every moving thing that moves upon the earth." So God created man in His image, in the image of God He created him, male and female He created them. (vv. 26–27)

And this is how it is stated in Genesis 9: "Whoever sheds the blood of man, by man shall his blood be shed; for in the image of God, He made man" (v. 6).

The difference here is fundamental. Genesis 1 tells me that *I* am in the image of God. Genesis 9 tells me that *the other person* is in the image of God. Genesis 1 speaks about the dominance of Homo sapiens over the rest of creation. Genesis 9 speaks about the sanctity of life and the prohibition of murder. The first chapter tells us about the potential power of human beings, while the ninth chapter tells us about the moral limits of that power. We may not use it to deprive another person of life.

This also explains why the keyword, repeated seven times, changes from "good" to "covenant." When we call something *good*, we are speaking about how it is in itself. But when we speak of *covenant*, we are talking about relationships. A covenant is a moral bond between persons.

What differentiates the world after the Flood from the world before is that the terms of the human condition have changed. God no longer expects people to be good because it is in their nature to be so. To the contrary, God now knows that "every inclination of the human heart is evil from childhood" (Gen. 8: 21) – and this despite the fact that we were created in God's image.

The difference is that there is only one God. If there were only one human being, he or she might live at peace with the world. But we know that this could not be the case because "it is not good for man to be alone" (ibid. 2:18). We are social animals. And when one human being thinks he or she has godlike powers vis-à-vis another human being, the result is violence. Therefore, thinking yourself godlike, if you are human, all-too-human, is very dangerous indeed.

That is why, with one simple move, God transformed the terms of the equation. After the Flood, He taught Noah and through him all humanity, that we should think, *not of ourselves but of the human other* as in the image of God. That is the only way to save ourselves from violence and self-destruction.

This really is a life-changing idea. It means that the greatest religious challenge is: Can I see God's image in one who is not in my image – whose colour, class, culture, or creed is different from mine?

People fear people not like them. That has been a source of violence for as long as there has been human life on earth. The stranger, the foreigner, the outsider, is almost always seen as a threat. But what if the opposite is the case? What if the people not like us enlarge rather than endanger our world?

There is a strange blessing we say after eating or drinking something over which we make the blessing *Shehakol*. It goes: *Borei nefashot rabot vehesronam*. God "creates many souls and their deficiencies." Understood literally, it is almost incomprehensible. Why should we praise God who creates deficiencies?

One beautiful answer[1] is that if we had no deficiencies, then lacking nothing, we would never need anyone else. We would be solitary rather than social. The fact that we are all different, and all have deficiencies, means that we need one another. What you lack, I may have, and what I lack, you may have. It is by coming together that we can each give the other something he or she lacks. It is our deficiencies and differences that bring us together in mutual gain, in a win-win scenario.[2] It is our diversity that makes us social animals.

---

1. I thank Mr Joshua Rowe of Manchester from whom I first heard this lovely idea.
2. This is what led thinkers like Montesquieu in the eighteenth century to conceptualise trade as an alternative to war. When two different tribes meet, they can either trade or fight. If they fight, one at least will lose and the other, too, will suffer losses. If they trade, both will gain. This is one of the most important contributions of the market economy to peace, tolerance, and the ability to see difference as a blessing, not a curse. See Albert O. Hirschman, *The Passions and the Interests: Political Arguments for Capitalism before Its Triumph* (Princeton: Princeton University Press, 2013).

This is the insight expressed in the famous rabbinic statement: "When a human being makes many coins in the same mint, they all come out the same. God makes us all in the same mint, the same image, His image, and we all come out different."[3] This is the basis of what I call – it was the title of one of my books – the dignity of difference.

This is a life-changing idea. Next time we meet someone radically unlike us, we should try seeing difference not as a threat but as an enlarging, possibility-creating gift. After the Flood, and to avoid a world "filled with violence" that led to the Flood in the first place, God asks us to see His image in one who is not in my image. Adam knew that he was in the image of God. Noah and his descendants are commanded to remember that the other person is in the image of God.

The great religious challenge is: Can I see a trace of God in the face of a stranger?

Life-Changing Idea #2

Next time you meet someone radically unlike you, try seeing difference not as a threat but as an enlarging, possibility-creating gift.

---

3. Mishna Sanhedrin 4:5.

Lekh Lekha

Inner-Directedness

I s character strictly personal – either you are or aren't calm, courageous, charismatic – or does culture have a part to play? Does when and where you live make a difference to the kind of person you become?

That was the question posed by three great American-Jewish sociologists, David Riesman, Nathan Glazer, and Reuel Denney in their 1950 classic, *The Lonely Crowd*.[1] Their argument was that particular kinds of historical circumstance give rise to particular kinds of people. It makes a difference, they said, whether you lived in a society with a high birth- and death-rate – where families had many children but life expectancy was short – or one on the brink of growth, or one in the early stages of decline. Each gave rise to its own type of character: not that everyone was the same but that you could discern certain traits in the population and culture as a whole.

---

1. David Riesman, Nathan Glazer, and Reuel Denney, *The Lonely Crowd: A Study of the Changing American Character* (New Haven: Yale University Press, 1950).

High birth- and death-rate societies, such as non-industrialised societies or Europe in the Middle Ages, tend to give rise to tradition-directed people: people who do what they do because that is how things have always been done. In these societies – often highly hierarchical – the primary struggle is to stay alive. Order is preserved by ensuring that people stick rigidly to rules and roles. Failure to do so gives rise to shame.

Societies on the brink of growth – transitional societies, such as Europe during the Renaissance and the Reformation – produce inner-directed types. Culture is in a state of change. There is high personal mobility. There is a mood of invention and exploration. This means that people have constantly to adapt to new challenges without losing a sense of where they are going and why. This means facing the future while keeping faith with the past. Such societies pay great attention to education. The young internalise the values of the group, which stay with them through life as a way of navigating change without disorientation or dislocation. They carry their inner world with them whatever they do and wherever they go. Failure in such societies is marked not by shame but by guilt.

Finally come the societies that have already achieved maximal growth and are on the brink of decline. Life expectancy has risen. The birth-rate falls. There is affluence. Much of the burden of care has been taken over by centralised agencies. There is less need for the driven, focused, resilient inner-directed types of an earlier age. The mood is no longer of scarcity but of abundance. The primary problem is not dealing with the material environment; it is getting on with and winning the approval of others. That is when the third character type emerges: the other-directed individual. Such people are more influenced by others in their age group, and by the media, than by their parents. Their source of direction in life is neither tradition nor internalised conscience but instead, contemporary culture. Other-directed people seek not so much to be esteemed but to be loved. When they fail, they feel not shame or guilt but anxiety.

Already by 1950, Riesman and his colleagues believed that this new, third character type was emerging in the America of their day. By now, thanks to the spread of social media and the collapse of structures of authority, the process has gone far further and has now spread throughout the West. Ours is the age of the Facebook profile, the vivid symbol of other-directedness.

Whether or not this is sustainable is an open question. But this insightful study helps us understand what is at stake in the opening of our *parasha*, the words that brought the Jewish people into being: "The Lord said to Abram, 'Go forth from your land, your birthplace, and your father's house to the land that I will show you'" (Gen. 12:1).

Abraham was commanded to leave behind the sources of both tradition-directedness ("your father's house") and other-directedness ("your land, your birthplace"). He was about to become the father of an inner-directed people.

His entire life was governed by an inner voice, the voice of God. He did not behave the way he did because that is how people had always acted, nor did he conform to the customs of his age. He had the courage to "be on one side while all the rest of the world was on the other."[2] His mission, as we read in the following *parasha*, was to "instruct his children and his household after him to keep the way of the Lord by doing what is right and just" (18:19), so that they too would carry with them the inner voice wherever they went. Theirs was a morality of righteousness and guilt, not honour and shame, or conformism and anxiety. Hence the centrality of education in Judaism, since Jews would have to hold fast to their values even when they were a minority in a culture whose values were diametrically opposed to their own.

Hence the astonishing resilience of Jews throughout the ages, and their ability to survive change, insecurity, even catastrophe. People whose values are indelibly engraved in their minds and souls can stand firm against the majority and persist in their identity even when others are losing theirs. It was that inner voice that guided the patriarchs and matriarchs throughout the book of Genesis – long before they had become a nation in their own right, and before the more public miracles of the book of Exodus.

Jewish identity *is* that inner voice, learned in childhood, reinforced by lifelong study, rehearsed daily in ritual and prayer. That is what gives us a sense of direction in life. It gives us the confidence of knowing

---

2. Genesis Rabba 42:8.

that Judaism, virtually alone among the cultures and civilisations of its day, has survived while the rest have been consigned to history. It is what allows us to avoid the false turns and temptations of the present, while availing ourselves of its genuine benefits and blessings.

Inner-directed people tend to be pioneers, exploring the new and unknown even while keeping faith with the old. Consider, for example, the fact that in 2015 *Time Magazine* identified Jerusalem, one of the world's most ancient religious centres, as one of the world's five fastest-growing centres for hi-tech start-ups. Tradition-directed people live in the past. Other-directed people live in the present. But inner-directed people carry the past into the present, which is how they have the confidence to build the future.

This life-changing idea of inner-directedness – the courage to be different – began with the words *Lekh lekha*, which could be translated as "Go to yourself." This means: Follow the inner voice, as did those who came before you, continuing their journey by bringing timeless values to a rapidly changing world.

Life-Changing Idea #3

Follow the inner voice, as did those who came before you, continuing their journey by bringing timeless values to a rapidly changing world.

Vayera

The Space Between Us

The stories told in Genesis chapters 21 and 22 – the sending away of Ishmael and the binding of Isaac – are among the hardest to understand in the whole of Tanakh. Both involve actions that strike us as almost unbearably harsh. But the difficulties they present go deeper even than that.

Recall that Abraham was chosen "so that he would instruct his children and his household after him to keep the way of the Lord by doing what is right and just" (Gen. 18:19). He was chosen to be a father. The first two letters of his name, *Av*, mean just that. *Avram* means "a mighty father." *Avraham*, says the Torah, means "a father of many nations."

Abraham was chosen to be a parental role model. But how can a man who banished his son Ishmael, sending him off with his mother Hagar into the desert, where they nearly died, be thought of as an exemplary father? And how could a man who was willing to sacrifice his son Isaac be a model for future generations?

These are not questions about Abraham. They are questions about the will of God. For it was not Abraham who wanted to send

Ishmael away. To the contrary, it "distressed Abraham greatly," because Ishmael was his son (21:11). It was God who told him to listen to Sarah and send the child away.

Nor was it Abraham who wanted to sacrifice Isaac. It was God who told him to do so, referring to Isaac as "your son, your only one, the one you love" (22:2). Abraham was acting on both occasions against his emotions, his paternal instincts. What is the Torah telling us about the nature of fatherhood? It seems very difficult indeed to draw a positive message from these events.

There is an even deeper problem, and it is hinted at in the words God spoke to Abraham in summoning him to the binding of his son: "Take your son, your only son, the one you love, Isaac, and go (*lekh lekha*) to the region of Moriah. Sacrifice him there as a burnt offering on a mountain I will show you." These words inevitably remind us of God's first summons: "Go forth (*Lekh lekha*) from your land, your birthplace, and your father's house" (12:1). These are the only two places in which this phrase occurs in the Torah. Abraham's last trial echoed his first.

But note that the first trial meant that Abraham had to abandon his father, thereby looking as if he were neglecting his duties as a son.[1] So, whether as a father to his sons or as a son to his father, Abraham was commanded to act in ways that seem the exact opposite of what we would expect and how we should behave.

This is too strange to be accidental. There is a mystery here to be decoded.

The barrier to our understanding of these events lies in the sheer abyss of time between then and now. Abraham, as the pioneer of a new kind of faith and way of life, was instituting a new form of relationship between the generations. Essentially, what we are seeing in these events is *the birth of the individual.*

In ancient times, and in antiquity in Greece and Rome, the basic social unit was not the individual but the family. Religious rituals were performed around the fire in the family hearth, with the father serving as priest, offering sacrifices, libations, and incantations to the spirits of dead ancestors. The power of the father was absolute. Wives and children

---

1. See Rashi on Gen. 11:32.

had no rights and no independent legal personalities. They were mere property and could be killed by the head of the household at will. Each family had its own gods, and the father was the sole intermediary with the ancestral spirits, whom he would one day join. There were no individuals in the modern sense. There were only families, under the absolute rule of its male head.

The Torah was a radical break with this entire mindset. The anthropologist Mary Douglas points out that the Torah was unique in the ancient world in making no provision for sacrifices to dead ancestors, and forbidding the attempt to communicate with the spirits of the dead.[2]

Monotheism was more than simply the belief in one God. Because each human was in His image, and because each could be in direct relationship with Him, the individual was suddenly given significance – not just fathers but also mothers, and not just parents but also children. No longer were they fused into a single unit, with a single controlling will. They were each to become persons in their own right, with their own identity and integrity.[3]

Such changes do not happen overnight, and they do not happen without wrenching dislocations. That is what is happening at both ends of the Abraham story. At the beginning of his mission, Abraham was told to separate himself from his father, and towards the end he was told to separate himself, in different ways, from each of his two sons. These painful episodes represent the agonising birth-pangs of a new way of thinking about humanity.

First separate, then connect. That seems to be the Jewish way. That is how God created the universe, by first separating domains – day and night, upper and lower waters, sea and dry land – then allowing them to be filled. And that is how we create real personal relationships. By separating and leaving space for the other. Parents should not seek to control children. Spouses should not seek to control one another. It is the carefully calibrated distance between us in which relationship allows each party to grow.

---

2. Mary Douglas, *Leviticus as Literature* (Oxford: Oxford University Press, 1999).
3. See Peter Berger, *The Sacred Canopy* (New York: Doubleday, 1967), 117, where he speaks of "the highly individuated men" (and women) who "populate the pages of the Old Testament to a degree unique in ancient religious literature."

In his recent book on sporting heroes, *The Greatest*, Matthew Syed notes how important the encouragement of parents is to the making of champions, but he adds:

> Letting go – that is the essential paradox of parenthood. You care, you nurture, you sacrifice, and then you watch as the little ones fly into the great unknown, often shouting recriminations as they depart. You will experience the stomach clenching pain of separation, but you do so with a smile and a hug, aware that the desire to protect and love must never morph into the tyranny of mollycoddling.[4]

It is this drama of separation that Abraham symbolically enacts in his relationship both to his father and to his two sons. In this world-transforming moment of the birth of the individual, God is teaching him the delicate art of making space, without which no true individuality can grow.

In the lovely words of Irish poet John O'Donohue our challenge is: "To bless the space between us."[5]

Life-Changing Idea #4

First separate, then connect; it is the carefully calibrated distance that allows us to grow as individuals and create stronger relationships together.

4. Matthew Syed, *The Greatest: The Quest for Sporting Perfection* (London: John Murray, 2017), 9.
5. John O'Donohue, *To Bless the Space Between Us* (New York: Doubleday, 2008).

Ḥayei Sara

The World's Oldest Man

On August 11, 2017, the world's oldest man passed away, just a month short of his 114th birthday – making him one of the ten longest-lived men since modern record-keeping began. If you knew nothing else about him than this, you would be justified in thinking that he had led a peaceful life, spared of fear, grief, and danger.

The actual truth is the opposite. The man in question was Yisrael Kristal, Holocaust survivor. Born in Poland in 1903, he survived four years in the Lodz ghetto, and was then transported to Auschwitz. In the ghetto, his two children died. In Auschwitz, his wife was killed. When Auschwitz was liberated, he was a walking skeleton weighing a mere 37 kilos. He was the only member of his family to survive.

He was raised as a religious Jew and stayed so all his life. When the war was over and his entire world destroyed, he married again, this time to another Holocaust survivor. They had children. They made *aliya* to Haifa. There he began again in the confectionery business, as he had done in Poland before the war. He made sweets and chocolate. He became an innovator. If you have ever had Israeli orange peel covered in chocolate, or liqueur chocolates shaped like little bottles and covered with silver foil, you are enjoying one of the products he originated. Those who knew him said he was a man with no bitterness in his soul. He wanted people to taste sweetness.

In 2016, at the age of 113, he finally celebrated his bar mitzva. A hundred years earlier, this had proved impossible. By then, his mother was dead and his father was fighting in the First World War. With an almost poetic sense of fittingness, Yisrael died on the eve of Shabbat *Parashat Ekev*, the *parasha* that includes the second paragraph of the *Shema* with its commands to wear tefillin and teach Torah to your children, "so that you and your children may live long in the land that the Lord swore to your ancestors."

Yisrael Kristal faithfully did both. On his bar mitzva he joked that he was the world's oldest tefillin-wearer. He gathered his children, grandchildren, and great-grandchildren under his tallit and said, "Here's one person, and look how many people he brought to life. As we're all standing here under my tallit, I'm thinking: six million people. Imagine the world they could have built." This was an extraordinary man.

His life sheds light on one of the most tantalising verses in the Torah. Describing the death of Abraham, our *parasha* says that he "breathed his last and died in good old age, old and satisfied" (Gen. 25:8). His is the most serene death in the Torah. Yet consider his life, fraught as it was with trial after trial.

To pursue the call of God, he had to say goodbye to his land, his birthplace, and his father's house and travel to an unknown destination. Twice, famine forced him into exile, where his life was in danger. Promised countless children – as many as the dust of the earth and the stars of the sky – he remained childless until old age. Then God told him to send away his son by Sarah's handmaid Hagar. And if that trial were not heart-breaking enough, God then told him to sacrifice his only son from Sarah, Isaac, the one who God had told him would be his spiritual heir and bearer of the covenant into the future.

Seven times promised a land, when Sarah died he owned not a single square inch of territory in which to bury her, and had to entreat the Hittites to let him buy a field and burial cave. This was a life of disappointed hopes and delayed fulfilments. What kind of man was this that the Torah can say that he died "in good old age, old and satisfied"?

I learned the answer to this question through a series of life-changing encounters with Holocaust survivors. They were among the strongest, most life-affirming people I have ever met. For years I wondered how they were able to survive at all, having seen what they saw and known what they knew. They had lived through the deepest darkness ever to have descended on a civilisation.

Eventually I realised what they had done. When the war was over, most focused with single-minded intensity on the future, or if not on the future then on the present, taking it day by day. They did not look back. Instead, strangers in a strange land, they built homes and careers, married and had children, and brought new life into the world.

It is impossible to generalise. Every life was different, every story unique. But this is what I discovered: In most cases, they did not talk about their experiences during the *Shoah*, even to their spouses, their children, and their closest friends. This silence lasted, in many cases, for as long as fifty years. Only then, when the future they had built was secure, did they allow themselves to look back and bear witness to what they had suffered and seen. Some of them wrote books. Many of them went around schools, telling their story so that the Holocaust could not be denied.[1] First they built a future. Only then did they allow themselves to remember the past.

That is what Abraham did in this *parasha*. He had received three promises from God: children, a land, and the assurance that he would be the father, not of one nation but of many nations (17:4–5). At the age of 137, he had one unmarried son, no land, and had fathered no nations. He uttered not a single word of complaint. It seems that he realised that God wanted him to act, not to wait for God to do the work for him.

So, when Sarah died, he bought the first plot in what would become the Holy Land, the field and cave of Machpelah. Then he instructed his servant to find a wife for Isaac, his son, so that he might

---

1. For two fascinating portraits of how encounters with the Holocaust and its survivors were transformative for young Americans, see the films *Paper Clips* (2004) and *Freedom Writers* (2007).

live to see the first Jewish grandchildren. Lastly, in his old age, he married again and had six sons, who would eventually become progenitors of many nations. He did not, except briefly, sit and mourn the past. Instead he took the first steps towards building the future.

That, in his own way, is what Yisrael Kristal did – and that is how a survivor of Auschwitz lived to become the world's oldest man. He too died "in good old age, old and satisfied."

That is what the Jewish people did collectively when, a mere three years after standing eyeball-to-eyeball with the angel of death at Auschwitz, David Ben-Gurion proclaimed the Jewish State in our people's ancient homeland, the land of Israel. Had world Jewry sat passively and wept from then till now for the murdered generations of European Jewry, it would have been an understandable reaction. But it did not. It was as if the Jewish people had said collectively, in the words of King David, "I will not die but live" (Ps. 118:17), thereby giving testimony to the God of life. That is why the West's oldest nation is still young, a world leader in life-saving medicine, disaster relief, and life-enhancing technology.

This is a transformative idea. To survive tragedy and trauma, first build the future. Only then, remember the past.

Life-Changing Idea #5

To survive tragedy and trauma, first build the future.
Only then, remember the past.

Toledot

Why Isaac? Why Jacob?

Why Isaac, not Ishmael? Why Jacob, not Esau? These are among the most searing questions in the whole of Judaism.

It is impossible to read Genesis 21, with its description of how Hagar and her son were cast out into the wilderness, how their water ran out, how Hagar placed Ishmael under a bush and sat at a distance so she would not see him die, without feeling intensely for both of them, mother and child. They are both crying. The Torah tells us that God heard Ishmael's tears and sent an angel to comfort Hagar, show her a well of water, and assure her that God would make her son "*a great nation*" (v. 18) – the very promise he gave Abraham himself at the start of his mission (12:2).

Likewise in the case of Esau. The emotional climax of the *parasha* occurs in chapter 27, at the point when Jacob leaves Isaac's presence, having deceived him into thinking that he was Esau. Then Esau enters, and slowly both father and son realise what has happened. This is what we read:

> Then Isaac trembled with a very great trembling, and said, "Who then was it who hunted game and brought it to me and I ate it

before you came and I blessed him? – and he will be blessed." When Esau heard his father's words, he cried an intensely loud and bitter cry, and said to his father, "Bless me, me too, my father!" (vv. 33–34)

These are among the most powerful descriptions of emotion in the whole of the Torah, and they are precisely the opposite of what we would expect. We would expect the Torah to enlist our sympathies for the chosen: Isaac and Jacob. Instead it almost forces us to empathise with the rejected: Hagar, Ishmael, and Esau. We feel their pain and sense of loss.

So, why Isaac and not Ishmael? Why Jacob and not Esau? To this there are two types of answer. The first is given by Midrash. On this reading Isaac and Jacob were righteous. Ishmael and Esau were not.

Ishmael worshipped idols.[1] He violated married women.[2] He tried to kill Isaac with his bow and arrow while making it look as if it was an accident.[3] Esau was attracted, even in the womb, to idolatrous shrines.[4] He trapped not only animals but also his father Isaac by pretending to be pious when he was not.[5] God cut short Abraham's life by five years so that he would not live to see his grandson violate a betrothed woman, commit murder, deny God, deny the resurrection of the dead, and despise the birthright.[6] Such is the way of Midrash. It helps us see Isaac and Jacob as perfectly good, Ishmael and Esau as dangerously bad. That is an important part of our tradition.

But it is not the way of the written Torah itself, at least insofar as we seek what Rashbam called *omek peshuto shel mikra*, the "deep plain sense of Scripture."[7] The Torah does not portray Ishmael and Esau as wicked. The worst it has to say about Ishmael is that Sarah saw him *metzaḥek* (Gen. 21:9), a word with many meanings, most of them not negative. Literally, it means, "he was laughing." But Abraham and Sarah also laughed (17:17, 18:12). So did Isaac (26:8). Indeed Isaac's name,

1. Genesis Rabba 53:11; Exodus Rabba 1:1.
2. Genesis Rabba 53:11.
3. Ibid.
4. Ibid. 63:6.
5. *Tanḥuma, Toledot* 8.
6. Bava Batra 16b.
7. Rashbam on Gen. 37:2, 28; Ex. 3:14, 13:9.

chosen by God Himself (17:19), means, "He will laugh." There is nothing in the word itself that implies improper conduct.[8]

In the case of Esau, the most pointed verse is the one in which
he agrees to part with his birthright in return for a bowl of soup
(Gen. 25:34). In a staccato series of five consecutive verbs, the Torah
says that he "ate, drank, rose, went, and despised" his birthright. Yet this
tells us that he was impetuous, not that he was evil.

If we seek the "deep plain sense," we must rely on the explicit testimony of the Torah itself – and what it tells us is fascinating. An angel
told Hagar before Ishmael was born that he would be "a wild donkey
of a man, his hand against everyone, and everyone's hand against him"
(Gen. 16:12). He became an expert archer (21:20). Esau, red-haired,
physically mature at a young age, was "a skilful hunter, a man of the
field" (25:27). Ishmael and Esau were at home in nature. They were
strong, adroit, unafraid of the wild. In any other culture they might
have emerged as heroes.

And that is the point. We will only understand the Torah if we
recall that every other religion in the ancient world worshipped nature.
That is where they found God, or more precisely, the gods: in the sun,
the moon, the stars, the storm, the rain that fed the earth, and the earth
that gave forth food.

Even in the twenty-first century, people for whom science has
taken the place of religion still worship nature. For them we are physical beings. For them there is no such thing as a soul, merely electrical
impulses in the brain. For them there is no real freedom: we are what
we are because of genetic and epigenetic causes over which we have no
real control. Free will, they say, is an illusion. Human life, they believe,
is not sacred, nor are we different in kind from other animals. Nature is
all there is. Such was the view of Lucretius in ancient Rome and Epicu-
rus in pre-Christian Greece, and it is the view of scientific atheists today.

The faith of Abraham and his descendants is different. God, we
believe, is beyond nature, because He created nature. And because He

---

8. Robert Alter makes the ingenious suggestion that it means that Ishmael was "Isaac-ing,"
imitating his younger brother (Robert Alter, *The Five Books of Moses: A Translation
with Commentary* [New York: Norton, 2004], 103).

made us in His image, there is something in us that is beyond nature also. We are free. We are creative. We can conceive of possibilities that have not yet existed, and act so as to make them real. We can adapt to our environment, but we can also adapt our environment to us. Like every other animal we have desires, but unlike any other animal we are capable of standing outside our desires and choosing which to satisfy and which not. We can distinguish between what is and what ought to be. We can ask the question "Why?"

After the Flood God was reconciled to human nature and vowed never again to destroy the world (Gen. 9:11). Yet He wanted humanity to know that there is something beyond nature. That is why He chose Abraham and his descendants as His "witnesses."[9]

Not by accident were Abraham and Sarah, Isaac and Rebecca, and Jacob and Rachel, unable to have children by natural means. Nor was it mere happenstance that God promised the Holy Land to a landless people. He chose Moses, the man who said, "I am not a man of words," to be the bearer of His word. When Moses spoke God's words, people knew they were not his own.

God promised two things to Abraham, Isaac, and Jacob: children and a land. Throughout history, most people at most times have taken children and a land for granted. They are part of nature. They constitute the two most basic natural drives: the Darwinian imperative and the territorial imperative. All animals have children, and many have their own territory that they mark and defend.

Jews – one of the world's smallest people – have rarely been able to take children for granted. Abraham's first recorded words to God were, "O Lord God, what can You give me seeing that I go childless?" (15:2), and even today we ask, will we have Jewish grandchildren? Nor have they been able to take their land for granted. They were often surrounded by enemies larger and more powerful than themselves. For many centuries they suffered exile. Even today they find the State of Israel's very right to exist being called into question in a way that applies to no other sovereign people. As David Ben-Gurion said, "In Israel, to be a realist you have to believe in miracles."

9. Is. 43:10–12, 44:8.

Isaac and Jacob were not men of nature: the field, the hunt, the gladiatorial game of predator-and-prey. They were not Ishmael and Esau, people who could survive by their own strength and skill. They were men who needed God's spirit to survive. Israel is the people who in themselves testify to something beyond themselves.

Jews have consistently shown that you can make a contribution to humanity out of all proportion to your numbers, and that a small nation can outlive every empire that sought its destruction. They have shown that a nation is strong when it cares for the weak, and rich when it cares for the poor. Jews are the people through whom God has shown that the human spirit can rise above nature, testifying that there is something real that transcends nature.

That is a life-changing idea. We are as great as our ideals. If we truly believe in something beyond ourselves, we will achieve beyond ourselves.

Life-Changing Idea #6

You are as great as your ideals. If you truly believe in something beyond yourself, you will achieve beyond yourself.

Vayetzeh

Out of the Depths

What did Jacob add to the Jewish experience? What is it that we find in him that we do not find to the same measure in Abraham and Isaac? Why is it his name – Jacob/Israel – that we carry in our identity? How was it that all his children stayed within the faith? Is there something of him in our spiritual DNA? There are many answers. I explore one here, and another in the next *parasha, Vayishlaḥ*.

Jacob was the man whose deepest spiritual encounters happened when he was on a journey, alone and afraid at the dead of night, fleeing from one danger to another. In this *parasha*, we see him fleeing from Esau and about to meet Laban, a man who would cause him great grief. In the following *parasha* we see him fleeing in the opposite direction, from Laban to Esau, a meeting that filled him with dread: he was "very afraid and distressed" (Gen. 32:7). Jacob was supremely the lonely man of faith.

Yet it is precisely at these moments of maximal fear that he had spiritual experiences that have no parallel in the lives of either Abraham or Isaac – nor even Moses. In this *parasha* he has a vision of a ladder stretching from earth to heaven, with angels ascending and descending, at the end of which he declares: "Surely God is in this place and I did not know it.... How awesome is this place! This is nothing other than the house of God, and this, the gate of heaven!" (28:16–17).

In *Parashat Vayishlaḥ*, caught between his escape from Laban and his imminent encounter with Esau, he wrestles with a stranger – variously described as a man, an angel, and God Himself – receives a new name, Israel, and says, naming the place of the encounter Peniel, "I have seen God face to face and my life was spared" (32:31).

This was no small moment in the history of faith. We normally assume that the great spiritual encounters happen in the desert, or a wilderness, or a mountain top, in an ashram, a monastery, a retreat, a place where the soul is at rest, the body calm, and the mind in a state of expectation. But that is not Jacob, nor is it the only, or even the primary, Jewish encounter. We know what it is to encounter God in fear and trembling. Through much – thankfully not all, but much – of Jewish history, our ancestors found God in dark nights and dangerous places. It is no accident that Rabbi Joseph Soloveitchik called his most famous essay *The Lonely Man of Faith*,[1] nor that Rabbi Adin Steinsaltz called one of his books about Judaism *The Strife of the Spirit*.[2]

Sometimes it is when we feel most alone that we discover we are not alone. We can encounter God in the midst of fear or a sense of failure. I have done so at the very points when I felt most inadequate, overwhelmed, abandoned, looked down on by others, discarded, and disdained. It was then that I felt the hand of God reaching out to save me the way a stranger did when I was on the point of drowning in an Italian sea on my honeymoon.[3] That is the gift of Jacob/Israel, the man who found God in the heart of darkness.

Jacob was the first but not the last. Recall Moses in his moment of crisis, when he said the terrifying words, "If this is what You are going to do to me, please kill me now if I have found favour in Your sight, and let me not see my misery" (Num. 11:15). That is when God

---

1. Rabbi Joseph B. Soloveitchik, *The Lonely Man of Faith* (Jerusalem: Maggid Books, 2018).
2. Rabbi Adin Steinsaltz, *The Strife of the Spirit* (Jerusalem: Maggid Books, 2011).
3. I have told the story in the video *Understanding Prayer: Thanking and Thinking*. I also give an account of it in my book *Celebrating Life* (London: Fount, 2000).

allowed Moses to see the effect of his spirit on seventy elders, one of the rare cases of a spiritual leader seeing the influence he has had on others in his lifetime.

It is when Elijah was weary to the point of asking to die that God sent him the great revelation at Mount Horeb: the whirlwind, the fire, the earthquake, and the still, small voice (I Kings 19). There was a time when Jeremiah felt so low that he said: "Cursed be the day on which I was born, let not the day on which my mother gave birth to me be blessed.... Why did I come out from the womb, to see toil, and sorrow, and to end my days in shame?" (Jer. 20:14, 18). It was after this that he had his most glorious hope-filled prophecies of the return of Israel from exile, and of God's everlasting love for His people, a nation that would live as long as the sun, the moon, and the stars (Jer. 31).

Perhaps no one spoke more movingly about this condition than King David in his most agitated psalms. In psalm 69 he speaks as if he were drowning: "Save me, O God, for the waters have come up to my neck. I sink in the miry depths, where there is no foothold" (Ps. 69:2–3).

Then there is the line as famous to Christians as to Jews: "My God, my God, why have You forsaken me?" (Ps. 22:2). And the equally famous, "Out of the depths I cry to You, Lord" (Ps. 130:1).

This is the heritage of Jacob who discovered that you can find God, not just when you are peacefully tending your sheep, or joining others in prayer at the Temple or in the synagogue, but also when you are in danger, far from home, with peril in front of you and fear behind.

These two encounters, in this *parasha* and the next, also provide us with powerful metaphors of spiritual life. Sometimes we experience it as climbing a ladder, rung by rung. Each day, week, month, or year, as we study and understand more, we come a little closer to heaven as we learn to stand above the fray, rise above our reactive emotions, and begin to sense the complexity of the human condition. That is faith as a ladder.

Then there is faith as a wrestling match, as we struggle with our doubts and hesitations, above all with the fear (it's called the "impostor syndrome") that we are not as big as people think we are or as God wants us to be.[4] Out of such experiences we, like Jacob, can emerge limping. Yet it is out of such experiences that we too can discover that we have been wrestling with an angel who forces us to a strength we did not know we had.

The great musicians have the power to take pain and turn it into beauty.[5] The spiritual experience is slightly different from the aesthetic one. What matters in spirituality is truth not beauty: existential truth as the almost-infinitesimal me meets the Infinite-Other and I find my place in the totality of things, and a strength-not-my-own runs through me, lifting me to safety above the raging waters of the troubled soul.

That is the gift of Jacob, and this is his life-changing idea: That out of the depths we can reach the heights. The deepest crises of our lives can turn out to be the moments when we encounter the deepest truths and acquire our greatest strengths.

Life-Changing Idea #7

The deepest crises of your life can turn out to be the moments when you encounter the deepest truths and acquire your greatest strengths.

---

4. There is, of course, the opposite phenomenon, of those who think they've outgrown Judaism, that they are bigger than the faith of their fathers. Sigmund Freud seems to have suffered from this condition.

5. For me the supreme example is the Adagio of Schubert's String Quintet in C Major op. 163, written just two months before the composer's death.

Vayishlaḥ

The Struggle of Faith

Thereare Mozarts and there are Beethovens. Which are you?

I have only the most amateur knowledge of music, but the impression one gets about Mozart is that, from him, music flowed. There is something effortless and effervescent about his compositions. He wrote at speed. He carried the worries of the world lightly.

Not so Beethoven, for whom it sometimes took years for an idea to crystallise into its final form, with countless drafts and revisions and crossings-out. This was a man who could be angry with himself and with the world, for whom creativity was a struggle from which he emerged triumphant with work that is rarely less than strenuous and full of conflict until its final majestic resolution. The ethereal, mystical, almost otherworldly quality of his last compositions, the sublime late piano sonatas and string quartets, are the creation of one who has finally found peace after a life of wrestling with his own angels and demons.

All of this is, for me, a way of coming to understand Jacob, the man who became Israel, our father-in-faith. Jacob is not the most obvious choice of religious hero. He does not appear – at least on the surface of the biblical text – as a man with Abraham's courage or kindness, Isaac's faithfulness and self-restraint, Moses' vigour and passion, David's politics and poetry, or Isaiah's lyricism and hope.

He was a man surrounded by conflict: with his brother Esau, his father-in-law Laban, his wives, Leah and Rachel, and his children, whose sibling rivalry eventually brought the whole family into exile in Egypt. His life seems to have been a field of tensions.

Then there were his transactions: the way he purchased Esau's birthright, took his blessing, and eventually outwitted his wily father-in-law Laban. In each case he seems to have won, but then his situation deteriorates. The episode in which, at Rebecca's request, he dressed up as Esau and deceived his blind father, forced him to leave home and – as we see in this *parasha* – left him traumatised with fear at the prospect of meeting Esau again. Almost the same deception he practised on Isaac, he suffered at the hand of Laban. Even his escape from Laban might have ended in tragedy, had God not warned him not to harm Jacob (hence the passage in the Haggada: "Go and learn what Laban the Aramean sought to do to our father Jacob"). His life as portrayed in the Torah seems to be a constant series of escapes from one trouble to the next.

So who and what was Jacob?

To this there are two radically different answers. There is the Jacob of Midrash who even in the womb longed for a synagogue,[1] who spent his years as a young man studying in the *bet midrash*,[2] who looked like Abraham,[3] and whose arms were like pillars of marble.[4] His motives were always pure. He bought Esau's birthright because he could not bear to see Esau offering sacrifices (the privilege of the firstborn) to idols.[5] As for his father's blessing, the very reason Isaac became blind in old age was so that this could be possible.[6] Esau was the opposite, a violent and mercurial character who had deceived his father into thinking he was ultra-pious,[7]

---

1. Genesis Rabba 63:6.
2. Ibid. 63:10.
3. *Midrash Lekaḥ Tov*, Gen. 47:18.
4. Genesis Rabba 65:17.
5. Ibid. 63:13.
6. Ibid. 65:8.
7. See Rashi on Gen. 25:27.

but who had – on the day he came in "tired" from the field – committed a whole series of crimes including murder.[8]

This is an extreme portrayal, but not without scriptural basis. Jacob is called an *ish tam*, which conveys the sense of simplicity, integrity, and single-mindedness. The plain sense of the oracle Rebecca received before the twins were born was that "the elder will serve the younger." She knew Jacob was the son destined to prevail. Besides which, as Maharatz Chajes says in his "Introduction to the Aggadic Literature,"[9] Midrash paints biblical characters in moral black-and-white for obvious moral and educational reasons. It is difficult to teach children how to behave if all you have to offer is a series of studies in ambiguity, complexity, and shades of grey.

The other Jacob, though, is the one we read in the plain sense of the text. The obvious question is: Why did the Torah choose to portray the third of the patriarchs in this way? The Torah is highly selective in the details it chooses to relate. Why not paint Jacob in more attractive colours?

It seems to me that the Torah is delivering, here as elsewhere, an extraordinary message: If we can truly relate to God as God, in His full transcendence and majesty, then we can relate to humans as humans in all their fallibility. In every other religious literature known to me, heroes are idealised until they no longer seem human at all. They are divine or semi-divine, perfect and infallible. There is no one like that in the whole of Tanakh. Even Noah (righteous, perfect) is seen drunk and dishevelled. Even Job (blameless, upright) eventually curses his fate. The man who, more than any other, epitomises fallibility is Jacob.

And perhaps that is the point. Jacob was a Beethoven, not a Mozart. His life was a series of struggles. Nothing came easily to him. He, alone of the patriarchs, was a man who chose to be chosen. Abraham was called by God. Isaac was chosen before his birth. Moses, Joshua, Samuel, David, Isaiah, and Jeremiah were all singled out by God for their mission. Not so Jacob. It was he who bought the

---

8. Bava Batra 16b. See above on *Parashat Toledot*.
9. Rabbi Zvi Hirsch Chajes, *Mevo HaAggadot* (printed at the beginning of standard editions of *Ein Yaakov*).

birthright and took the blessing, he who chose to carry Abraham's destiny into the future.

Not until he was running away from home did God appear to him. Not until years later, alone, at night, terrified at the prospect of meeting Esau, did God or an angel wrestle with him. He alone was given, by God or the angel, a completely new name, not an enhancement of his old one but a completely new identity: Israel. Even more strikingly, despite the fact that he was told "Your name shall no more be called Jacob,"[10] the Torah continues to call him Jacob, suggesting that his struggle was lifelong – as, often, is ours.

Were I to choose a soundtrack for the Jacob I have come to know, it would be Beethoven's *Hammerklavier* sonata or his *Grosse Fugue*, music of such overwhelming tension that it seems on the verge of bursting through all form and structure. Yet it was through these epic struggles that Beethoven eventually reached his own version of serenity, and it was through Jacob's extended wrestling match with destiny that he eventually achieved what neither Abraham nor Isaac accomplished: all his children stayed within the faith. "According to the pain is the reward," said the Sages.[11] That is Jacob.

There are saintly people for whom spirituality comes as easily as did music to Mozart. But God does not reach out only to saints. He reaches out to all of us. That is why He gave us Abraham for those who love, Isaac for those who fear, and Jacob/Israel for those who struggle.

Hence this *parasha*'s life-changing idea: If you find yourself struggling with faith, you are in the company of Jacob who became Israel, the father-in-faith of us all.

Life-Changing Idea #8

If you find yourself struggling with faith, you are in the company of Jacob who became Israel, the father-in-faith of us all.

---

10. He is told this twice, first by the angel, then by God Himself: Gen. 32:29, 35:10.
11. Mishna Avot 5:23.

Vayeshev

Improbable Endings and the Defeat of Despair

We live life looking forward but we understand it only looking back.

As we live from day to day, our life can seem like a meaningless sequence of random events, a series of accidents and happenstances that have no shape or inner logic. A traffic jam makes us late for an important meeting. A stray remark we make offends someone in a way we never intended. By a hair's-breadth we fail to get the job we so sought. Life as we experience it can sometimes feel like Joseph Heller's definition of history: "a trashbag of random coincidences blown open in a wind."[1]

Yet looking back, it begins to make sense. The opportunity we missed here led to an even better one there. The shame we felt at our unintentionally offensive remark makes us more careful about what we say in the future. Our failures, seen in retrospect many years later, turn

---

1. *Good as Gold* (London: Vintage Books, 2011), 78.

out to have been our deepest learning experiences. Our hindsight is always more perceptive than our foresight. We live life facing the future, but we understand life only when it has become our past.

Nowhere is this set out more clearly than in the story of Joseph in this *parasha*. It begins on a high note: "Now Israel loved Joseph more than all his sons, because he was a son of his old age, and he made a richly embroidered robe" (Gen. 37:3). But with dramatic speed, that love and that gift turn out to be Joseph's undoing. His brothers began hating him. When he told them his dream, they hated him even more. His second dream offended even his father. Later, when he went to see his brothers tending their flocks, they first plotted to kill him, and eventually sold him as a slave.

At first, in Potiphar's house, he seemed to be favoured by fortune. But then his master's wife tried to seduce him and when he refused her advances she accused him of attempted rape and he was sent to prison with no way of proving his innocence. He seemed to have reached his nadir. There was nowhere lower for him to fall.

Then came an unexpected ray of hope. Interpreting the dream of a fellow prisoner, who had once been Pharaoh's cupbearer, he predicted his release and return to his former elevated role. And so it happened. Joseph asked only one thing in return: "Remember me when it goes well with you, and please show me kindness: mention me to Pharaoh, and get me out of this place. For I was forcibly taken from the land of the Hebrews, and here also I have done nothing to deserve being put in this pit" (40:14).

The last line of the *parasha* is one of the cruellest blows of fate in the Torah: "The chief cupbearer did not remember Joseph; he forgot him" (v. 23). Seemingly his one chance of escape to freedom is now lost. Joseph, the beloved son in his magnificent robe has become Joseph, the prisoner bereft of hope. This is as near the Torah gets to Greek tragedy. It is a tale of Joseph's hubris leading, step after step, to his nemesis. Every good thing that happens to him turns out to be only the prelude to some new and unforeseen misfortune.

Yet a mere two years later, at the beginning of the next *parasha*, we discover that all this has been leading to Joseph's supreme elevation. Pharaoh makes him viceroy over Egypt, the greatest empire of the ancient world. He gives him his own signet ring, has him dressed in royal robes and a gold chain, and has him paraded in a chariot to the acclaim of the crowds. A mere thirty years old, he has become the second most powerful man in the world. From the lowest pit he has risen to dizzying heights. He has gone from zero to hero overnight.

What is stunning about the way this story is told in the Torah is that it is constructed to lead us, as readers, in precisely the wrong direction. *Parashat Vayeshev* has the form of a Greek tragedy. *Parashat Miketz* then comes and shows us that the Torah embodies another worldview altogether. Judaism is not Athens. The Torah is not Sophocles. The human condition is not inherently tragic. Heroes are not fated to fall.

The reason is fundamental. Ancient Israel and the Greece of antiquity – the two great influences on Western civilisation – had profoundly different understandings of time and circumstance. The Greeks believed in *moira* or *ananke*, blind fate. They thought that the gods were hostile, or at best indifferent, to humankind, so there was no way of avoiding tragedy if that is what fate had decreed. Jews believed, and still believe, that God is with us as we travel through time. Sometimes we feel as if we are lost, but then we discover, as Joseph did, that He has been guiding our steps all along.

Initially Joseph had flaws in his character. He was vain about his appearance;[2] he brought his father evil reports about his brothers;[3] his narcissism led directly to the advances of Potiphar's wife.[4] But the story of which he was a part was not a Greek tragedy. By its end – the death of Joseph in the final chapter of Genesis – he had become a different human being entirely, one who forgave his brothers the crime they committed against him, the man who saved an entire region from famine and starvation, the one Jewish tradition calls "the *tzaddik*."[5]

Don't think you understand the story of your life at half-time. That is the lesson of Joseph. At the age of twenty-nine he would have been justified in thinking of his life as an abject failure: hated by his brothers, criticised by his father, sold as a slave, imprisoned on a false charge and with his one chance of freedom gone.

2. Genesis Rabba 84:7; see Rashi on Gen. 37:2.
3. Gen. 37:2, and see Genesis Rabba 84:7.
4. *Tanḥuma, Vayeshev* 8.
5. Yoma 35b.

The second half of the story shows us that Joseph's life was not like that at all. His became a tale of unprecedented success, not only politically and materially, but also morally and spiritually. He became the first person in recorded history to forgive. By saving the region from famine, he became the first in whom the promise made by God to Abraham came true: "Through you, all the families of the land will be blessed" (Gen. 12:3). There was no way of predicting how the story would end on the basis of the events narrated in *Parashat Vayeshev*. The turning point in his life was a highly improbable event that could not have been predicted but which changed all else, not just for him but for large numbers of people and for the eventual course of Jewish history. God's hand was at work, even when Joseph felt abandoned by every human being he had encountered.

We live life forward but we see the role of providence in our lives only looking back. That is the meaning of God's words to Moses, "You will see My back" (Ex. 33:23), meaning, "You will see Me only when you look back."

Joseph's story is a precise reversal of the narrative structure of Sophocles' *Oedipus*. Everything Laius and his son Oedipus do to *avert* the tragic fate announced by the oracle in fact brings it closer to fulfilment, whereas in the story of Joseph, every episode that seems to be leading to tragedy turns out in retrospect to be a necessary step to saving lives and the fulfilment of Joseph's dreams.

Judaism is the opposite of tragedy. It tells us that every bad fate can be averted (hence our prayer on the High Holy Days that "penitence, prayer, and charity avert the evil decree") – while every positive promise made by God will never be undone.[6]

Hence the life-changing idea: Despair is never justified. Even if your life has been scarred by misfortune, lacerated by pain, and your chances of happiness seem gone forever, there is still hope. The next chapter of your life can be full of blessings. You can be, in Wordsworth's lovely phrase, "surprised by joy."

Every bad thing that has happened to you thus far may be the necessary prelude to the good things that are about to happen because

---

6. Shabbat 55a.

you have been strengthened by suffering and given courage by your ability to survive. That is what we learn from the heroes of endurance from Joseph to the Holocaust survivors of today, who kept going, had faith, refused to despair, and were privileged to write a new and different chapter in the book of their lives.

Seen through the eye of faith, today's curse may be the beginning of tomorrow's blessing. That is a thought that can change a life.

Life-Changing Idea #9

Seen through the eye of faith, today's curse may be the beginning of tomorrow's blessing.

Miketz

Jews and Economics

We know that Jews have won a disproportionate number of Nobel Prizes: over 20 per cent of them from a group that represents 0.2 per cent of the world population, an over-representation of 100 to one. But the most striking disproportion is in the field of economics. The first Nobel Prize in economics was awarded in 1969. By 2017, of the seventy-nine laureates, twenty-nine were Jews; that is, over 36 per cent.

Among famous Jewish economists, one of the first was David Ricardo, inventor of the theory of comparative advantage, which Paul Samuelson called the only true and non-obvious theory in the social sciences. Then there was John von Neumann, inventor of Game Theory (creatively enlarged by Nobel Prize winner Robert Aumann). Milton Friedman developed monetary economics, Kenneth Arrow welfare economics, and Joe Stiglitz and Jeffrey Sachs, development economics. Daniel Kahneman and the late Amos Tversky created the field of behavioural economics. Garry Becker applied economic analysis to other areas of decision making, as did Richard Posner to the interplay of economics and law. To these we must add outstanding figures in economic and financial policy: Larry Summers, Alan Greenspan, Sir James Wolfensohn, Janet Yellen, Stanley Fischer, and others too numerous to mention.

It began with Joseph who, in this *parasha*, became the world's first economist. Interpreting Pharaoh's dreams, he develops a theory of trade cycles – seven fat years followed by seven lean years – a cycle that still seems approximately to hold. Joseph also intuited that when a head of state dreams about cows and ears of corn, he is probably unconsciously thinking about macro-economics. The disturbing nature of the dreams suggested that God was sending an advance warning of a "black swan,"[1] a rare phenomenon for which conventional economics is unprepared.

So, having diagnosed the problem, he immediately proceeds to a solution: Use the good years to build up resources for the lean times, a sound instance of long-term economic planning:

> Let Pharaoh appoint commissioners over the land to take a fifth of the harvest of Egypt during the seven years of abundance. They should collect all the food of these good years that are coming and store up the grain under the authority of Pharaoh, to be kept in the cities for food. This food should be held in reserve for the country, to be used during the seven years of famine that will come upon Egypt, so that the country may not be ruined by the famine. (Gen. 41:34–36)

This turned out to be life-saving advice. His later economic policies, narrated in *Parashat Vayigash* (47:11–26), are more questionable. When the people ran out of money during the lean years, Joseph told them to trade their livestock. When this too ran out, he arranged for them to sell their land to Pharaoh with the sole exception of the land belonging to the priests. The Egyptians were now, in essence, Pharaoh's serfs, paying him a tax of 20 per cent of their produce each year.

This nationalisation of livestock, labour, and land meant that power was now concentrated in the hands of Pharaoh, and the people themselves

---

1. Nassim Nicholas Taleb, *The Black Swan: The Impact of the Highly Improbable* (London: Allen Lane, 2011).

reduced to serfdom. Both of these developments would eventually be used against Joseph's own people, when a new Pharaoh arose and enslaved the Israelites. It cannot be by accident that the Torah twice uses about the Egyptians the same phrase it will later use about the Israelites: *avadim lePharo*, they have become "Pharaoh's slaves" (47:19, 25). There is already here a hint that too much economic power in the hands of the state leads to what Friedrich Hayek called "the road to serfdom"[2] and the eclipse of liberty.

So a reasonable case could be made that Joseph was the first economist. But why the predominance of Jews in economics in the modern age? I do not want to argue that Jews created capitalism. They didn't. Max Weber famously argued that it was the Protestant (primarily Calvinist) ethic that shaped "the spirit of capitalism."[3] Rodney Stark argued that it was the Catholic Church that did so, prior to the Reformation.[4] The author of the first great text of market economics, Adam Smith's *The Wealth of Nations* (1776), was a leading member of the Scottish Enlightenment whose religious views hovered between conventional Christianity and Deism. Those who have claimed a special kinship between Jews and capitalism – most notably Karl Marx and Werner Sombart – tended to like neither Jews nor capitalism.

Clearly, though, there is a strong affinity between the market economy and what is broadly known as the Judaeo-Christian ethic, because it was only in such cultures that it emerged. China, for example, led the West in almost every aspect of technology until the seventeenth century, yet it failed to generate science, a free economy, or an industrial revolution, and fell far behind until recent times. What was it about biblical values that proved so fruitful for economic thought, institutions, and growth?

The Harvard historian and economist David Landes offered insight in his magisterial work *The Wealth and Poverty of Nations*.[5] First

---

2. Friedrich Hayek, *The Road to Serfdom* (Chicago: University of Chicago Press, 1946).
3. Max Weber, *The Protestant Ethic and the Spirit of Capitalism* (London: G. Allen & Unwin, 1930).
4. Rodney Stark, *The Victory of Reason: How Christianity Led to Freedom, Capitalism and Western Success* (New York: Random House, 2007).
5. David Landes, *The Wealth and Poverty of Nations* (London: Little, Brown and Co., 1998), 45–59.

is the biblical insistence on property rights. He quotes Moses' words during the Koraḥ revolt: "I have not taken so much as a donkey from them, nor have I wronged any one of them" (Num. 16:15). Likewise, the prophet Samuel rhetorically asks the people who have come asking for a king: "Whose ox have I taken, or whose ass have I taken?" (I Sam. 12:3). Landes says that these remarks set the Israelites apart from any other culture of the time. Elsewhere, the king's right to appropriate other people's property was taken for granted.[6] The philosopher John Locke understood that private property rights are an essential element of a free society.

A second feature was Judaism's respect for the dignity of labour. God saved Noah from the flood, but Noah had to build the ark. Third was the Judaic sense of linear time: time not as a series of cycles in which everything eventually returns to the way it was, but rather as an arena of change, development, and progress. We are so familiar with these ideas – they form the bedrock of Western culture – that we are not always aware that they are not human universals. Jonathan Haidt calls them WEIRD: that is, they belong to societies that are Western, Educated, Industrialised, Rich, and Democratic.[7]

To my mind, the most decisive single factor – the great break of Judaism from the ancient world of magic, mystery, and myth – was the deconsecration of nature that followed from the fact that God created nature by an act of will, and by making us in His image, gave us too the creative power of will. That meant that for Jews, holiness lies not in the way the world is but in the way it ought to be. Poverty, disease, famine, injustice, and the exploitation of the powerless by the powerful are not the will of God. They may be part of human nature, but we have the power to rise above nature.[8] God wants us not to accept but to heal, to

---

6. To be sure, a king of Israel was entitled to appropriate land for national necessities, but not for private gain. Hence Elijah's denunciation of Ahab's seizure of Naboth's vineyard (I Kings 21). For a fine account of the halakhic and conceptual issues involved, see "Din Melekh BeYisrael" in *Kol Kitvei Maharatz Chajes* (Jerusalem, 1958), I:43–49.

7. Jonathan Haidt, *The Righteous Mind: Why Good People Are Divided by Politics and Religion* (London: Penguin, 2013).

8. See above on *Parashat Toledot*.

cure, to prevent. So Jews have tended to become, out of all proportion to their numbers, lawyers fighting injustice, doctors fighting disease, teachers fighting ignorance, economists fighting poverty, and (especially in modern Israel) agricultural technologists finding new ways to grow food in environments where it has never grown before.

All of this is brilliantly portrayed in this *parasha*. First Joseph diagnoses the problem. There will be a famine lasting seven years. It is what he does next that is world-changing. He sees this not as a fate to be endured but as a problem to be solved. Then, without fuss, he solves it, saving a whole region from death by starvation.

What can be changed need not be endured. Human suffering is not a fate to be borne, but a challenge to be overcome. This is Joseph's life-changing idea. What can be healed is not holy. God does not want us to accept poverty and pain, but to cure them.

Life-Changing Idea #10

What can be healed is not holy. God does not want us to accept poverty and pain but to cure them.

Vayigash

The First Psychotherapist

The phrase "Jewish thinker" may mean two very different things. It may mean a thinker who just happens to be Jewish by birth or descent – a Jewish physicist, for example – or it may refer to someone who has contributed specifically to Jewish thought: like Judah Halevi or Maimonides.

The interesting question is: Is there a third kind of Jewish thinker, one who contributes to the universe of knowledge, but does so in a recognisably Jewish way? The answer to this is never straightforward, yet we instinctively feel that there is such a thing. To give an analogy: There is often something recognisably Jewish about a certain kind of humour. Ruth Wisse has interesting things to say about it in her book, *No Joke*.[1] So does Peter Berger in his *Redeeming Laughter*.[2] Humour is universal, but it speaks in different accents in different cultures.

---

1. Ruth Wisse, *No Joke: Making Jewish Humor* (Princeton: Princeton University Press, 2013).
2. Peter Berger, *Redeeming Laughter: The Comic Dimension of Human Experience* (Boston: De Gruyter, 2014).

I believe that something similar applies to psychoanalysis and psychotherapy. So many of the early practitioners of psychoanalysis, with the marked exception of Jung, were Jewish that it became known in Nazi Germany as the "Jewish science." I have argued – though my views on this have been challenged – to the contrary, that by taking the Greek myth of Oedipus as one of his key models, Freud developed a tragic view of the human condition that is more Hellenistic than Jewish.[3]

By contrast, three of the most significant post-war psychotherapists were not merely Jewish by birth but profoundly Jewish in their approach to the human soul. Viktor Frankl, a survivor of Auschwitz, developed on the basis of his experiences there an approach he called logotherapy, based on "man's search for meaning."[4] Though the Nazis took away almost every vestige of humanity from those they consigned to the death factories, Frankl argued that there was one thing they could never take away from their prisoners: the freedom to decide how to respond.

Aaron T. Beck was the founder of what is widely regarded as one of the most effective forms of psychotherapy: Cognitive Behavioural Therapy.[5] Among patients suffering from depression, he found that their feelings were often linked to highly negative thoughts about themselves, the world, and the future. By getting them to think more realistically, he found that their mood tended to improve.

Martin Seligman is the founder of Positive Psychology, which aims not just to treat depression but actively to promote what he calls "authentic happiness" and "learned optimism."[6] Depression, Seligman argued, is often linked to pessimism, which comes from interpreting

---

3. There were undeniably Jewish elements in Freud's work, most notably the fact that though he himself called psychoanalysis the "speaking cure," it is in fact the "listening cure," and listening is a key feature of Jewish spirituality.
4. Frankl wrote many books, but the most famous is *Man's Search for Meaning* (Boston: Beacon Press, 2017), one of the most influential works of the twentieth century.
5. See Aaron T. Beck, *Cognitive Therapy and the Emotional Disorders* (London: Penguin, 1989). See also his *Prisoners of Hate: The Cognitive Basis of Anger, Hostility and Violence* (New York: HarperCollins, 1999).
6. Martin Seligman, *Authentic Happiness* (New York: Free Press, 2002); *Learned Optimism* (New York: Vintage Books, 2008).

events in a particular kind of way that he calls "learned helplessness." Pessimists tend to see misfortune as permanent ("It's always like this"), personal ("It's my fault"), and pervasive ("I always get things wrong"). This leaves them feeling that the bad they suffer is inevitable and beyond their control. Optimists look at things differently. For them, negative events are temporary, the result of outside factors, and exceptions rather than the rule. So, within limits,[7] you can unlearn pessimism, and the result is greater happiness, health, and success.

What links all three thinkers is their belief that, first of all, there is always more than one possible interpretation of what happens to us; secondly, we can choose between different interpretations; and finally, the way we think shapes the way we feel. This gives all three a marked resemblance to a particular kind of Jewish thought, namely Chabad (Ḥabad) Ḥasidut, as developed by the first Lubavitcher Rebbe, Rabbi Schneur Zalman of Liadi (1745–1812). The word Ḥabad stands for the initial letters of the three intellectual virtues, *ḥokhma*, *bina*, and *daat*, "wisdom, understanding, and knowledge," which influence the more emotional attributes of *ḥesed*, *gevura*, and *tiferet*, "kindness, self-restraint, and beauty or emotional balance." Unlike the other hasidic movements, which emphasised the emotional life, Chabad Hasidism focused on the power of the intellect to shape emotion. It was, in its way, an anticipation of cognitive behavioural therapy.

Its origins, however, lie far earlier. In the previous *parasha* I argued that Joseph was the first economist. Here I want to suggest that he was the first cognitive therapist. He was the first to understand the concept of reframing, that is, seeing the negative events of his life in a new way, thereby liberating himself from depression and learned helplessness.

The moment at which he does so comes when, moved by Judah's passionate plea to let Benjamin return home to their father Jacob, he finally reveals himself to his brothers:

I am your brother Joseph, whom you sold into Egypt. And now, do not be distressed and do not be angry with yourselves for

7. Seligman admits that there are things about us that we can't change, but there is much about us that we can. See Martin Seligman, *What You Can Change and What You Can't* (London: Nicolas Brealey, 2007).

selling me here, because it was to save lives that God sent me ahead of you. For two years now there has been famine in the land, and for the next five years there will be no ploughing and reaping. But God sent me ahead of you to preserve for you a remnant on earth and to save your lives by a great deliverance. So then, it was not you who sent me here, but God. (Gen. 45:4–8)

Note what Joseph is doing here. He is reframing events so that the brothers will not have to live under an unbearable burden of guilt for having sold Joseph as a slave and deceived their father, causing him years of undiminished grief. But he is only able to do so for them because he has already done so for himself. When it happened, we cannot be sure. Was Joseph aware, all along, that the many blows of misfortune he suffered were all part of a divine plan, or did he only realise this when he was taken from prison to interpret Pharaoh's dreams, and then made viceroy of Egypt?

The text is silent on this point, but it is suggestive. More than any other character in the Torah, Joseph attributes all his achievements to God. This allows him to do what, in secular terms, Frankl, Beck, and Seligman would all have advised him to do if he had been one of their patients: think of a mission he was being called on to fulfil (Frankl), reinterpret misfortune as possibility (Beck), and see the positive elements of his situation (Seligman). Not only was Joseph freed from a physical prison, he freed himself from an emotional prison, namely resentment towards his brothers. He now saw his life not in terms of a family drama of sibling rivalry, but as part of a larger movement of history as shaped by divine providence.

That is what makes me think that the work of Frankl, Beck, and Seligman is Jewish in a way that Freudian psychoanalysis is not. At the heart of Judaism is the idea of human freedom. We are not prisoners of events but active shapers of them. To be sure, we may be influenced by unconscious drives, as Freud thought, but we can rise above them by "habits of the heart" that hone and refine our personality.

Joseph's life shows that we can defeat tragedy by our ability to see our life not just as a sequence of unfair events inflicted on us by others, but also as a series of divinely intended moves, each of which brings us closer to a situation in which we can do what God wants us to do.

We can't all be Joseph, but thanks to Rabbi Schneur Zalman of Liadi in spiritual terms, and to Frankl, Beck, and Seligman in secular ones, we can learn what it is to change the way we feel by changing the way we think, and the best way of doing so is to ask, "What does this bad experience enable me to do that I could not have done otherwise?" That can be life-transforming.

Life-Changing Idea #11

We are not prisoners of events but their active shapers.

What It Takes to Forgive

Joseph forgives. That, as I have argued above, was a turning point in history. For this was the first recorded act of forgiveness in literature.

It is important here to make a key distinction between forgiveness, which is characteristic of the Judaeo-Christian tradition, and the appeasement of anger, which is a human universal. People are constantly harming others, who then become angry, indignant, and "disrespected." If the offender does nothing to turn away their wrath, they will take revenge.

Revenge is one way of restoring the social order, but it is a very costly and dangerous one because it can lead to a circle of retaliation that has no natural stopping point.[1] One of my family offends one of your family (think of Montagues and Capulets, or Corleones and Tattaglias), so one of your family takes revenge, for which one of my family must retaliate for the sake of family honour, and so it goes, sometimes

---

1. Rene Girard, in *Violence and the Sacred* (Baltimore, MD: Johns Hopkins Press, 1977), argues that religion was born in the attempt to find a way to stop cycles of retaliation and revenge.

for generations. The cost is often so great that it is in everyone's interest to find a way of stopping the cycle. That is universal. It exists in every human group, and some non-human ones as well.[2]

The general way of bringing this kind of conflict to an end is what the ancient Greeks called *sungnome*, often translated as "forgiveness," but which actually – as David Konstan shows in his masterly study, *Before Forgiveness*[3] – means something like pardon, appeasement, a willingness to make allowances, or accept an excuse, or grant an indulgence. The end result is that the victim forgoes revenge. The offender does not atone. Instead he or she makes some kind of plea in mitigation: I couldn't help it; it wasn't that bad; it's human nature; I was carried away. In addition the offender must show, in words or body language, some form of humility or submission.

One classic example in the Torah is Jacob's conduct towards Esau when they meet again after more than twenty years, during which time Jacob had been away in the home of Laban. He knew that Esau felt wronged by him and had declared his intention to take revenge after their father Isaac died. That is why Jacob fled in the first place. When they meet again, Jacob does not mention the earlier incident. But he does attempt to appease[4] Esau by sending him an enormous gift of livestock, and by abasing himself, bowing down to him seven times, and calling him "my lord," and himself "your servant" (Gen. 32). For his part, Esau does not mention the earlier episode, whether because he had forgotten it, or it no longer rankled with him, or because he was mollified by Jacob's self-abasement. This was not remorse and forgiveness, but submission and appeasement.

---

2. See Frans de Waal, *Peacemaking among Primates* (Cambridge, MA: Harvard University Press, 1989).

3. David Konstan, *Before Forgiveness: The Origins of a Moral Idea* (Cambridge: Cambridge University Press, 2010).

4. Note that the word Jacob uses to himself (Gen. 32:21) comes from the verb K-P-R which will later be used in Leviticus to mean atonement, and is the source of the phrase Yom Kippur. It means literally to "cover over." It is what Noah does when he covers the ark with pitch (Gen. 6:14). It also means a ransom (Num. 35:32) such as might be paid to compensate a family for the murder of one of its members, a payment forbidden in Jewish law.

What Joseph does towards his brothers is different. When he first reveals himself to them, he says, "And now, do not be distressed and do not be angry with yourselves for selling me here, because it was to save lives that God sent me ahead of you" (Gen. 45:5). This sounds like forgiveness, but, as this *parasha* makes clear, it is not necessarily so. The word "forgiveness" is not used. And the brothers may well have assumed that, as in the case of Esau, Joseph intended to take revenge but not during the lifetime of their father. That is what provokes the drama at the end of this *parasha*: When Joseph's brothers saw that their father was dead, they said, "What if Joseph holds a grudge against us and pays us back for all the wrongs we did to him?" So they sent word to Joseph, saying,

> Your father left these instructions before he died: "This is what you are to say to Joseph: Please forgive (*sa*) your brothers' wrong and the sin they committed in treating you so badly." Now please forgive the sins of the servants of the God of your father. (Gen. 50:15–17)

This was Joseph's response:

> Joseph said to them, "Don't be afraid. Am I in the place of God? You intended to harm me, but God intended it for good to accomplish what is now being done, the saving of many lives. So then, don't be afraid. I will provide for you and your children." And he reassured them and spoke kindly to them. (vv. 19–21)

This is forgiveness. Joseph does not use the word, but he makes it clear that he forgoes all thought of revenge. What is happening here and why did it not happen in other cultures? This is one of the most fascinating features of Judaism, and why it eventually made such a difference to the world.

Note what has to happen for forgiveness to be born. First, Joseph engages in an elaborate plan, hiding his identity, to make sure the brothers were capable of remorse and atonement. This happens on their first encounter in Egypt, when he accuses them of being spies, and they say in his presence – not knowing that he could understand them – "Surely we are guilty because of our brother. We saw how distressed he was when he pleaded with us for his life, but we would not listen; that's why this distress has come upon us" (42:21). They know they have done wrong. They acknowledge their guilt.

Second, Joseph arranges a trial that will test whether Judah, the brother who proposed selling him into slavery in the first place, is indeed a changed person. He has Benjamin brought before him on a false charge, and is about take him as his slave when Judah intervenes and offers to become a slave in his place so that Benjamin can go free. This is what the Sages and Maimonides defined as complete repentance, that is, you have changed to the extent that you are now a different person. These two elements tell us what has changed in the brothers so that they, the wrongdoers, can be forgiven.

There is a change in Joseph too, as we noted in *Parashat Vayigash*. He has reframed his life, so that the entire story of his relationship with his brothers has now become utterly secondary to the drama of divine providence that is still unfolding. As he explains: "You intended to harm me, but God intended it for good." This is what allows the victim, Joseph, to forgive.

These, though, are details. What is absolutely fundamental is that Judaism represents, for the first time in history, a morality of guilt rather than shame. In our essay on *Parashat Lekh Lekha* we explored some of the elements that made it possible. We discussed the difference between tradition-directed cultures and – what the call to Abraham initiates – inner-directed ones. Tradition-directed individuals, when they break the rules, feel shame. Inner-directed personalities feel guilt.

In *Parashat Ekev*, below, we discuss the difference between cultures of the eye and of the ear. Visual cultures are almost always shame cultures. Shame is what you feel when you imagine other people seeing what you are doing. The first instinct when you feel shame is to try to hide or to wish you were invisible.[5] In cultures of hearing, however, morality is represented by an inner voice, the voice of guilt that you cannot hide from even if you are invisible to the world.

---

5. That is what, I suggest, was at stake in the Garden of Eden, which is all about shame and hiding. Adam and Eve followed their eyes rather than their ears.

The key difference between the two is that in shame cultures, wrongdoing is like a stain on the person. Hence the only way to be rehabilitated is to have the stain covered up somehow (the meaning, as we noted, of the verb K-P-R). You do this by placating the victim of your wrong so that in effect he "turns a blind eye" to what you did. His resentment, indignation, and desire for revenge have been appeased.

In guilt cultures, however, there is a fundamental distinction between the person and his or her acts. It was the act that was wrong, not the person. That is what makes forgiveness possible. I forgive you because, when you admit you did wrong, express remorse, and do all you can to make amends, especially when I see that, given the opportunity (as was Judah) to repeat the crime, you do not do so because you have changed, then I see that you have distanced yourself from your deed. Forgiveness means I fundamentally reaffirm your worth as a person, despite the fact that we both know your act was wrong.[6]

Forgiveness exists in righteousness-and-guilt cultures. It does not exist in honour-and-shame cultures like those of ancient Greece and pre-Christian Rome.

Contemporary culture in the West, often thought by secularists to be morally superior to the ethics of the Hebrew Bible, is in fact – for good or bad – a regression to pre-Christian Greece and Rome. That is why, nowadays, people who are found to have done wrong are publicly shamed. Examples are not necessary: they abound in every day's news. In a shame culture, the main thing to do is not to be found out, because once you are, there is no way back. There is no place in such a culture for forgiveness. At best you seek to appease. As in ancient Greece, the culprit argues, "I couldn't help it; it wasn't that bad; it's human nature; I was carried away." They undergo some ritual of self-abasement. Eventually

---

6. Note that in certain cultures, forgiveness does not require remorse, atonement, and the like. Maimonides himself says (*Hilkhot Deot* 6:9) that if you regard the person who wronged you as incapable of handling criticism, then you may forgive him unilaterally. Note however that this kind of forgiveness does not signal that you reaffirm the moral worth of the person you forgive. To the contrary, you regard him as beneath contempt. Judaism seems always to have known this. The Christian theologian who understood it best was Dietrich Bonhoeffer, who called it "cheap grace."

they hope, not that people will forgive but that they will forget. This is an ugly kind of culture.

Which is why Judaism remains the eternal alternative. What matters is not outward appearances but the inner voice. And when we do wrong, as we all do, there is a way forward: to confess, express remorse, atone, make amends, and, like Judah, change. To know that however wrong our deeds, "the soul You gave me is pure," and that if we work hard enough on ourselves, we can be forgiven, is to inhabit a culture of grace and hope. And that is a life-changing idea.

Life-Changing Idea #12

Judaism allows us to inhabit a culture of grace and hope. If we work hard enough on ourselves, we can be forgiven.

Exodus
שמות

Shemot

God Loves Those Who Argue

I have become increasingly concerned about the assault on free speech taking place throughout the West, particularly in university campuses.[1] This is being done in the name of "safe space," that is, space in which you are protected against hearing views which might cause you distress, "trigger warnings,"[2] and "micro-aggressions" – namely, any remark that someone might find offensive even if no offence is meant.

So far has this gone that at the beginning of the 2017 academic year, students at an Oxford College banned the presence of representatives of the Christian Union on the grounds that some might find their

---

1. I first wrote about this in my book *The Home We Build Together* (London: Continuum, 2007), in the chapter entitled "The Defeat of Freedom in the Name of Freedom," 37–48. The situation has become significantly worse since then.
2. See on this, Mick Hume, *Trigger Warning: Is the Fear of Being Offensive Killing Free Speech?* (London: William Collins, 2016).

presence alienating and offensive.[3] Increasingly, speakers with controversial views are being disinvited. The number of such incidents on American college campuses rose from six in 2000 to forty-four in 2016.[4]

Undoubtedly this entire movement was undertaken for the highest of motives, to protect the feelings of the vulnerable. That is a legitimate ethical concern. Jewish law goes to extremes in condemning *lashon hara*, hurtful or derogatory speech, and the Sages were careful to use what they called *lashon sagi nahor*, euphemism, to avoid language that people might find offensive.

But a safe space is not one in which you silence dissenting views. To the contrary: It is one in which you give a respectful hearing to views opposed to your own, knowing that your views too will be listened to respectfully. That is academic freedom, and it is essential to a free society.[5] As George Orwell said, "If liberty means anything at all, it means the right to tell people what they do not want to hear."[6]

John Stuart Mill likewise wrote that one of the worst offences against freedom is "to stigmatise those who hold the contrary opinion as bad and immoral men."[7] That is happening today in institutions that are supposed to be the guardians of academic freedom. We are coming perilously close to what Julian Benda called, in 1927, "the treason of the intellectuals." He claimed that academic life had been degraded to the extent that it had allowed itself to become an arena for "the intellectual organisation of political hatreds."[8]

What is striking about Judaism, and we see this starkly in this *parasha*, is that argument and the hearing of contrary views is of the

3. See http://www.telegraph.co.uk/education/2017/10/10/oxford-college-bans-harmful-christian-union-freshers-fair.
4. Jean M. Twenge, *iGen* (New York: Atria, 2017), 253.
5. I salute the University of Chicago, Princeton, and other universities that have taken a strong stand in defence of free speech on campus; and Professor Jonathan Haidt and his colleagues at the Heterodox Academy, founded to promote intellectual diversity in academic life.
6. From Orwell's proposed preface to *Animal Farm*, first published in the *Times Literary Supplement* on September 15, 1972.
7. John Stuart Mill, *On Liberty and Other Essays* (Oxford: Oxford University Press, 1998), ch. 2.
8. Julian Benda, *The Treason of the Intellectuals* (New Jersey: Transaction, 2007), 27.

essence of religious life. Moses argues with God. That is one of the most striking things about him. He argues with Him on their first encounter at the burning bush. Four times he resists God's call to lead the Israelites to freedom, until God finally gets angry with him (Ex. 3:1–4:7). More significantly, at the end of the *parasha* he says to God:

> Lord, why have You brought trouble on this people? Why did You send me? Since I came to Pharaoh to speak in Your name, he has brought trouble on this people, and You have not rescued Your people at all. (5:22–23)

This is extraordinary language for a human being to use to God. But Moses was not the first to do so. The first was Abraham, who said, on hearing of God's plan to destroy the cities of the plain, "Shall the Judge of all the earth not do justice?" (Gen. 18:25).

Similarly, Jeremiah, posing the age-old question of why bad things happen to good people and good things to bad people, asked: "Why does the way of the wicked prosper? Why do all the faithless live at ease?" (Jer. 12:1). In the same vein, Habakkuk challenged God: "Why do You tolerate the treacherous? Why are You silent while the wicked swallow up those more righteous than themselves?" (Hab. 1:13). Job who challenges God's justice is vindicated in the book that bears his name, while his friends who defended divine justice are said not to have spoken correctly (Job 42:7–8). Heaven, in short, is not a safe space in the current meaning of the phrase. To the contrary: God loves those who argue with Him – so it seems from Tanakh.

Equally striking is the fact that the Sages continued the tradition and gave it a name: argument for the sake of Heaven,[9] defined as debate for the sake of truth as opposed to victory.[10] The result is that Judaism is, perhaps uniquely, a civilisation all of whose canonical texts are anthologies of arguments. Midrash operates on the principle that there are "seventy faces" to Torah and thus that every verse is open to multiple interpretations. The Mishna is full of paragraphs in

9. Mishna Avot 5:17.
10. Meiri on Avot ad loc.

the form of "Rabbi X says this, while Rabbi Y says that." The Talmud says in the name of God Himself, about the conflicting views of the schools of Hillel and Shammai, that "these and those are the words of the living God."[11]

A standard edition of *Mikraot Gedolot* consists of the biblical text surrounded by multiple commentaries and even commentaries on the commentaries. The standard edition of the Babylonian Talmud has the text surrounded by the often conflicting views of Rashi and the Tosafists. Moses Maimonides, writing his masterpiece of Jewish law, the *Mishneh Torah*, took the almost unprecedented step of presenting only the halakhic conclusion without the accompanying arguments. The ironic but predictable result was that the *Mishneh Torah* was eventually surrounded by an endless array of commentaries and arguments. In Judaism there is something holy about argument.

Why so? First, because only God can see the totality of truth. For us, mere mortals who can see only fragments of the truth at any one time, there is an irreducible multiplicity of perspectives. We see reality now one way, now another. The Torah provides us with a dramatic example in its first two chapters, which give us two creation accounts, both true, from different vantage points. The different voices of priest and prophet, Hillel and Shammai, philosopher and mystic, historian and poet, each capture something essential about the spiritual life. Even within a single genre, the Sages noted that "no two prophets prophesy in the same style."[12] Torah is a conversation scored for many voices.

Second, because justice presupposes the principle that in Roman law is called *audi alteram partem,* "hear the other side." That is why God wants an Abraham, a Moses, a Jeremiah, and a Job to challenge Him, sometimes to plead for mercy or, as in the case of Moses at the end of this *parasha,* to urge Him to act swiftly in defence of His people.[13] Both the case for the prosecution and for the defence must be heard if justice is to be done and seen to be done.

---

11. Eiruvin 13b.
12. Sanhedrin 89a.
13. See Pesaḥim 87a–b for a remarkable passage in which God criticises the prophet Hosea for not coming to the defence of his people.

The pursuit of truth and justice requires the freedom to disagree. Netziv (Rabbi Naftali Zvi Yehudah Berlin, 1816–1893, dean of Volozhyn Yeshiva, Russia) argued that it was the prohibition of disagreement that was the sin of the builders of Babel.[14] What we need, therefore, is not "safe spaces" but rather, civility, that is to say, giving a respectful hearing to views with which we disagree. In one of its loveliest passages the Talmud tells us that the views of the school of Hillel became law "because they were pleasant and did not take offence, and because they taught the views of their opponents as well as their own, indeed they taught the views of their opponents before their own."[15]

And where do we learn this from? From God Himself, who chose as His prophets people who were prepared to argue with Heaven for the sake of Heaven in the name of justice and truth.

When you learn to listen to views different from your own, realising that they are not threatening but enlarging, then you have discovered the life-changing idea of argument for the sake of Heaven.

Life-Changing Idea #13

When you learn to listen to views different from your own, realising that they are not threatening but enlarging, then you have discovered the life-changing idea of argument for the sake of Heaven.

---

14. *Haamek Davar* on Gen. 11:4.
15. Eiruvin 13b.

Va'era

Free Will – Use It or Lose It

In *Parashat Va'era* we read for the first time, not of Pharaoh hardening his heart but of God doing so: "I will harden Pharaoh's heart," said God to Moses, "and multiply My signs and wonders in the land of Egypt" (Ex. 7:3). And so indeed we find in the sixth plague, boils (9:12), the eighth, locusts (10:1, 20), and the tenth, the firstborn (11:10). In each case the hardening is attributed to God.

Hence the problem that troubled the Sages and later commentators: If God was the cause and Pharaoh merely His passive vehicle, what was his sin? He had no choice, therefore no responsibility, therefore no culpability. The commentators give a broad range of answers. One: Pharaoh's loss of free will during the last five plagues was a punishment for his obstinacy in the first five, where he acted freely.[1] Two: The relevant verb, CH-Z-K, does not mean "to harden" but "to strengthen." God was

---

1. This is roughly the position of Maimonides, who argues that after the first five refusals, God "closed the door of repentance" to Pharaoh. See *Mishneh Torah, Hilkhot Teshuva* 5:2–3, 6:1–3.

not taking away Pharaoh's free will but, to the contrary, preserving it in the face of the overwhelming disasters that were hitting Egypt.[2] Three: God is a partner in all human action, but we only usually attribute an act to God if it seems inexplicable in ordinary human terms. Pharaoh acted freely throughout, but it was only during the last five plagues that his behaviour was so strange that it was attributed to God.[3]

Note how reluctant the commentators were to take the text at face value – rightly so, because free will is one of the fundamental beliefs of Judaism. Maimonides explains why: If we had no free will there would be, he says, no point to the commands and prohibitions, since we would behave as we were predestined to, regardless of what the law is. Nor would there be any justice in reward or punishment since neither the righteous nor the wrongdoer is free to be other than what they are.[4]

So the problem is an ancient one.[5] But it has become much more salient in modern times because of the sheer accumulation of challenges to the belief in human freedom. Marx said history is formed by the play of economic forces. Freud argued that we are what we are because of unconscious drives. Neo-Darwinians say that however we rationalise our behaviour, we do what we do because people who behaved this way in the past survived to hand on their genes to future generations. Most recently, neuroscientists have shown, using fMRI scans, that in some cases our brain registers a decision up to seven seconds before we are consciously aware of it.[6]

All of this is interesting and important, but contemporary secularists usually fail to see what the ancient Sages knew: If we genuinely lack free will, our entire sense of what it is to be human will crumble into dust. There is a glaring contradiction at the heart of our culture. On the one hand, secularists believe that nothing should constrain our freedom to choose to do whatever we want to do, or be whatever we want to be, so long as we do not harm others. Their supreme value is autonomous

2. This is the view of Sforno on Ex. 7:3.
3. This is the view of Samuel David Luzzatto on Ex. 7:3.
4. Maimonides, *Mishneh Torah, Hilkhot Teshuva* 5:4.
5. It was raised by Aristotle also.
6. See https://www.nature.com/news/2008/080411/full/news.2008.751.html.

choice. On the other hand, secularists tell us that human freedom does not exist. Why then should we invoke freedom to choose as a value if it is, according to science, an illusion?

If hard determinism is true, there is no reason to honour liberty or create a free society. To the contrary: We should embrace Aldous Huxley's *Brave New World*, where children are conceived and hatched in laboratories, and adults programmed to stay happy by a regime of drugs and pleasure. We should implement the scenario of Anthony Burgess' *The Clockwork Orange*, in which criminals are reformed by brain surgery or conditioning. If freedom does not exist, why be bothered by the addictive nature of computer games and social media? Why prefer genuine reality to virtual reality? It was Nietzsche who rightly observed that the greater our scientific achievements, the lower our view of the human person. No longer the image of God, we have become mere incarnated algorithms.

The truth is that the more we understand about the human brain, the better able we are to describe what free action really is. At present, scientists distinguish between the amygdala, the most primitive part of the brain, conditioned to sensitise us to potential danger; the limbic system, sometimes called the "social brain," which is responsible for much of our emotional life; and the prefrontal cortex, which is analytical and capable of dispassionately weighing the consequences of alternative choices.[7] The tensions between these three form the arena within which personal freedom is won or lost.

Patterns of behaviour are shaped by neural pathways connecting different parts of the brain, but not all of them are good for us. So, for instance, we might turn to drugs, or binge eating, or thrill-seeking to distract us from some of the unhappy chemicals – fears and anxieties, for instance – that are also part of the architecture of the brain. The more often we do so, the more myelin gets wrapped around the pathway, and the more rapid and instinctive the behaviour. So the more often we behave in certain ways, the harder it is to break the habit and create a new and different pathway. To do so requires the acquisition of new

---

7. The amygdala and the limbic system are what the Zohar and other Jewish mystical texts call the *nefesh habehemit*, the "animal soul" within us.

habits, acted on consistently for an extended period of time. Current scientific thinking suggests that a minimum of sixty-six days is needed to form a new habit.[8]

So we now have a scientific way of explaining the hardening taking place in Pharaoh's heart. Having established a pattern of response to the first five plagues, he would find it progressively more difficult at every level – neuro-scientifically, psychologically, and politically – to change. The same is true of every bad habit and political decision. Almost all our structures, mental and social, tend to reinforce previous patterns of behaviour. So our freedom diminishes every time we fail to exercise it.

If so, then this *parasha* and contemporary science tell the same story: Freedom is not a given, nor is it an absolute. We have to work for it. We acquire it slowly in stages, and we can lose it, as Pharaoh lost his, and as drug addicts, workaholics, and people addicted to computer games lose theirs. In one of the most famous opening lines in all literature, Jean-Jacques Rousseau wrote, at the beginning of *The Social Contract*, that "man is born free and everywhere he is in chains." In fact, the opposite is true. Our early character is determined partly by DNA – the genetic heritage of our parents, partly by our home and upbringing, partly by our friends,[9] and partly by the surrounding culture. We are not born free. We have to work hard to achieve freedom.

That takes rituals, whose repeated performance creates new neural pathways and new rapid-response behaviour. It requires a certain calibrated distance from the surrounding culture, if we are not to be swept away by social fads and fashions that seem liberating now but destructive in retrospect. It needs a mental mindset that pauses before any significant action and asks, "Should I do this? May I do this? What rules of conduct should I bring to bear?" It involves an internalised narrative of identity, so that we can ask of any course of action, "Is this who I am and what I stand for?"

---

8. One easily accessible recent book on the subject is Loretta Graziano Breunin, *Habits of a Happy Brain: Retrain Your Brain to Boost Your Serotonin, Dopamine, Oxytocin, & Endorphin Levels* (Avon, MA: Adams Media, 2016).

9. See Judith Harris, *The Nurture Assumption* (New York: Free Press, 2009).

It is no accident that the elements listed in the previous paragraph are all prominent features of Judaism, which turns out to be an ongoing seminar in willpower and impulse control. Now that we are beginning to understand the plasticity of the brain, we know at least a little of the neuroscience that lies behind the ability to overcome bad habits and addictions. Keeping Shabbat, for example, has the power to liberate us and our children from smartphone addiction and all that goes with it. The religion whose first festival, Pesaḥ, celebrates collective freedom, gives us, in its rituals, the skills we need for personal freedom.

Freedom is less a gift than an achievement. Even a Pharaoh, the most powerful man in the ancient world, could lose it. Even a nation of slaves could, with the help of God, acquire it. Never take freedom for granted. It needs a hundred small acts of self-control daily, which is what halakha, Jewish law, is all about.

Freedom is a muscle that needs to be exercised: use it or lose it. That is a life-transforming idea.

Life-Changing Idea #14

Freedom is an achievement. It is a muscle that needs to be exercised daily: use it or lose it.

Bo

The Story We Tell

It remains one of the most counterintuitive passages in all of religious literature. Moses is addressing the Israelites just days before their release. They have been exiles for 210 years. After an initial period of affluence and ease, they have been oppressed, enslaved, and their male children killed in an act of slow genocide. Now, after signs and wonders, and a series of plagues that have brought the greatest empire of the ancient world to its knees, they are about to go free.

Yet Moses does not talk about freedom, or the land flowing with milk and honey, or the journey they will have to undertake through the desert. Instead, three times, he turns to the distant future, when the journey is complete and the people – free at last – are in their own land. And what he talks about is not the land itself, or the society they will have to build, or even the demands and responsibilities of freedom.[1]

Instead, he talks about education, specifically about the duty of parents to their children. He speaks about the questions children may

---

1. That, of course, is a primary theme of the book of Deuteronomy.

ask when the epic events that are about to happen are, at best, a distant memory. He tells the Israelites to do what Jews have done from then to now. Tell your children the story. Do it in the maximally effective way. Re-enact the drama of exile and exodus, slavery and freedom. Get your children to ask questions. Make sure that you tell the story as your own, not as some dry account of history. Say that the way you live and the ceremonies you observe are "because of what God did for me" – not my ancestors but me. Make it vivid, make it personal, and make it live.

He says this not once but three times:

> It shall be that when you come to the land which God will give you as He said, and you observe this ceremony, and your children say to you, "What does this service mean to you?" you shall say, "It is a Passover sacrifice to the Lord, who passed over the houses of the Israelites in Egypt when He struck the Egyptians and spared our homes." (Ex. 12:25–27)

> On that day you shall tell your child, "It is because of what the Lord did for me when I came out of Egypt." (13:8)

> In the future, when your child asks you, "What is this?" you shall tell him, "With a mighty hand, the Lord brought us out from Egypt, from the land of slavery." (13:14)

Why was this the most important thing he could do in this intense moment of redemption? Because freedom is the work of a nation; nations need identity, identity needs memory, and memory is encoded in the stories we tell. Without narrative, there is no memory, and without memory, we have no identity. The most powerful link between the generations is the tale of those who came before us – a tale that becomes ours, and that we hand on as a sacred heritage to those who will come after us. We are the story we tell ourselves about ourselves, and identity begins in the story parents tell their children.

That narrative provides the answer to the three fundamental questions every reflective individual must ask at some stage in their lives: Who am I? Why am I here? How then shall I live? There are many answers to these questions, but the Jewish ones are: I am a member of the people whom God rescued from slavery to freedom. I am here to build a society that honours the freedom of others, not just my own. And I must live in conscious knowledge that freedom is the gift of God, honoured by keeping His covenant of law and love.

Twice in the history of the West this fact was forgotten, or ignored, or rebelled against. In the seventeenth and eighteenth centuries, there was a determined effort to create a world without identities. This was the project called the Enlightenment. It was a noble dream. To it we owe many developments whose value is beyond question and that we must strive to preserve. However, one aspect of it failed and was bound to fail: the attempt to live without identity.

The argument went like this. Identity throughout the Middle Ages was based on religion. But religion had for centuries led to war between Christians and Muslims. Then, following the Reformation, it led to war between Christian and Christian, Protestant and Catholic. Therefore, to abolish war one had to move beyond identity. Identities are particular. Therefore, let us worship only the things that are universal: reason and observation, philosophy and science. Let us have systems, not stories. Then we will become one humanity, like the world before Babel. As Schiller put it, and Beethoven set to music in the last movement of the Ninth Symphony: *Alle Menschen werden Brüder,* "All men will be brothers."

It cannot be done, at least as humanity is presently constituted. The reaction, when it came, was fierce and disastrous. The nineteenth century saw the return of the repressed. Identity came back with a vengeance, this time based not on religion but on one of three substitutes for it: the nation state, the (Aryan) race, and the (working) class. In the twentieth century, the nation state led to two world wars. Race led to the Holocaust. The class struggle led to Stalin, the Gulag, and the KGB. A hundred million people were killed in the name of three false gods.

For the past fifty years the West has been engaged in a second attempt to abolish identity, this time in the opposite direction. What the secular West now worships is not the universal but the individual: the self, the "Me," the "I." Morality – the thick code of shared values binding society together for the sake of the common good – has been dissolved into the right of each individual to do or be anything he or she chooses, so long as they do not directly harm others.

Identities have become mere masks we wear temporarily and without commitment. For large sections of society, marriage is an anachronism, parenthood delayed or declined, and community a faceless crowd. We still have stories, from *Harry Potter* to *Lord of the Rings* to *Star Wars*, but they are films, fictions, fantasies – a mode not of engagement but of escapism. Such a world is supremely tolerant, until it meets views not to its liking, when it quickly becomes brutishly intolerant, and eventually degenerates into the politics of the mob. This is populism, the prelude to tyranny.

Today's hyper-individualism will not last. We are social animals. We cannot live without identities, families, communities, and collective responsibility. Which means we cannot live without the stories that connect us to a past, a future, and a larger group whose history and destiny we share. The biblical insight still stands. To create and sustain a free society, you have to teach your children the story of how we achieved freedom and what its absence tastes like: the unleavened bread of affliction and the bitter herbs of slavery. Lose the story and eventually you lose your freedom. That is what happens when you forget who you are and why.

The greatest gift we can give our children is not money or possessions, but a story – a real story, not a fantasy, one that connects them to us and to a rich heritage of high ideals. We are not particles of dust blown this way or that by the passing winds of fad and fashion. We are heirs to a story that inspired a hundred generations of our ancestors and eventually transformed the Western world. What you forget, you lose. The West is forgetting its story. We must never forget ours.

With the hindsight of thirty-three centuries we can see how right Moses was. A story told across the generations is the gift of an identity, and when you know who you are and why, you can navigate the wilderness of time with courage and confidence. That is a life-changing idea.

Life-Changing Idea #15

Know your own story, because a story told across the generations is a gift.
When you know who you are and why, you can navigate the wilderness
of time with courage and confidence.

Beshallaḥ

The Longer, Shorter Road

At the end of his new book, *Tribe of Mentors*,[1] Timothy Ferris cites the following poem by Portia Nelson. It's called "Autobiography in Five Short Chapters":

> Chapter 1: I walk down the street. There is a deep hole in the sidewalk. I fall in. I am lost…. I am helpless. It isn't my fault. It takes forever to find a way out.

> Chapter 2: I walk down the same street. There is a deep hole in the sidewalk. I pretend I don't see it. I fall in again. I can't believe I am in this same place. But it isn't my fault. It still takes a long time to get out.

> Chapter 3: I walk down the same street. There is a deep hole in the sidewalk. I see it is there. I still fall in…. It's a habit…. But,

---

1. Timothy Ferris, *Tribe of Mentors: Short Life Advice from the Best in the World* (Boston: Houghton Mifflin Harcourt, 2017).

my eyes are open. I know where I am. It is my fault. I get out immediately.

Chapter 4: I walk down the same street. There is a deep hole in the sidewalk. I walk around it.

Chapter 5: I walk down another street.

That is probably how life is like for many of us. It certainly was for me. We set off, confident that we know where we are going, only to find that it is rarely that simple. "Life," said John Lennon in "Beautiful Boy," "is what happens while we are making other plans." We fall into holes. We make mistakes. Then we make them again. Eventually we avoid them, but by then we may have the growing suspicion that we took the wrong turning to begin with. If we are lucky, we find another road.

Hence the opening of this *parasha*:

> When Pharaoh let the people leave, God did not lead them by way of the land of the Philistines, although that was nearby, for God said, "Lest the people change their minds when they encounter war and return to Egypt." So God brought the people by a round-about route by way of the desert to the Red Sea... (Ex. 13:17–18)

This is actually quite a difficult text to understand. In and of itself it makes eminent sense. God did not want the people immediately to face battle with the seven nations in the land of Canaan since, as newly liberated slaves, they were psychologically unprepared for war. We now know also that there was an additional factor. There were Egyptian forts at various points along the sea route to Canaan, so the Israelites would come up against them even before reaching the land.

Three facts, though, still need to be reckoned with. First, the Torah itself says that God "hardened Pharaoh's heart" (14:4), leading him to pursue the Israelites with a force of six hundred chariots. This so demoralised the Israelites that they cried, "Were there not enough graves in Egypt that you had to bring us out here to die in the desert?... It would have been better to be slaves in Egypt than to die in the desert" (14:11–12). Why did God cause Pharaoh to pursue the Israelites if He did not want them to think of going back? He should surely have made the first stage of their journey as undemanding as possible.

Second, the people *did* face war long before they came anywhere near the land of Canaan. They did so almost immediately after crossing the Red Sea, when they were attacked by the Amalekites (17:8). The strange fact is that when they had to fight a battle on their own, without any miraculous intervention from God, they expressed no fear. Inspired by Moses' upraised arms, they fought and won (17:10–13).

Third, the roundabout route failed to prevent the people's response to the report of the spies. Terrified by their account of the strength of the native population and the well-fortified nature of their cities, they said, "Let us appoint a [new] leader and return to Egypt" (Num. 14:4).

It seems, therefore, that the circuitous route by which God led the Israelites was not to prevent their *wanting* to return, but rather, to prevent their being *able* to return. Leading them miraculously through the Red Sea was like Caesar crossing the Rubicon, or Cortes burning his boats before his conquest of the Aztecs. It made retreat impossible. Whatever their doubts and fears, the Israelites had no real choice. They had to continue onward, even if in the end it took forty years and a new generation to reach their destination.

What this meant was that almost from the dawn of their history as a nation, Jews were forced to learn that *lasting achievement takes time.* You can never get there by the shortest road. Thanks to the work of Anders Ericsson, popularised by Malcolm Gladwell, we know that greatness in many fields takes 10,000 hours of practice.[2] The history of all too many nations born after the Second World War and the end of empire shows that you can't create a democracy by United Nations decree, or freedom by a Universal Declaration of

2. See Anders Ericsson, *Peak: Secrets from the New Science of Expertise* (Boston: Houghton Mifflin Harcourt, 2016); Malcolm Gladwell, *Outliers* (New York: Little, Brown and Co., 2013). Of course, as many have pointed out, this is not true in all fields, nor is it the only relevant factor.

Human Rights. People who try to get rich fast often discover that their wealth is like Jonah's gourd: it appears overnight and disappears the next day. When you try to take a shortcut, you find yourself, like the poet, falling into a hole.

The Talmud tells the story of R. Yehoshua ben Ḥananya who asked a young man sitting at a crossroad, "Which is the way to the town?" The young man pointed to one of the paths and said, "This way is short but long. The other way is long but short." Yehoshua ben Ḥananya set out on the first path, quickly arrived at the town, but found his way blocked by gardens and orchards. He then returned to the young man and said, "Didn't you tell me that this path was short?" "I did," said the young man, "but I also warned you that it was long."[3] Better to take the long road that eventually gets you to your destination than the short one that doesn't, even though it looks as if it does.

Today's world is full of books, videos, and programmes promising a fast track to almost anything from weight loss to riches to success and fame. The life-changing idea symbolised by the route God led the Israelites on when they left Egypt is that *there are no fast tracks*. The long way is short; the short way is long. Better by far to know at the outset that the road is long, the work is hard, and there will be many setbacks and false turnings. You will need grit, resilience, stamina, and persistence. In place of a pillar of cloud leading the way, you will need the advice of mentors and the encouragement of friends. But the journey is exhilarating, and there is no other way. The harder it gets, the stronger you become.

Life-Changing Idea #16

There are no fast tracks. Lasting achievement takes time. You can never get there by the shortest road. The harder it gets, the stronger you become.

---

3. Eiruvin 53b.

Yitro

The Bond of Loyalty
and Love

In the course of any life there are moments of awe and amazement when, with a full heart, you thank God *sheheheyanu vekiyemanu vehigiyanu lazeman hazeh,* "who has kept us alive and sustained us and brought us to this day."

Two that particularly stand out in my own memory were separated by almost ten years. The first was the Lambeth Conference at Canterbury in 2008. The conference is the gathering, every ten years, of the bishops of the Anglican Communion – that is, not just the Church of England but the entire worldwide structure, much of it based in America and Africa. It is the key event that brings this global network of churches together to deliberate on directions for the future. That year I became, I believe, the first rabbi to address a plenary session of the conference. The second, much more recent, took place in October 2017 in Washington when I addressed the friends and supporters of the American Enterprise Institute, one of the world's great economic think tanks.

The two gatherings could not have been less alike. One was religious, Christian, and concerned with theology. The other was secular, American, and concerned with economics and politics. Both of them, though, were experiencing some kind of crisis. In the case of the Anglican Church it had to do with gay bishops.[1] Could the Church accommodate such people? The question was tearing the Church apart, with many of the American bishops in favour and most of the African ones against. There was a real sense, before the conference, that the communion was in danger of being irreparably split.

In Washington in 2017, the issue at the forefront of people's minds was quite different. A year earlier there had been a sharply divisive American presidential election. New phrases had been coined to describe some of the factors involved – post-truth, fake news, flyover states, alt-right, identity politics, competitive victimhood, whatever – as well as the resurfacing of an old one: populism. It all added up to what I termed the politics of anger. Was there a way of knitting together the unravelling strands of American society?

The reason these two events are connected in my mind is that on both occasions I spoke about the same concept – the one that is central to this *parasha*, and to biblical Judaism as a whole, namely *brit*, covenant. This was, in the seventeenth century especially, a key concept in the emerging free societies of the West, especially in Calvinist or Puritanical circles.

To grossly simplify a complex process, the Reformation developed in different directions in different countries, depending on whether Luther or Calvin was the primary influence. For Luther the key text was the New Testament, especially the letters of Paul. For Calvin and his followers, however, the Hebrew Bible was the primary text, especially in relation to political and social structures. That is why covenant played a large part in the (Calvinist) post-Reformation politics of Geneva, Holland, Scotland, England under Cromwell, and especially the Pilgrim Fathers, the first European settlers in North America. It lay at the heart of the Mayflower Compact (1620) and John Winthrop's famous "City upon a Hill" speech aboard the *Arbella* in 1630.

---

1. One, Gene Robinson, had already been appointed and was serving in New Hampshire.

Over time however, and under the influence of Jean-Jacques Rousseau, the word "covenant" was gradually supplanted by the phrase "social contract." Clearly there is something similar between the two, but they are not the same thing at all. In fact, they operate on different logics and they create different relationships and institutions.[2]

In a contract, two or more people come together, each pursuing their self-interest, to make a mutually advantageous exchange. In a covenant, two or more people, each respecting the dignity and integrity of the other, come together in a bond of loyalty and trust to do together what neither can achieve alone.[3] It isn't an exchange; it's a moral commitment. It is more like a marriage than a commercial transaction. Contracts are about interests; covenants are about identity. Contracts benefit; covenants transform. Contracts are about "Me" and "You"; covenants are about "Us."

What makes the Hebrew Bible revolutionary in political terms is that it contains not one founding moment but two. One is set out in I Samuel 8, when the people come to the prophet Samuel and ask for a king. God tells Samuel to warn the people what the consequences will be. The king will take the people's sons to ride with his chariots and their daughters to work in his kitchens. He will take their property as taxation, and so on. Nonetheless, the people insist that they still want a king, so Samuel appoints Saul.

Commentators have long been puzzled by this chapter. Does it represent approval or disapproval of monarchy? The best answer ever given was provided by Rabbi Zvi Hirsch Chajes, who explained that what Samuel was doing at God's behest was proposing a social contract precisely on the lines set out by Thomas Hobbes in *The Leviathan*. People are willing to give up certain of their rights, transferring them to a central power – a king or a government – who undertakes in return to ensure the defence of the realm externally and the rule of law within.[4] The book of Samuel thus contains the first recorded instance of a social contract.

---

2. I have set out the philosophy of this in *The Politics of Hope* (London: Jonathan Cape, 1997). Most recently I have summarised this argument in a whiteboard animation video: http://rabbisacks.wpengine.com/the-politics-of-hope/.

3. One might ask: What is there that God cannot do alone? The answer, given the theology of the Hebrew Bible, is: to live within the human heart. That requires our free assent.

4. *Kol Kitvei Maharatz Chajes*, I:43–49.

However, this was the *second* founding moment of Israel as a nation, not the first. The first took place in our *parasha*, on Mount Sinai, several centuries earlier, when the people made with God, not a contract but a covenant. What happened in the days of Samuel was the birth of Israel as a kingdom. What happened in the days of Moses – long before they had even entered the land – was the birth of Israel as a nation under the sovereignty of God.

The two central institutions of modern Western liberal democracies are both contractual. There are commercial contracts that create the *market*; and there is the social contract that creates the *state*. The market is about the creation and distribution of wealth. The state is about the creation and distribution of power. But a covenant is about neither wealth nor power, but rather about the bonds of belonging and collective responsibility. As I put it in *The Politics of Hope*, a social contract creates a state. A social covenant creates a society. A society is the totality of relationships that do not depend on exchanges of wealth and power, namely marriages, families, congregations, communities, charities, and voluntary associations. The market and the state are arenas of competition. Society is an arena of cooperation. And we need both.

The reason that the concept of covenant proved helpful to the Anglican bishops on the one hand, and the American Enterprise Institute on the other, is that it is the supreme example of a bond that brings together, in a single cooperative enterprise, individuals and groups that are profoundly different. They could not be more different than the parties at Mount Sinai: God and the children of Israel; the one infinite and eternal; the other, finite and mortal.

In fact the very first human relationship, between the first man and the first woman, contains a two-word definition of covenant: *ezer kenegdo*, meaning on the one hand "a helper," but on the other, someone "over-and-against."[5] In a marriage, neither husband nor wife sacrifice their distinctive identities. At Sinai, God remained God and the Israelites remained human. A symbol of covenant is the Havdala candle: multiple wicks that stay separate but produce a single flame.

---

5. Gen. 2:18 and Rashi ad loc., based on Yevamot 63a.

So covenant allowed the Anglican Communion to stay together despite the deep differences between the American and African churches. The American covenant held the nation together despite, in Lincoln's day, a civil war, and at other times, civil and economic strife; and its renewal will do likewise in the future. In Moses' day it allowed the Israelites to become "one nation under God" despite their division into twelve tribes. Covenants create unity without uniformity. They value diversity but, rather than allowing a group to split into competing factions, they ask each to contribute something uniquely theirs to the common good. Out of multiple "Me's" they create an overarching "Us."

What made these two experiences in Canterbury and Washington so moving to me was that they showed how prophetic Moses' words were when he told the Israelites that the Torah and its commands "will show your wisdom and understanding to the nations, who will hear about all these decrees and say, 'Surely this great nation is a wise and understanding people'" (Deut. 4:6). Torah continues to inspire not only Jews but all who seek guidance in hard times.

So, if you find yourself in a situation of conflict that threatens to break something apart, whether a marriage, a family, a business, a community, a political party, or an organisation, framing a covenant will help keep people together, without any side claiming victory or defeat. All it needs is recognition that there are certain things we can do together that none of us can do alone.

Covenant lifts our horizon from self-interest to the common good. There is nothing wrong with self-interest. It drives economics and politics, the market and the state. But there are certain things that cannot be achieved on the basis of self-interest alone, among them trust, friendship, loyalty, and love. Covenant really is a life- and world-changing idea.

Life-Changing Idea #17

If you find yourself in a situation of conflict that threatens to break something apart, framing a covenant will help keep people together. There are certain things we can do together that none of us can do alone.

Mishpatim

The Power of Empathy

W illiam Ury, founder of the Harvard Program of Negotiation, tells a marvellous story in one of his books.[1] A young American, living in Japan to study aikido, was sitting one afternoon in a train in the suburbs of Tokyo. The carriage was half empty. There were some mothers with children, and elderly people going shopping.

Then at one of the stations, the doors opened, and a man staggered into the carriage, shouting, drunk, dirty, and aggressive. He started cursing the people, and lunged at a woman holding a baby. The blow hit her and sent her into the lap of an elderly couple. They jumped up and ran to the other end of the carriage. This angered the drunk, who went after them, grabbing a metal pole and trying to wrench it out of its socket. It was a dangerous situation, and the young student readied himself for a fight.

---

1. Adapted from William Ury, *The Power of a Positive No* (New York: Bantam Books), 77–80.

Before he could do so, however, a small, elderly man in his seventies, dressed in a kimono, shouted "Hey" to the drunk in a friendly manner. "Come here and talk to me." The drunk came over, as if in a trance. "Why should I talk to you?" he said. "What have you been drinking?" asked the old man. "Sake," he said, "and it's none of your business!"

"Oh that's wonderful," said the old man. "You see, I love sake too. Every night, me and my wife (she's 76, you know), we warm up a little bottle of sake and take it out into the garden and we sit on an old wooden bench. We watch the sun go down, and we look to see how our persimmon tree is doing. My great-grandfather planted that tree..."

As he continued talking, gradually the drunk's face began to soften and his fists slowly unclenched. "Yes," he said, "I love persimmons too." "And I'm sure," said the old man, smiling, "you have a wonderful wife."

"No," replied the drunk. "My wife died." Gently, he began to sob. "I don't got no wife. I don't got no home. I don't got no job. I'm so ashamed of myself." Tears rolled down his cheeks.

As the train arrived at the student's stop and he was leaving the train, he heard the old man sighing sympathetically, "My, my. This is a difficult predicament indeed. Sit down here and tell me about it." In the last glimpse he saw of them, the drunk was sitting with his head in the old man's lap. The man was softly stroking his hair.

What he had sought to achieve by muscle, the old man had achieved with kind words.

A story like this illustrates the power of empathy, of seeing the world through someone else's eyes, entering into their feelings, and of acting in such a way as to let them know that they are understood, that they are heard, that they matter.[2]

If there is one command above all others that speaks of the power and significance of empathy it is the line in this *parasha*: "Do not oppress a stranger, because you know what it feels like to be a stranger: you were strangers in the land of Egypt" (Ex. 23:9).

---

2. Two good recent books on the subject are Roman Krznaric, *Empathy* (New York: A Perigee Book, 2014), and Peter Bazalgette, *The Empathy Instinct* (London: John Murray, 2017). See also Simon Baron-Cohen's fascinating book, *The Essential Difference* (London: Penguin, 2004), on why women tend to be better at this than men.

Why *this* command? The need for empathy surely extends way beyond strangers. It applies to marriage partners, parents and children, neighbours, colleagues at work, and so on. Empathy is essential to human interaction generally. Why then invoke it specifically about strangers?

The answer is that "empathy is strongest in groups where people identify with each other: family, friends, clubs, gangs, religions or races."[3] The corollary to this is that the stronger the bond within the group, the sharper the suspicion and fear of those outside the group. It is easy to "love your neighbour as yourself." It is very hard indeed to love, or even feel empathy for, a stranger. As primatologist Frans de Waal puts it:

> We've evolved to hate our enemies, to ignore people we barely know, and to distrust anybody who doesn't look like us. Even if we are largely cooperative within our communities, we become almost a different animal in our treatment of strangers.[4]

Fear of the one-not-like-us is capable of disabling the empathy response. That is why this specific command is so life-changing. Not only does it tell us to empathise with the stranger because you know what it feels like to be in his or her place. It even hints that this was part of the purpose of the Israelites' exile in Egypt in the first place. It is as if God had said, your sufferings have taught you something of immense importance. You have been oppressed; therefore come to the rescue of the oppressed, whoever they are. You have suffered; therefore you shall become the people who are there to offer help when others are suffering.

And so it has proved to be. There were Jews helping Gandhi in his struggle for Indian independence; Martin Luther King in his efforts for civil rights for African Americans; Nelson Mandela in his campaign to end apartheid in South Africa. An Israeli medical team is usually one of the first to arrive whenever and wherever there is a natural disaster today. The religious response to suffering is to use it to enter into the mindset of others who suffer. That is why I found so often that it was

---

3. Bazalgette, *The Empathy Instinct*, 7.
4. Frans de Waal, "The Evolution of Empathy," in Keltner, Marsh, and Smith (eds.), *The Compassionate Instinct: the Science of Human Goodness* (New York: Norton, 2010), 23.

the Holocaust survivors in our community who identified most strongly with the victims of ethnic war in Bosnia, Rwanda, Kosovo, and Darfur.

I have argued, in *Not in God's Name*,[5] that empathy is structured into the way the Torah tells certain stories – about Hagar and Ishmael when they are sent away into the desert, about Esau when he enters his father's presence to receive his blessing only to find that Jacob has taken it, and about Leah's feelings when she realises that Jacob loves Rachel more. These stories *force us into recognising the humanity of the other*, the seemingly unloved, unchosen, rejected.

Indeed, it may be that *this is why the Torah tells us these stories in the first place*. The Torah is essentially a book of law. Why then contain narrative at all? Because law without empathy equals justice without compassion. Rashi tells us: "Originally God planned to create the world through the attribute of justice but saw that it could not survive on that basis alone. Therefore He prefaced it with the attribute of compassion, joined with that of justice."[6] That is how God acts and how He wants us to act. Narrative is the most powerful way in which we enter imaginatively into the inner world of other people.

Empathy is not a lightweight, touchy-feely, add-on extra to the moral life. It is an essential element in conflict resolution. People who have suffered pain often respond by inflicting pain on others. The result is violence, sometimes emotional, sometimes physical, at times directed against individuals, at others, against whole groups. The only genuine, non-violent alternative is to enter into the pain of the other in such a way as to ensure that the other knows that he, she, or they have been understood, their humanity recognised, and their dignity affirmed.

Not everyone can do what the elderly Japanese man did, and certainly not everyone should try disarming a potentially dangerous individual that way. But active empathy is life-changing, not only for you but for the people with whom you interact. Instead of responding with anger to someone else's anger, try to understand where the anger might be coming from. In general, if you seek to change anyone's behaviour,

5. Jonathan Sacks, *Not in God's Name: Confronting Religious Violence* (Jerusalem: Maggid Books, 2015).
6. Rashi on Gen. 1:1.

you have to enter into their mindset, see the world through their eyes and try to feel what they are feeling, and then say the word or do the deed that speaks to their emotions, not yours. It's not easy. Very few people do this. Those who do, change the world.

Life-Changing Idea #18

If you seek to change anyone's behaviour, you have to enter into their mindset, and then say the word or do the deed that speaks to their emotions, not yours.

Teruma

Why We Value
What We Make

The behavioural economist Dan Ariely did a series of experiments on what is known as the IKEA effect, or "Why we overvalue what we make." The name comes, of course, from the store that sells self-assembly furniture. For practically challenged people like me, putting an item of furniture together is usually like doing a giant jigsaw puzzle in which various pieces are missing, and others are in the wrong place. But in the end, even if the item is amateurish, we tend to feel a certain pride in it. We can say, "I made this," even if someone else designed it, produced the pieces, and wrote the instructions. There is, about something in which we have invested our labour, a feeling like that expressed in Psalm 128: "When you eat the fruit of the labour of your hands, you will be happy, and it will go well with you."[1]

---

1. On the pleasures of physical work generally, especially craftsmanship, see Matthew
   Crawford, *The Case for Working with Your Hands* (London: Viking, 2010); published

Ariely wanted to test the reality and extent of this added value. So he got volunteers to make origami models by elaborate folding of paper. He then asked them how much they were prepared to pay to keep their own model. The average answer was 25 cents. He asked other people in the vicinity what they would be prepared to pay. The average answer was five cents. In other words, people were prepared to pay five times as much for something they had made themselves. His conclusions were: The effort that we put into something does not just change the object. It changes us and the way we evaluate that object. And the greater the labour, the greater the love for what we have made.[2]

This is part of what is happening in the long sequence about the building of the Sanctuary that begins in our *parasha* and continues, with few interruptions, to the end of the book of Exodus. There is no comparison whatsoever between the *Mishkan* – the holy and the Holy of Holies – and something as secular as self-assembly furniture. But at a human level, there are psychological parallels.

The *Mishkan* was the first thing the Israelites made in the wilderness, and it marks a turning point in the Exodus narrative. Until now God had done all the work. He had struck Egypt with plagues. He had taken the people out to freedom. He had divided the sea and brought them across on dry land. He had given them food from heaven and water from a rock. And, with the exception of the Song at the Sea, the people had not appreciated it. They were ungrateful. They complained.

Now God instructed Moses to take the people through a role reversal. Instead of His doing things for them, He commanded them to make something for Him. This was not about God. God does not need a sanctuary, a home on earth, for God is at home everywhere. As Isaiah said in His name: "Heaven is My throne and the earth My footstool.

---

in America as *Shop Class as Soul Craft*. Among the early Zionists there was a strong sense, best expressed by A. D. Gordon, that working on the land was itself a spiritual experience. Gordon was influenced here not only by Tanakh but also by the writings of Leo Tolstoy.

2. Dan Ariely, *The Upside of Irrationality* (New York: Harper Perennial, 2011), 83–106. His TED lecture on this subject can be seen at: https://www.ted.com/talks/dan_ariely_what_makes_us_feel_good_about_our_work.

What house, then, can you build for Me?" (Is. 66:1). This was about humans and their dignity, their self-respect.

With an extraordinary act of *tzimtzum*, self-limitation, God gave the Israelites the chance to make something with their own hands, something they would value because, collectively, they had made it. Everyone who was willing could contribute, from whatever they had: "Gold, silver or bronze, blue, purple or crimson yarns, fine linen, goat hair, red-dyed ram skins, fine leather, acacia wood, oil for the lamp, balsam oils for the anointing oil and for the fragrant incense" (Ex. 3–6), jewels for the breastplate, and so on. Some gave their labour and skills. Everyone had the opportunity to take part: women as well as men, the people as a whole, not just an elite.

For the first time God was asking them not just to follow His pillar of cloud and fire through the wilderness, or obey His laws, but to be active: to become builders and creators. And because it involved their work, energy, and time, they invested something of themselves in it, individually and collectively. To repeat Ariely's point: We value what we create. The effort that we put into something does not just change the object. It changes us.

Few places in the Torah more powerfully embody R. Yoḥanan's saying that "wherever you find God's greatness, there you find His humility."[3] God was giving the Israelites the dignity of being able to say, "I helped build a house for God." The Creator of the universe was giving His people the chance to become creators also – not just of something physical and secular, but of something profoundly spiritual and sacred.

Hence the unusual Hebrew word for contribution, *teruma*, which means not just something we give but something we lift up. The builders of the Sanctuary lifted up their gift to God, and in the process of lifting, discovered that they themselves were lifted. God was giving them the chance to become "His partners in the work of creation,"[4] the highest characterisation ever given of the human condition.

---

3. Megilla 31a.
4. Shabbat 10a, 119b.

This is a life-changing idea. The greatest gift we can give people is to give them the chance to create. This is the one gift that turns the recipient into a giver. It gives them dignity. It shows that we trust them, have faith in them, and believe they are capable of great things.

We no longer have a Sanctuary in space, but we do have Shabbat, the "sanctuary in time."[5] Recently, a senior figure in the Church of England spent Shabbat with us in the Marble Arch Synagogue. He was with us for the full twenty-five hours, from *Kabbalat Shabbat* to Havdala. He prayed with us, learned with us, ate with us, and sang with us.[6] "Why are you doing this?" I asked him. He replied, "One of the greatest gifts you Jews gave us Christians was the Sabbath. We are losing it. You are keeping it. I want to learn from you how you do it."

The answer is simple. To be sure, it was God who at the dawn of time made the seventh day holy.[7] But it was the Sages who, making "a fence around the law," added many laws, customs, and regulations to protect and preserve its spirit.[8] Almost every generation contributed something to the heritage of Shabbat, if only a new song, or even a new tune for old words. Not by accident do we speak of "making Shabbat." The Jewish people did not create the day's holiness, but they did co-create its *hadrat kodesh*, its sacred beauty. Ariely's point applies here as well: The greater the effort we put into something, the greater the love for what we have made.

Hence the life-changing lesson: If you want people to value something, get them to participate in creating it. Give them a challenge and give them responsibility. The effort we put into something does not just change the object: it changes us. The greater the labour, the greater the love for what we have made.

---

5. Abraham Joshua Heschel, *The Sabbath: Its Meaning for Modern Man* (New York: Farrer, Straus and Giroux, 2005).
6. He was not, of course, observing all the Shabbat laws; both Jews and Christians agree that these are imperatives for Jews alone.
7. As opposed to the festivals, whose date is dependent on the calendar that was determined by the Sanhedrin. This difference is reflected in the liturgy.
8. Halakhically, this is the concept of *shevut* that Nahmanides saw as essentially biblical in origin.

Life-Changing Idea #19

*The effort you put into something does not just change
the object: it changes you. The greater the labour,
the greater the love for what you have made.*

Tetzaveh

Crushed for the Light

There are lives that are lessons. The late Henry Knobil's was one. He was born in Vienna in 1932. His father had come there in the 1920s to escape the rising tide of anti-Semitism in Poland, but like Jacob fleeing from Esau to Laban, he found that he had fled one danger only to arrive at another.

After the Anschluss and Kristallnacht it became clear that, if the family were to survive, they had to leave. They arrived in Britain in 1939, just weeks before their fate would have been sealed had they stayed. Henry grew up in Nottingham, in the Midlands. There he studied textiles, and after his army service went to work for one of the great British companies, eventually starting his own highly successful textile business.

He was a passionate, believing Jew and loved everything about Judaism. He and his wife Renata were a model couple, active in synagogue life, always inviting guests to their home for Shabbat or the festivals. I came to know Henry because he believed in giving back to the community, not only in money but also in time and energy and leadership. He became the chairperson of many Jewish organisations including the national Israel (UJIA) appeal, British Friends of Bar Ilan University, the Jewish Marriage Council, the British-Israel Chamber of Commerce, and the Western Marble Arch Synagogue.

He loved learning and teaching Torah. He was a fine raconteur with an endless supply of jokes, and regularly used his humour to bring "laughter therapy" to cancer patients, Holocaust survivors, and the residents of Jewish Care homes. Blessed with three children and many grandchildren, he had retired and was looking forward, with Renata, to a serene last chapter in a long and good life.

Then, seven years ago, he came back from morning service in the synagogue to find that Renata had suffered a devastating stroke. For a while her life hung in the balance. She survived, but their whole life now had to change. They gave up their magnificent apartment in the centre of town for a place with easier wheelchair access. Henry became Renata's constant carer and life support. He was with her day and night, attentive to her every need.

The transformation was astonishing. Before, he had been a strong-willed businessman and communal leader. Now he became a nurse, radiating gentleness and concern. His love for Renata and hers for him bathed the two of them in a kind of radiance that was moving and humbling. And though he might, like Job, have stormed the gates of heaven to know why this had happened to them, he did the opposite. He thanked God daily for all the blessings they had enjoyed. He never complained, never doubted, never wavered in his faith.

Then, a year ago, he was diagnosed with an inoperable condition. He had, and knew he had, only a short time to live. What he did then was a supreme act of will. He sought one thing: to be given the grace to live as long as Renata did, so that she would never find herself alone. Three months ago, as I write these words, Renata died. Shortly thereafter, Henry joined her.[1] "Beloved and pleasant in their lives, and in their death undivided."[2] Rarely have I seen such love in adversity.

Henry taught us about the power of faith to turn pain into ḥesed, loving-kindness. Faith was at the very heart of what he stood for. He

---

1. Henry Knobil passed away on December 10, 2017.
2. II Sam. 1:23.

believed that God had spared him from Hitler for a purpose. He had given Henry business success for a purpose also. I never heard him attribute any of his achievements to himself. For whatever went well, he thanked God. For whatever did not go well, the question he asked was simply: What does God want me to learn from this? What, now that this has happened, does He want me to do? That mindset had carried him through the good years with humility. Now it carried him through the painful years with courage.

Our *parasha* begins with the words: "Command the Israelites to bring you clear olive oil, crushed for the light, so that the lamp may always burn" (Ex. 27:20). The Sages drew a comparison between the olive and the Jewish people:

> R. Yehoshua ben Levi asked, why is Israel compared to an olive? Just as an olive is first bitter, then sweet, so Israel suffers in the present but great good is stored up for them in the time to come. And just as the olive only yields its oil by being crushed – as it is written, "clear olive oil, crushed for the light" – so Israel fulfils [its full potential in] the Torah only when it is pressed by suffering.[3]

The oil was, of course, for the Menora, whose perpetual light – first in the Sanctuary, then in the Temple, and now that we have no Temple, the more mystical light that shines from every holy place, life, and deed – symbolises the divine light that floods the universe for those who see it through the eyes of faith. To produce this light, something has to be crushed. And here lies the life-changing lesson.

Suffering is bad. Judaism makes no attempt to hide this fact. The Talmud gives an account of various sages who fell ill. When asked, "Are your sufferings precious to you?" they replied, "Neither they nor their reward."[4] When they befall us or someone close to us, they can lead us to despair. Alternatively, we can respond stoically. We can practise the attribute of *gevura*, strength in adversity. But there is a third possibility. We can respond as Henry responded, with compassion, kindness, and

3. *Midrash Pitron Torah*, Num. 13:2.
4. Berakhot 5b.

love. We can become like the olive which, when crushed, produces the pure oil that fuels the light of holiness.

When bad things happen to good people, our faith is challenged. That is a natural response, not a heretical one. Abraham asked, "Shall the Judge of all the earth not do justice?" (Gen. 18:25). Moses asked, "Why have You done harm to this people?" (Ex. 5:22). Yet in the end, the wrong question to ask is, "Why has this happened?" We will never know. We are not God, nor should we aspire to be. The right question is, "Given that this has happened, what then shall I do?" To this, the answer is not a thought but a deed. It is to heal what can be healed, medically in the case of the body, psychologically in the case of the mind, spiritually in the case of the soul. Our task is to bring light to the dark places of our and other people's lives.

That is what Henry did. Renata still suffered. So did he. But their spirit prevailed over their body. Crushed, they radiated light. Let no one imagine this is easy. It takes a supreme act of faith. Yet it is precisely here that we feel faith's power to change lives. Great faith can turn pain into love and holy light.

Life-Changing Idea #20

When you experience suffering, the question to ask is, "Given this has happened, what then shall I do?" for this has an answer not of thought but of deed.

Ki Tissa

Anger – Its Uses and Abuses

Comparing two of the most famous events in the Torah, we face what seems like a glaring contradiction. In this *parasha*, Moses on the mountain is told by God to go down to the people. They have made a golden calf. Moses descends, holding in his hands the holiest object of all time, the two tablets carved and inscribed by God Himself.

As he reached the foot of the mountain, he saw the people dancing around the calf. In his anger, he threw down the tablets and broke them to pieces (Ex. 32:19). It was a public display of anger. Yet Moses was not criticised for this act, done entirely of his own accord.[1] Resh Lakish, commenting on the verse in which God commands Moses to carve a new set of tablets to replace the ones "which you broke" (34:1), says that God was, in effect, giving His approval to Moses' deed.[2]

The Sages went further. The concluding verses of the Torah state, "No other prophet has arisen in Israel like Moses, whom the

---

1. Shabbat 87a.
2. Ibid.

Lord knew face to face...or in any of the mighty hand and awesome wonders Moses displayed in the sight of all Israel" (Deut. 34:10–12). Of the phrase "mighty hand," they said that it refers to the breaking of the tablets.[3] In other words, it is seen as one of his greatest acts of courage and leadership.

Many years later Moses was faced with another crisis. The people had arrived at Kadesh. There was no water. The people complained. Once again, Moses displayed anger. Told by God to speak to the rock, he struck it twice, and water gushed out. This time, however, instead of being praised for what he did, God said to him, "Because you did not trust in Me to sanctify Me in the sight of the Israelites, you will not bring this assembly into the land I have given them" (Num. 20:12).

The difficulties in this passage are well known. What was Moses' sin? And was not the punishment disproportionate? My concern here, though, is simply with the comparison between the two events. In both cases, the people were running out of control. In both cases, Moses performed a gesture of anger. Why was one commended, the other condemned? Why was a show of anger appropriate in one case but not in the other? Is anger always wrong when shown by a leader, or is it sometimes necessary?

The answer is provided by Maimonides in his law code, the *Mishneh Torah*. In *Hilkhot Deot*, he tells us that in general we should follow the middle way in the emotional life. But there are two emotions about which Maimonides says that we should not follow the middle way, but should instead strive to eliminate them entirely from our emotional life: pride and anger. About anger he says this:

> Anger is an extremely bad attribute, and one should distance one-self from it by going to the other extreme. One should train one-self not to get angry, even about something to which anger might be the appropriate response.... The ancient Sages said, "One who yields to anger is as if he has worshipped idols." They also said, "Whoever yields to anger, if he is wise, his wisdom deserts him, and if he is a prophet, his prophecy leaves him." And "The life of an irascible person is not a life." Therefore they have instructed

---

3. Y. Taanit 4:5.

us to keep far from anger, training ourselves to stay calm even in the face of provocation. This is the right way.[4]

However he adds an important qualification:

> If one wants to instil reverence in his children and family, or in public if he is the head of the community, and his desire is to show them his anger so as to bring them back to the good, he should appear to be angry with them so as to reprove them, but he must inwardly remain calm as if he were acting the part of an angry man, but in reality he is not angry at all.[5]

According to Maimonides, the emotion of anger is always the wrong response. We may not be able to help feeling it, but we should be aware that while it lasts we are in the grip of an emotion we cannot control. That is what makes anger so dangerous. It is, to use Daniel Kahneman's terminology, thinking fast when we ought to be thinking slow.

What then are we to do? Maimonides, here and elsewhere, adopts a position that has been strikingly vindicated by neuroscientists' discovery of the plasticity of the brain. Intensive training over a prolonged period rewires our neural circuitry. We can develop new patterns of response, initially through intense self-control, but eventually through habit.[6] This is particularly hard to do in the case of anger, which is why we have to work so hard to eliminate it from our emotional repertoire.

But, says Maimonides, there is a fundamental difference between *feeling* anger and *showing* it. Sometimes it is necessary for a parent, teacher, or leader to *demonstrate* anger – to look angry even if you aren't. It has a shock effect. When someone in authority displays anger, the person or group it is directed against is in danger, and knows it. It is almost like administering an electric shock, and it is often effective in bringing a person or group to order. It is, though, a very high-risk strategy. There

---

4. Maimonides, *Mishneh Torah, Hilkhot Deot* 2:3.
5. Ibid.
6. For more on the plasticity of the brain, see above on *Parashat Va'era*.

is a danger it will provoke an angry response, making the situation worse, not better.[7] It is a weapon to be used only rarely, but sometimes it is the only way.

The key question then becomes: Is this a moment when anger is called for, or not? That calls for careful judgment. When people are dancing around an idol, anger is the right response. But when there is no water and the people are crying out in thirst, it is the wrong one.[8] Their need is real, even if they do not express it in the right way.

So, to summarise: We should never feel anger. But there are times when we should show it. These are few and far between, but they exist. I say this because of one of my own most life-changing experiences.

There was a time when I smoked a pipe. It was the wrong thing to do and I knew it. There is a mitzva to take care of your health, and smoking harms you badly in multiple ways. Yet there is such a thing as addiction, and it can be very hard to cure even when you are fully aware of how badly you are injuring yourself and others. For years I tried to give it up, and repeatedly failed. Then someone I respected greatly became angry with me. It was a cool anger, but it felt like a slap in the face.

It cured me. The shock was so great that I stopped and never smoked again. The experience of being on the receiving end of someone's anger changed my life. It may even have saved my life.

This was a difficult discovery. When you are a leader, you are often at the receiving end of people's anger. You learn to live with it and not let it depress or deflect you. However when someone who clearly cares for you gets angry with you, not because he or she disagrees with you, but simply because they see you doing yourself harm, it can change your life in a way few other things can.

You come to see the point of Maimonides' distinction as well. Therapeutic anger, if we can call it that, is done not out of emotion but out of careful, deliberate judgment that this is what the situation calls for right now. The person who delivers the shock is not so much feeling anger as showing it. That is what makes it all the more shocking.

---

7. For one example of this see Maimonides *Mishneh Torah, Hilkhot Mamrim* 6:9.
8. See Maimonides' introduction to Tractate Avot, *Shemona Perakim*, ch. 4.

There are families and cultures where anger is used all too often. This is abusive and harmful. Anger is bad for the person who feels it and often for the one who receives it. But sometimes there are situations that demand it, where putting up with someone's bad behaviour is damaging, and where making excuses for it can become a form of co-dependency. Friends and family, intending no more than to be tolerant and kind, in effect make it easy for the person to stay addicted to bad habits, at a cost to his and others' happiness.

Maimonides on Moses teaches us that we should try to conquer our feelings of anger. But when we see someone or a group acting wrongly, we may have to show anger even if we don't feel it. People sometimes need that shock to help them change their lives.

Life-Changing Idea #21

We should never feel anger, but there are times when we should show it. People sometimes need that shock to help them change their lives

Vayak'hel

Beyond the Self

Ⅰn the bookshops in the part of London where I live, there used to be a substantial section of works about religion. Nowadays these sections have shrunk, downsized in some cases to non-existence. In their place have come books on self-help. There is something deep about this, but also something quite perplexing.

It is clear that the secular societies of the West have found a new god. It is not any of the many gods of ancient times. It isn't the one God of monotheism. It is not even any of the three substitutes for religion dreamed up in the nineteenth century: nationalism, racism, and Marxism. The god of our time is the self.

In 2017 I read about a new medical condition, called "selfitis."[1] The term was coined as a joke in 2014 to describe people who feel compelled to keep taking selfies and posting them on social media. Three years later, researchers in Nottingham and India had produced evidence that the condition actually exists. Typical "selfitis" sufferers, they say,

---

1. *The Telegraph* (London), December 15, 2017.

113

are "attention seekers, often lacking in self-confidence," and hoping to "boost their social standing."

The self now rules in one domain after another. Politics is about individual rights; above all, the right to choose. Morality is about doing whatever you want so long as you don't harm others. People once turned to religious leaders in their quest for the good, the holy, and the transcendent. Now, often, they pay coaches to help them reach their life goals, preferences, and the holy grail of self-esteem.

Instead of turning to faith in something beyond ourselves, millennials turn to books, mentors, or gurus who teach us how to help ourselves. The new religion tells us we can achieve anything we want if we know "the secret." We can awaken the giant within, win friends and influence people, think and grow rich, feel the fear and do it anyway, and discover the life-changing magic of tidying up. We can learn to "love yourself like your life depends on it."[2]

In one way, there's nothing wrong or strange about this. These works are the twentieth- and twenty-first-century equivalents of what used to be called "wisdom literature" – common sense guides to life by those with insight and experience. In fact, the most recent trend in self-help books is to turn back to wisdom writers from ancient Greece and Rome, in particular Seneca, Epictetus, and Marcus Aurelius, the sages of Stoicism. What people tend to forget, though, is that Stoicism appeared as a philosophy in Greece and Rome when those two great civilisations had passed their prime. People had lost faith in the old gods and not yet found new ones. Stoicism is a superb recipe for finding calm when the world is falling apart. It is, though, supremely self-centred.[3]

That is the problem. The trouble with self-help is that the things that really change your life almost always come from the outside. The Talmud tells a story about R. Yoḥanan, who had great powers of healing. Visiting people who were sick, he would cure them by the touch of his hand. One day, he himself became ill, and R. Ḥanina

---

2. From the title of the book by Kamal Ravikant, *Love Yourself Like Your Life Depends on It* (CreateSpace, 2012).
3. See Thomas Joiner, "Mindfulness would be good for you. If it weren't so selfish," *Washington Post*, August 25, 2017.

came and cured him. The Talmud asks the obvious question: Why did R. Yoḥanan not cure himself? It answers: "A prisoner cannot release himself from prison."[4]

That is what is missing from the new religion of the self. Oddly enough in an age that venerates Darwin, it ignores the most salient truth of Darwinism, that what makes humans different is that we are supremely social animals. Aristotle knew this. So did Maimonides. The Torah says so loudly and clearly at the very beginning of the human story: "It is not good for man to be alone" (Gen. 2:18). Happiness, meaning, fulfilment, blessing, the gifts of a life well lived, are not – at least for most people – to be found in the self, but beyond the self, in relationships, families, and communities.

That is why the first thing Moses did after his long stay up the mountain, winning forgiveness for the people after the sin of the Golden Calf, was *vayak'hel*: to turn them back into a community.

He did so, as our *parasha* elaborates, in two ways. One was to begin the work of constructing the *Mishkan*, the Sanctuary. The best way of creating community is to get a group of people to build something together. If you have ever been engaged with others in bringing to fruition an innovative project, you will know the exhilaration that comes from bonding with a team while working together. That is what the Israelites experienced while they were making the Sanctuary. It is the one extended episode in the Torah's account of the wilderness years in which there were no complaints or rebellions.

The other way – stated in our *parasha* ahead of the Sanctuary-building – was Shabbat. Shabbat is the antidote to "selfitis." It's the day in which we lay aside our private projects of working, earning, spending, and striving, and simply celebrate together the things that are not about "Me" but about "Us": family, community, congregation, praying together, learning together, eating together, and singing together.

Judaism is a supremely social faith, built around the concept of *vayak'hel*, the act of gathering together as a community. Our holiest prayers cannot be said without a community. On the High Holy Days we confess publicly, together, not "my sins" but "ours." We pray for the

---

4. Berakhot 5b.

sick, and comfort mourners, by grouping them with "the others" who are similarly afflicted. Maimonides writes about one who "separates himself from the community":

> Even though he commits no transgression, he remains separated from the congregation of Israel, does not observe the commandments together with them, does not include himself in their troubles, nor afflict himself on their fast-days, but follows his own path as if he were one of the nations and not [a member of the Jewish people]. He has no share in the World to Come.[5]

To be a Jew, in other words, is not just a matter of believing or behaving, but also of belonging. Martin Buber wrote a famous book about spirituality called *I and Thou*. It had a huge impact on Christian theologians, much less so on Jewish ones. The reason is self-evident. Judaism is less about I-and-thou than about we-and-thou. It is constructed in the first-person plural of togetherness. We know perfectly well that we are imperfect; that we all lack something. Even Moses needed an Aaron and Miriam. That is why *davar shebikedusha*, a holy act or prayer, requires a community,[6] because what we lack individually, we hope to achieve collectively. All-of-us is greater than any-of-us.

That is something we are in grave danger of forgetting, especially with the spread of smartphones and social media. The evidence is rapidly accumulating that virtual relationships are not the same as face-to-face ones and that social media-generated crowds are quite different from communities. As Susan Pinker writes in *The Village Effect*, "Digital networks and screen media have the power to make the world seem much smaller. But when it comes to certain life-changing transformations, they're no match for face-to-face."[7] As she and others have

---

5. *Mishneh Torah, Hilkhot Teshuva* 3:11.
6. Berakhot 21a.
7. Susan Pinker, *The Village Effect: Why Face-to-Face Contact Matters* (London: Atlantic Books, 2015), 8.

documented,[8] being part of a community is good for health, happiness, and the successful negotiation of life's challenges.

This is why self-help has its limits. A prisoner cannot release himself from prison. The self cannot cure its own sicknesses. We need the presence of others to heal, to grow, to help us through the hard times, and to remind us of our responsibilities when times are hard for others. Hence the life-changing idea: Happiness lies beyond the self, in the strength of our relationships, our connections to community, and in what we give to and are given by others.

Life-Changing Idea #22

Happiness lies beyond the self, in the strength of our relationships, our connections to community, and in what we give to and are given by others.

---

8. See also Matthew Lieberman, *Social: Why Our Brains Are Wired to Connect* (Portland: Broadway Books, 2014); John Cacioppo and William Patrick, *Loneliness: Human Nature and the Need for Social Connection* (New York: Norton, 2009).

Pekudei

Making Space

This double *parasha*,[1] with its long account of the construction of the Sanctuary – one of the longest narratives in the Torah, taking a full thirteen chapters – comes to a magnificent climax:

> Then the cloud covered the Tent of Meeting, and the glory of the Lord filled the Sanctuary. Moses could not enter the Tent of Meeting because the cloud had settled on it, and the glory of the Lord filled the Sanctuary. (Ex. 40:34–35)

That is what the building of the Sanctuary was about: how to bring God, as it were, from heaven to earth, or at least from the top of the mountain to down in the valley, from the remote God of awe-inspiring power to the *Shekhina*, the indwelling presence, God as *shakhen*, a neighbour, intimate, close, within the camp, in the midst of the people.

---

1. *Parashot Vayak'hel* and *Pekudei* are very often combined.

Yet for all this, we wonder why the Torah has to go on at such length in its details of the *Mishkan*, taking up the whole of *Parashot Teruma* and *Tetzaveh*, half of *Parashat Ki Tissa*, and then again *Parashot Vayak'hel* and *Pekudei*. After all, the *Mishkan* was at best a temporary dwelling for the *Shekhina*, suited to the years of wandering and wilderness. In Israel, it was superseded by the Temple. For two thousand years in the absence of a Temple its place was taken by the synagogue. Why, if the Torah is timeless, does it devote such space to what was essentially a time-bound structure?

The answer is deep and life-transforming, but to reach it we have to note some salient facts. First, the language the Torah uses in *Pekudei* is highly reminiscent of the language used in the narrative of the creation of the universe:

Genesi 1–2	**Exodus 39–40**
And God *saw* all that He had made and *behold* it was very good. (1:31)	Moses *saw* all the skilled work and *behold* they had done it; as God had commanded it they had done it. (39:43)
The heavens and earth and all their array were *completed*. (2:1)	All the work of the Tabernacle of the Tent of Meeting was *completed*. (39:32)
And God *completed* all the *work* that He had done. (2:2)	And Moses *completed* the *work*. (40:33)
And God *blessed*... (2:3)	And Moses *blessed*... (39:43)
And *sanctified* it. (2:3)	And you shall *sanctify* it and all its vessels. (40:9)

Clearly the Torah wants us to connect the birth of the universe with the building of the *Mishkan*, but how and why?

The numerical structure of the two passages heightens the connection. We know that the key number of the creation narrative is seven. There are seven days, and the word "good" appears seven times. The first verse of the Torah contains seven Hebrew words, and the second, fourteen. The word *eretz*, "earth," appears twenty-one times, the word *Elokim*, "God," thirty-five times, and so on.

So too in *Parashat Pekudei*, the phrase "as the Lord commanded Moses" appears seven times in the account of the making of the priestly garments (Ex. 39:1–31), and another seven times in the description of Moses setting up the Sanctuary (40:17–33).

Note also one tiny detail, the apparently odd and superfluous "And" at the very beginning of the book of Exodus: "*And* these are the names…" The presence of this connective suggests that the Torah is telling us that the books of Genesis and Exodus are inherently connected. They are part of the same extended narrative.

The final relevant fact is that one of the Torah's most significant stylistic devices is the chiasmus, or "mirror-image symmetry" – a pattern of the form $ABCC^1B^1A^1$, as in "(A) He who sheds (B) the blood (C) of man, (C^1) by man (B^1) shall his blood (A^1) be shed" (Gen. 9:6). This form can be the shape of a single sentence, as here, or a paragraph, but it can also exist at larger levels of magnitude.

What it means is that a narrative reaches a certain kind of closure when the end takes us back to the beginning – which is precisely what happens at the end of Exodus. It reminds us, quite precisely, of the beginning of all beginnings, when God created heaven and earth. The difference is that this time human beings have done the creating: the Israelites, with their gifts, their labour, and their skills.

To put it simply: Genesis begins with God creating the universe as a home for humankind. Exodus ends with human beings, the Israelites, creating the Sanctuary as a home for God.

But the parallel goes far deeper than this – telling us about the very nature of the difference between *kodesh* and *ḥol*, sacred and secular, the holy and the mundane.

We owe to the great mystic, Rabbi Isaac Luria, the concept of *tzimtzum*, "self-effacement" or "self-limitation." Luria was perplexed by the question: If God exists, how can the universe exist? At every point in time and space, the Infinite should crowd out the finite. The very existence of God should act as does a black hole to everything in its vicinity. Nothing, not even light waves, can escape a black hole, so overwhelming is its gravitational pull. Likewise, nothing physical or material should be able to survive for even a moment in the presence of the pure, absolute being of God.

Luria's answer was that, in order for the universe to exist, God had to hide Himself, screen His presence, limit His being. That is *tzimtzum*.

Now let us come back to the key words *kodesh* and *ḥol*. One of the root meanings of *ḥol*, and the related root ḥ-l-l, is "empty." *Ḥol* is the space vacated by God through the process of self-limitation so that a physical universe can exist. It is, as it were, "emptied" of the pure divine light.

Kodesh is the result of a parallel process in the opposite direction. It is the space vacated by us so that God's presence can be felt in our midst. It is the result of our own *tzimtzum*. We engage in self-limitation every time we set aside our devices and desires in order to act on the basis of God's will, not our own.

That is why the details of the Sanctuary are described at such length: to show that every feature of its design was not humanly invented but God-given. That is why the human equivalent of the word "good" in the Genesis creation account is "as the Lord commanded Moses." When we nullify our will to do God's will, we create something that is holy.

To put it simply: *Ḥol* is the space God makes for humankind; *kodesh* is the space humankind makes for God. And both spaces are created the same way: by an act of *tzimtzum*, self-effacement.

So the making of the Sanctuary that takes up the last third of the book of Exodus is not just about a specific construction, the portable shrine that the Israelites took with them on their journey through the wilderness. It is about an absolutely fundamental feature of religious life, namely the relationship between the sacred and the secular, *kodesh* and *ḥol*. *Ḥol* is the space God makes for us; *kodesh* is the space we make for God.

So, for six days a week – the days that are *ḥol* – God makes space for us to be creative. On the seventh day, the day that is *kadosh*, we make space for God by acknowledging that we are His creations. And what applies in time applies also in space. There are secular places where we pursue our own purposes. And there are holy places where we open ourselves, fully and without reserve, to God's purposes.

If this is so, we have before us an idea with life-transforming implications. The highest achievement is not self-expression, but self-limitation: making space for something other and different from us. The happiest marriages are those in which each spouse makes space for the other to be his- or herself. Great parents make space for their children. Great leaders make space for their followers. Great teachers make space for their pupils. They are there when needed, but they don't crush or inhibit or try to dominate. They practise *tzimtzum*, self-limitation, so that others have the space to grow. That is how God created the universe, and it is how we allow others to fill our lives with their glory.

Life-Changing Idea #23

The highest achievement is not self-expression but self-limitation: making space for something other and different from us.

Leviticus
ויקרא

Vayikra

The Call

It was never my ambition or aspiration to be a rabbi. I went to university to study economics. I then switched to philosophy. I also had a fascination with the great British courtroom lawyers, legendary figures like Marshall Hall, Rufus Isaacs, and F. E. Smith. To be sure, relatively late, I had studied for the rabbinate, but that was to become literate in my own Jewish heritage, not to pursue a career.

What changed me, professionally and existentially, was my second major *yeḥidut* – face-to-face conversation – with the Lubavitcher Rebbe, in January 1978. To my surprise, he vetoed all my career options: economist, lawyer, academic, even becoming a rabbi in the United States. My task, he said, was to train rabbis. There were too few people in Britain going into the rabbinate and it was my mission to change that.

What is more, he said, I had to become a congregational rabbi, not as an end in itself but so that my students could come and see how I gave sermons (I can still hear in my mind's ear how he said that word with a marked Russian accent: *sirmons*). He was also highly specific as to where I was to work: in Jews' College (today, the London School of

Jewish Studies), the oldest extant rabbinical seminary in the English-speaking world.

So I did. I became a teacher at the College, and later its principal. Eventually I became – again after consulting with the Rebbe – chief rabbi. For all this I have to thank not only the Rebbe, but also my wife Elaine. She did not sign up for this when we married. It was not even on our horizon. But without her constant support I could not have done any of it.

I tell this story for a reason: to illustrate the difference between a gift and a vocation, between what we are good at and what we are called on to do. These are two very different things. I have known great judges who were also brilliant pianists. Wittgenstein trained as an aeronautical engineer but eventually dedicated his life to philosophy. Ronald Heifetz qualified as a doctor and a musician but instead became the founder of the School of Public Leadership at the John F Kennedy School of Government at Harvard. We can be good at many things, but what gives a life direction and meaning is a sense of mission, of something we are called on to do.

That is the significance of the opening word of this *parasha* that gives its name to the entire book: *Vayikra*, "He called." Look carefully at the verse and you will see that its construction is odd. Literally translated it reads: "He called to Moses, and God spoke to him from the Tent of Meeting, saying…" The first phrase seems to be redundant. If we are told that God spoke to Moses, why say in addition, "He called"?

The answer is that God's call to Moses was something prior to and different from what God went on to say. The latter were the details. The former was the summons, the mission – not unlike God's first call to Moses at the burning bush where He invited him to undertake the task that would define his life: leading the people out of exile and slavery to freedom in the Promised Land.

Why this second call? Probably because the book of *Vayikra* has, on the face of it, nothing to do with Moses. The original name given to it by the Sages was *Torat Kohanim*, "the Law of the Priests"[1] – and Moses was not a priest. That role belonged to his brother Aaron. So it was as

---

1. Hence the Latin name Leviticus, meaning "pertaining to the Levites," i.e., the priestly tribe.

if God were saying to Moses: This too is part of your vocation. You are not a priest but you are the vehicle through which I reveal all My laws, including those of the priests.

We tend to take the concept of a vocation – the word itself comes from the Latin for a "call" – for granted as if every culture has such an idea. However, it is not so. The great German sociologist Max Weber (1864–1920) pointed out that the idea of vocation, so central to the social ethic of Western culture, is essentially "a religious conception, that of a task set by God."[2]

It was born in the Hebrew Bible. Elsewhere there was little communication between the gods and human beings. The idea that God might invite human beings to become His partners and emissaries was revolutionary. Yet that is what Judaism is about.

Jewish history began with God's call to Abraham, to leave his land and family. God called to Moses and the prophets. There is a particularly vivid account in Isaiah's mystical vision in which he saw God enthroned and surrounded by singing angels: "Then I heard the voice of the Lord saying, 'Whom shall I send? And who will go for us?' And I said, 'Here am I. Send me!'" (Is. 6:8).

The most touching account is the story of the young Samuel, dedicated by his mother Hannah to serve God in the Sanctuary at Shiloh where he acted as an assistant to Eli the priest. In bed at night he heard a voice calling his name. He assumed it was Eli. He ran to see what he wanted but Eli told him he had not called. This happened a second time and then a third, and by then Eli realised that it was God calling the child. He told Samuel that the next time the voice called his name, he should reply, "Speak, Lord, for Your servant is listening." It did not occur to the child that it might be God summoning him to a mission, but it was. Thus began his career as a prophet, judge, and anointer of Israel's first two kings, Saul and David (I Sam. 3).

These were all prophetic calls, and prophecy ended during the Second Temple period. Nonetheless the idea of vocation remains for all those who believe in divine providence. Each of us

---

2. Quoted in Michael Novak, *Business as a Calling: Work and the Examined Life* (New York: Free Press, 1996), 17.

is different, therefore we each have unique talents and skills to bring to the world. The fact that I am here, in this place, at this time, with these abilities, is not accidental. There is a task to perform, and God is calling us to it.

The man who did more than anyone to bring this idea back in recent times was Viktor Frankl, the psychotherapist who survived Auschwitz. There in the camp he dedicated himself to giving people the will to live. He did so by getting them to see that their lives were not finished, that they still had a task to perform, and that therefore they had a reason to survive until the war was over.

Frankl insisted that the call came from outside the self. He used to say that the right question was not "What do I want from life?" but "What does life want from me?" He quotes the testimony of one of his students who earlier in life had been hospitalised because of mental illness. He wrote a letter to Frankl containing these words:

> But in the darkness, I had acquired a sense of my own unique mission in the world. I knew then, as I know now, that I must have been preserved for some reason, however small; it is something that only I can do, and it is vitally important that I do it…. In the solitary darkness of the "pit" where men had abandoned me, He was there. When I did not know His name, He was there; God was there.[3]

Reading Psalms in the prison to which the KGB had sent him, Natan Sharansky had a similar experience.[4]

Frankl believed that "every human person constitutes something unique; each situation in life occurs only once. The concrete task of any person is relative to this uniqueness and singularity."[5] The essence of the task, he argued, is that it is self-transcending. It comes from outside the self and challenges us to live beyond mere self-interest. To discover such a task is to find that life – my life – has meaning and purpose.

---

3. Viktor Frankl, *The Unconscious God* (New York: Simon & Schuster, 1975), 11.
4. Natan Sharansky, *Fear No Evil* (New York: Vintage Books, 1989).
5. Viktor Frankl, *The Doctor and the Soul* (London: Souvenir Press, 1969), 57.

How do you discover your vocation? The late Michael Novak argued[6] that a calling has four characteristics. First, it is unique to you. Second, you have the talent for it. Third, it is something which, when you do it, gives you a sense of enjoyment and renewed energy. Fourth, do not expect it to reveal itself immediately. You may have to follow many paths that turn out to be false before you find the true one.

Novak quotes Logan Pearsall Smith who said, "The test of a vocation is the love of the drudgery it involves." All real achievement requires backbreaking preparation. The most common estimate is 10,000 hours of deep practice. Are you willing to pay this price? It is no accident that *Vayikra* begins with a call – because it is a book about sacrifices, and vocation involves sacrifice. We are willing to make sacrifices when we sense that a specific role or task is what we are called on to do.

Not all of us discover such a vocation. That does not make our lives any less good or worthwhile or valuable or beloved by God. There are lives lived day by day rather than towards any overarching purpose. The Talmud suggests that this is how the great Hillel lived.[7] But there is another possibility. There are lives that are answers to a call.

This is a life-changing idea. For each of us God may have a task: work to perform, a kindness to show, a gift to give, love to share, loneliness to ease, pain to heal, or broken lives to help mend. Discerning that task, hearing God's call, gives a life meaning and purpose. Where what we want to do meets what needs to be done, that is where God wants us to be.

Life-Changing Idea #24

For each of us God may have a task. Discerning that task, hearing God's call, is what gives a life meaning and purpose.

---

6. Novak, *Business as a Calling*, 17–40.
7. Beitza 16a.

Tzav

Giving Thanks

The first words we are taught to say each morning, immediately on waking, are *Modeh/Modah ani*, "I give thanks." We thank before we think. Note that the normal word order is inverted: *Modeh ani*, not *Ani modeh*, so that in Hebrew the "thanks" comes before the "I." Judaism is "gratitude with attitude." And this, according to recent scientific research, really is a life-enhancing idea.

The source of the command to give thanks is to be found in this *parasha*. Among the sacrifices it itemises is the *korban todah*, the thanksgiving offering:

> If he offers it [the sacrifice] as a thanksgiving offering, then along with this thanksgiving offering he is to offer unleavened loaves mixed with oil, unleavened wafers spread with oil, and loaves of fine flour well-kneaded and mixed with oil. (Lev. 7:12)

Though we have been without sacrifices for almost two thousand years, a trace of the thanksgiving offering survives to this day, in the form of the *HaGomel* blessing, "Who bestows good things on the unworthy," said in the synagogue, at the time of reading of the Torah, by one who has survived a hazardous situation. This is defined by the Sages (on the basis of Psalm 107) as one who has survived a sea-crossing, travelled across a desert, recovered from serious illness, or has been released from captivity.[1]

For me, the almost universal instinct to give thanks is one of the signals of transcendence[2] in the human condition. It is not just the pilot we want to thank when we land safely after a hazardous flight; not just the surgeon when we survive an operation; not just the judge or politician when we are released from prison or captivity. It is as if some larger force was operative, as if the hand that moves the pieces on the human chessboard were thinking of us; as if heaven itself had reached down and come to our aid.

Insurance companies sometimes describe natural catastrophes as "acts of God." Human emotion tends to do the opposite.[3] God is in the good news, the miraculous deliverance, the escape from catastrophe. That instinct – to offer thanks to a force, a presence, over and above natural circumstances and human intervention – is itself a signal of transcendence. Though not a proof of the existence of God, it is nonetheless an intimation of something deeply spiritual in the human heart. It tells us that we are not random concatenations of selfish genes, blindly reproducing themselves. Our bodies may be products of nature ("Dust you are, and to dust you will return"), but there is something within us that reaches out to Someone beyond us: the soul of the universe, the divine "You" to whom we offer our thanks. That is what was once expressed in the thanksgiving offering, and still is, in the *HaGomel* blessing.

Not until the early 1990s did a major piece of medical research reveal the dramatic physical effects of thanksgiving. It became known as the Nun Study. Some 700 American nuns, all members of the School

---

1. Berakhot 54b.
2. On this idea, see Peter Berger, *A Rumor of Angels* (New York: Doubleday, 1990).
3. Not always, of course. There was a memorable episode of *The Simpsons* in which Bart Simpson, before beginning his Thanksgiving meal, turns to heaven and says in place of grace, "We paid for all this stuff ourselves, so thanks for nothing."

Sisters of Notre Dame in the United States, agreed to allow their records to be accessed by a research team investigating the process of ageing and Alzheimer's Disease. At the start of the study the participants were aged between 75 and 102.[4]

What gave this study its unusual longitudinal scope is that in 1930 the nuns, then in their twenties, had been asked by the mother superior to write a brief autobiographical account of their life and their reasons for entering the convent. These documents were analysed by the researchers using a specially devised coding system to register, among other things, positive and negative emotions. By annually assessing the nuns' current state of health, the researchers were able to test whether their emotional state in 1930 had an effect on their health some sixty years later. Because they had all lived a very similar lifestyle during these six decades, they formed an ideal group for testing hypotheses about the relationship between emotional attitudes and health.

The results, published in 2001, were startling.[5] The more positive emotions – contentment, gratitude, happiness, love, and hope – the nuns expressed in their autobiographical notes, the more likely they were to be alive and well sixty years later. The difference was as much as seven years in life expectancy. So remarkable was this finding that it has led, since then, to a new field of gratitude research, as well as a deepening understanding of the impact of emotions on physical health.

Since the publication of the Nun Study and the flurry of further research it inspired, we now know of the multiple effects of developing an attitude of gratitude. It improves physical health and immunity against disease. Grateful people are more likely to take regular exercise and go for regular medical check-ups. Thankfulness reduces toxic emotions such as resentment, frustration, and regret, and makes depression less likely. It helps people avoid over-reacting to negative experiences by seeking revenge. It even tends to make people sleep better. It enhances self-respect,

---

4. See Robert Emmons, *Thanks!: How the New Science of Gratitude Can Make You Happier* (Boston: Houghton Mifflin, 2007).
5. Deborah D. Danner, David A. Snowdon, and Wallace V. Friesen, "Positive Emotions in Early Life and Longevity: Findings from the Nun Study," *Journal of Personality and Social Psychology* 80, no. 5 (2001): 804–13.

making it less likely that you will envy others for their achievements or success. Grateful people tend to have better relationships. Saying "thank you" enhances friendships and elicits better performance from employees. It is also a major factor in strengthening resilience. One study of Vietnam War veterans found that those with higher levels of gratitude suffered lower incidence of post-traumatic stress disorder. Remembering the many things we have to be thankful for helps us survive painful experiences, from losing a job to bereavement.[6]

Jewish prayer is an ongoing seminar in gratitude. *Birkot HaShaḥar*, "the dawn blessings" said at the start of morning prayers each day, are a litany of thanksgiving for life itself: the human body, the physical world, land to stand on, and eyes to see with.

Gratitude also lies behind a fascinating feature of the *Amida*. When the leader of prayer repeats the *Amida* aloud, we are silent other than for the responses of *Kedusha*, and saying Amen after each blessing, with one exception. When the leader says the words *Modim anaḥnu lakh*, "We give thanks to You," the congregation says a parallel passage known as *Modim DeRabbanan*. For every other blessing of the *Amida*, it is sufficient to assent to the words of the leader by saying Amen. The one exception is *Modim*, "We give thanks." Rabbi Elijah Spira (1660–1712), in his work *Eliyahu Rabba*,[7] explains that when it comes to saying thank you, we cannot delegate this to someone else to do it on our behalf. Thanks has to come directly from us.

Hence the transformative idea: Giving thanks is beneficial to the body and the soul. It contributes to both happiness and health. It is also a self-fulfilling attitude: The more we celebrate the good, the more good we discover that is worthy of celebration.

This is neither easy nor natural. We are genetically predisposed to paying more attention to the bad than the good.[8] For sound biological reasons, we are hyper-alert to potential threats and dangers. It takes

---

6. Much of the material in this paragraph is to be found in articles published in Greater Good: The Science of a Meaningful Life @ http://greatergood.berkeley.edu. See also Sonja Lyubomirsky, *The How of Happiness* (London: Sphere, 2007), 87–124.

7. *Eliyahu Rabba, Oraḥ Ḥayim* 127:1.

8. The classic study of this is Roy Baumeister et al., "Bad is stronger than good," *Review of General Psychology*, vol. 5, no. 4, (2001): 323–70.

focused attention to become aware of how much we have to be grateful for. That, in different ways, is the logic of prayer, of making blessings, of Shabbat, and many other elements of Jewish life.

It is also embedded in our collective name. The word *modeh*, "I give thanks," comes from the same root as *Yehudi*, meaning "Jew." We acquired this name from Jacob's fourth son, named by his mother Leah who, at his birth said, "This time I will thank God" (Gen. 29:35). Jewishness is thankfulness: not the most obvious definition of Jewish identity, but by far the most life-enhancing.

Life-Changing Idea #25

The more you celebrate the good, the more good you discover that is worthy of celebration.

Shemini

When Weakness Becomes Strength

Have you ever felt inadequate to a task you have been assigned or a job you have been given? Do you sometimes feel that other people have too high an estimate of your abilities? Has there been a moment when you felt like a faker, a fraud, and that at some time you would be found out and discovered to be the weak, fallible, imperfect human being you know in your heart you are?

If so, according to Rashi on this *parasha*, you are in very good company indeed. Here is the setting: The *Mishkan*, the Sanctuary, was finally complete. For seven days Moses had consecrated Aaron and his sons to serve as priests. Now the time had come for them to begin their service. Moses gives them various instructions. Then he says the following words to Aaron:

> Come near to the altar and offer your sin offering and your burnt offering, and make atonement for yourself and the people;

sacrifice the offering that is for the people and make atonement for them, as the Lord has commanded. (Lev. 9:7)

The Sages were puzzled by the instruction, "Come near." This seems to imply that Aaron had until then kept a distance from the altar. Why so? Rashi gives the following explanation: Aaron was ashamed and fearful of approaching the altar. Moses said to him: "Why are you ashamed? It was for this that you were chosen."

There is a name for this syndrome, coined in 1978 by two clinical psychologists, Pauline Clance and Suzanne Imes. They called it the impostor syndrome.[1] People who suffer from it feel that they do not deserve the success they have achieved. They attribute it not to their effort and ability but to luck, or timing, or to the fact that they have deceived others into thinking that they are better than they actually are. It turns out to be surprisingly widespread, and particularly so among high achievers. Research has shown that around 40 per cent of successful people do not believe they deserve their success, and that as many as 70 per cent have felt this way at some time or other.

However, as one might imagine, Rashi is telling us something deeper. Aaron was not simply someone lacking in self-confidence. There was something specific that he must have had in mind on that day that he was inducted into the role of high priest. For Aaron had been left in charge of the people while Moses was up the mountain receiving the Torah. That was when the sin of the Golden Calf took place.

Reading that narrative, it is hard to avoid the conclusion that it was Aaron's weakness that allowed it to happen. It was he who suggested that the people give him their gold ornaments, he who fashioned them into a calf, and he who built an altar before it (Ex. 32:1–6). When Moses saw the golden calf and challenged Aaron – "What did these people do to you, that you brought upon them this great sin?"– he replied, evasively, "They gave me the gold, and I threw it into the fire, and out came this calf!" (32:21, 24).

---

1. Pauline Clance and Suzanne Ament Imes, "The Imposter Phenomenon in High Achieving Women: Dynamics and Therapeutic Intervention," *Psychotherapy: Theory, Research and Practice* 15, no. 3 (1978): 241–47.

This was a man profoundly (and rightly) uncomfortable with his role in one of the most disastrous episodes in the Torah, and now he was being called to atone not only for himself but for the entire people. Was this not hypocrisy? Was he not himself a sinner? How could he stand before God and the people and assume the role of the holiest of men? No wonder he felt like an impostor and was ashamed and fearful of approaching the altar.

Moses, however, did not simply say something that would boost his self-confidence. He said something much more radical and life-changing: "It was for this that you were chosen." The task of a high priest is to atone for people's sins. It was his role, on Yom Kippur, to confess his wrongs and failings, then those of his household, then those of the people as a whole (Lev. 16:11–17). It was his responsibility to plead for forgiveness.

"That," implied Moses, "is why you were chosen. You know what sin is like. You know what it is to feel guilt. You more than anyone else understands the need for repentance and atonement. You have felt the cry of your soul to be cleansed, purified, and wiped free of the stain of transgression. What you think of as your greatest weakness will become, in this role you are about to assume, your greatest strength."

How did Moses know this? Because he had experienced something similar himself. When God told him to confront Pharaoh and lead the Israelites to freedom, he repeatedly insisted that he could not do so. Reread his responses to God's call to lead the Israelites out of Egypt (Ex. chs. 3–4), and they sound like someone radically convinced of his inadequacies. "Who am I?" "They won't believe in me." Above all, he kept repeating that he could not speak before a crowd, something absolutely necessary in a leader. He was not an orator. He did not have the voice of command:

> Then Moses said to the Lord, "Please, my Lord, I am not a man of words, not yesterday, not the day before, and not since You have spoken to Your servant. I am slow of speech and tongue." (Ex. 4:10)

> Moses said to the Lord, "Look, the Israelites do not listen to me. How then will Pharaoh listen to me? Besides, I have uncircumcised lips." (Ex. 6:12)

Moses had a speech defect. To him that was a supreme disqualification from being a mouthpiece for the divine word. What he did not yet understand is that this was one of the reasons God chose him. When Moses spoke the words of God, people knew he was not speaking his own words in his own voice. Someone else was speaking through him. This seems to have been the case for Isaiah and Jeremiah, both of whom were doubtful of their ability to speak and who became among the most eloquent of prophets.[2]

The people who can sway crowds with their oratory are, generally speaking, not prophets. Often they are, or become, dictators and tyrants. They use their power of speech to acquire more dangerous forms of power. God does not choose people who speak with their own voice, telling the crowds what they want to hear. He chooses people who are fully aware of their inadequacies, who stammer literally or metaphorically, who speak not because they want to but because they have to, and who tell people what they do not want to hear, but what they must hear if they are to save themselves from catastrophe. What Moses thought was his greatest weakness was, in fact, one of his greatest strengths.

The point here is not a simple "I'm OK, you're OK" acceptance of weakness. That is not what Judaism is about. The point is the struggle. Moses and Aaron in their different ways had to wrestle with themselves. Moses was not a natural leader. Aaron was not a natural priest. Moses had to accept that one of his most important qualifications was what nowadays we would call his low self-image, but what, operating from a completely different mindset, the Torah calls his humility. Aaron had to understand that his own experience of sin and failure made him the ideal representative of a people conscious of their own sin and failure.

---

2. There is a striking secular example: Winston Churchill had both a lisp and a stutter and though he fought against both, they persisted long into adulthood. Because of this, he had to think carefully in advance about his major speeches. He was fastidious in writing or dictating them beforehand, rewriting key phrases until the last moment. He used short words wherever possible, made dramatic use of pauses and silences, and developed an almost poetic use of rhythm. The result was not only that he became a great speaker. His speeches, especially over the radio during the Second World War, were a major factor in rousing the spirit of the nation. In the words of Edward Murrow, he "mobilised the English language and sent it into battle."

Feelings of inadequacy – the impostor syndrome – can be bad news or good news depending on what you do with them. Do they lead you to depression and despair? Or do they lead you to work at your weaknesses and turn them into strengths?

The key, according to Rashi in this *parasha*, is the role Moses played at this critical juncture in Aaron's life. He had faith in Aaron even when Aaron lacked faith in himself. That is the role God Himself played, more than once, in Moses' life. And that is the role God plays in all our lives if we are truly open to Him. I have often said that the mystery at the heart of Judaism is not our faith in God. It is God's faith in us.[3]

This then is the life-changing idea: What we think of as our greatest weakness can become, if we wrestle with it, our greatest strength. Think of those who have suffered tragedy and then devote their lives to alleviating the suffering of others. Think of those who, conscious of their failings, use that consciousness to help others overcome their own sense of failure.

What makes Tanakh so special is its total candour about humanity. Its heroes – Moses, Aaron, Isaiah, Jeremiah – all knew times when they felt like failures, "impostors." They had their moments of dark despair. But they kept going. They refused to be defeated. They knew that a sense of inadequacy can bring us closer to God, as King David said: "My sacrifice [i.e., what I bring as an offering to You], O God, is a broken spirit; a broken and contrite heart You, God, will not despise" (Ps. 51:19).

Better by far to know you are imperfect than to believe you are perfect. God loves us and believes in us despite, and sometimes because of, our imperfections. Our weaknesses make us human; wrestling with them makes us strong.

Life-Changing Idea #26

What you think of as your greatest weakness can become,
if you wrestle with it, your greatest strength.

---

3. See above on *Parashat Bereshit*.

Tazria

The Power of Bad

In their recent book *The Power of Bad*,[1] John Tierney and Roy Baumeister tell the following story. A young woman, Eliza Byington, took a job at a video production company on the West Coast of America. The office was open-plan, with individual cubicles, clearly designed to encourage interaction and collaboration, but it did not seem to work. The sales representatives who worked in the cubicles did not talk to one another. The managers, who had their own individual offices, kept their doors shut. People either went out to lunch alone or ate at their desks rather than using the communal recreation space. It was, she thought, a most unpleasant work environment.

Then one of the sales representatives developed a heart condition and started working at home for most of the week. Suddenly the whole atmosphere of the office changed. Sales representatives started wandering over to their colleagues to discuss progress and tactics. Managers started leaving their office doors open. Staff meetings were more creative. People

---

1. John Tierney and Roy Baumeister, *The Power of Bad* (Allen Lane, 2019), 135.

contributed more new ideas. Someone brought in home-made biscuits to share with the others. Someone else brought in a radio to play classical music. People started eating lunch together in the communal room. Some evenings a group would go out to drink together before going home. All this happened only on the days that this sales representative was at home. When he was present, the office reverted to its chilly unfriendliness.

As Tierney and Baumeister describe him, the individual in question was not antisocial. He mixed and chatted with others, but his conversation was profoundly negative. When talking about clients, he made fun of them and dismissed them as stupid or tiresome. At meetings, he mocked others for the mistakes they made or for their lack of experience. He criticised and complained. Despite all this, Byington had not seen him as a problem until she saw the difference between the functioning of the team when he was present and when he was absent. A single individual, simply by the negativity of his speech, was able to prevent an entire group of people from fulfilling their potential and thriving while doing so.

The connection between this story and our *parasha* is straightforward. *Parashot Tazria* and *Metzora* are both about a skin condition known as *tzaraat*, which is usually, though almost certainly incorrectly, translated as leprosy. The Sages were puzzled by the phenomenon. First, it accords with no known disease. We know of no illness whose symptoms apply not only to humans but also to garments and the walls of houses. Second, the Torah is not a book of medicine. If it deals with one illness, why not others? Third, the language it uses is not of illness and health but rather of impurity and purity, something else entirely.

They therefore sought the explanation by examining the most conspicuous instance of *tzaraat* in the Torah: that of Miriam who was struck with it for seven days after speaking negatively about her brother Moses (Num. 12). *Tzaraat* was not an illness but a punishment. The Talmud takes *metzora* to be an abbreviated form of the phrase *motzi shem ra,* meaning slander.[2] To be sure, some cited other sins that might lead to it. The Talmud mentions, in addition to malicious speech, bloodshed, an oath taken in vain, forbidden sexual relations, arrogance, theft, and stinginess.[3]

---

2. Arakhin 15b.
3. Ibid. 16a.

When a connection between *tzaraat* and evil speech is identified, certain features of the phenomenon begin to take on significance. First, the most obvious sign of *tzaraat* was a whitening of the skin. The phrase the Sages used to describe shaming someone was *malbin penei ḥavero*, someone who "causes his fellow's face to turn white."[4] Thus the punishment was measure-for-measure. Negative words that could turn someone else's face white are punished by the skin of the speaker turning white. Moreover, malicious speech is usually spoken in private, the fiction being that words conveyed confidentially will stay confidential. The punishment is the most public possible. No one, upon seeing a *metzora*, would doubt what they had witnessed. It was a visible mark of shame.

One particularly poignant detail in our *parasha* is: "He shall be unclean as long as the disease is on him. Being unclean, he shall dwell apart; his dwelling shall be outside the camp" (Lev. 13:46). If *tzaraat* were a disease, then this provision would clearly be a form of quarantine. But if it is a punishment for malicious speech, then the Talmud has a simple explanation: By his malicious speech he created division between husband and wife, or between one person and another. Therefore he is divided from the rest of society, condemned to live alone outside the camp as long as the condition lasts.[5]

Though *tzaraat* had long ceased to be a reality by the time of the Talmud, its insight into the destructive power of negative speech is well illustrated by Eliza Byington's story. One person, simply by the cynical and dismissive tone of his comments, was able to disrupt the normal functioning of what otherwise would have been a creative and successful team. His absence from the office – the behavioural equivalent of the *metzora*'s banishment outside the camp – allowed the group to thrive again.

This matters greatly in Judaism. Jews have always been a small and vulnerable people, whether as a tiny nation surrounded by great empires, or as a minority in exile surrounded by a majority population whose religion and culture were different from, and often hostile to, their own. High morale was essential to survival. The Torah makes

---

4. Mishna Avot 3:11.
5. Arakhin 16b.

just this point when it tells us how, in the battle against the Amalekites, when Moses lifted his hands and the people looked up to heaven, they prevailed. When they looked down, they began to falter. Speaking badly about people destroys morale and the entire group suffers.

Tierney and Baumeister cite another case of a clothing company that dismissed one of its most successful salespeople. His results were outstanding, but he often antagonised his fellow salespeople, refusing to help them, and at times tried to usurp them. After he was ousted from the company, none of the remaining salespeople reached his level of success, but the company's sales nonetheless rose by some 30 per cent.

These are purely economic propositions. But Tierney and Baumeister have a much larger point, which is that bad is more powerful than good. We are predisposed to notice negative phenomena. They generate responses of freeze, fight, or flight, and these reactions are powerful and very fast acting. We notice threats more than reassurance. Bad news has greater impact than good news. In fact, often the good news does not count as news at all. It is easier to make someone believe something negative about another person or group than something positive. John Gottman, the doyen of marriage research, argues that for a marriage to succeed it must contain five times as many positive experiences as negative ones, since the negatives are felt so intensely. That is the *ra* in *metzora*, the evil of evil speech. Words have power, but bad words have the greatest power. They are a genuinely destructive force.

Bad speech has always been destructive. But its negative force has grown exponentially with the development of the internet, smartphones, and social media. These have fundamentally changed the nature of interpersonal communication. It is far easier to be rude, negative, critical, offensive, scathing, and destructive when communicating electronically because of the so-called "disinhibition effect" which occurs when people are not speaking face-to-face. They are not constrained by the humanising influence of personal contact. They can hide behind some form of anonymity. They are not around to see the effect of their words. So visible and vulnerable are we on social media that almost anyone can take or give offence and deliver a devastating comment with no forethought or self-restraint. A new and unlovely world is emerging, overwhelmed by cyberbullying, depression, anxiety, sleep disturbance, low self-esteem, loneliness, and withdrawal.

A 2018 survey in the United States, for example, showed that 59 per cent of teenagers have experienced online abuse, 42 per cent have been called offensive names, 32 per cent have had false rumours spread about them, and 63 per cent believe that online harassment is a serious problem.[6]

Data compiled in 2018 by the Office for National Statistics showed that the suicide rate in Britain among children and young people aged fifteen to nineteen almost doubled in the course of eight years, a rise attributed by Dame Sally Davies, chief medical officer for England, to the effect of media such as Facebook, Instagram, and Snapchat.[7] A particularly frightening figure is that 22 per cent of fourteen-year-old girls in Britain have self-harmed.[8]

Imagine a world in which those who posted negative, hurtful, or malicious remarks about others on social media were publicly exposed, carried a visible mark of shame, and for a period were excluded from public places and the company of others – in short, suffered the fate of the *metzora*. This would be a world in which people would think twice before using speech to harm or damage other people. The by now well-documented negative effects of social media have made us vividly aware of how easily people can use evil speech if they think they can do so without paying the costs themselves, and how harmful that can be.

---

6. Pew Research Center: Internet and Technology, "A Majority of Teens Have Experienced Some Form of Cyberbullying," https://www.pewresearch.org/internet/2018/09/27/a-majority-of-teens-have-experienced-some-form-of-cyberbullying/.

7. "Suicide rate almost doubles among teenagers," https://inews.co.uk/news/health/suicide-rates-teenagers-young-people-social-media-141803.

8. NHS, "Nearly a quarter of 14-year-old girls in UK 'self-harming', charity reports," https://www.nhs.uk/news/mental-health/nearly-quarter-14-year-old-girls-uk-self-harming-charity-reports/.

Hence the life-changing idea that the way we use words shapes our social environment. Speaking negatively about others harms them, harms us, and damages the delicate strands of relationship that constitute our common life.

Life-Changing Idea #27

The way we use words shapes our social environment.

Metzora

The Power of Praise

From time to time couples come to see me before their wedding. Sometimes they ask me whether I have any advice to give them as to how to make their marriage strong. In reply I give them a simple suggestion. It is almost magical in its effects. It will make their relationship strong and in other unexpected ways it will transform their lives.

They have to commit themselves to the following ritual. Once a day, usually at the end of the day, they must each praise the other for something the other has done that day, no matter how small: an act, a word, a gesture that was kind, sensitive, generous, or thoughtful. The praise must be focused on that one act, not generalised. It must be genuine; it must come from the heart. And the other must learn to accept the praise.

That is all they have to do. It takes at most a minute or two. But it has to be done, not sometimes, but every day. I learned this in a most unexpected way.

I have written elsewhere[1] about the late Lena Rustin: one of the most remarkable people I have ever met. She was a speech therapist specialising in helping stammering children. She founded the Michael Palin Centre for Stammering in London, and she had a unique approach to her work. Most speech therapists focus on speaking and breathing techniques, and on the individual child (those she worked with were on average around five years old). Lena did more. She focused on relationships, and worked with parents, not just children.

Her view was that to cure a stammer, she had to do more than help the child to speak fluently. She had to change the entire family environment. Families tend to create an equilibrium. If a child stammers, everyone in the family adjusts to it. Therefore if the child is to lose its stammer, all the relationships within the family will have to be renegotiated. Not only must the child change. So must everyone else.

But change at that basic level is hard. We tend to settle into patterns of behaviour until they become comfortable like a well-worn armchair. How do you create an atmosphere within a family that encourages change and makes it unthreatening? The answer, Lena discovered, was praise. She told the families with which she was working that every day they must catch each member of the family doing something right, and say so, specifically, positively, and sincerely. Every member of the family, but especially the parents, had to learn to give and receive praise.

Watching her at work I began to realise that she was creating, within each home, an atmosphere of mutual respect and continuous positive reinforcement. She believed that this would generate self-confidence not just for the stammering child but for all members of the family. The result would be an environment in which people felt safe to change and to help others do so likewise.

I filmed Lena's work for a documentary I made for BBC television on the state of the family in Britain. I also interviewed some of the parents whose children she had worked with. When I asked them whether Lena had helped their child, not only did each of them say "Yes," but they went on to say that *she had helped save their marriage.* This was extraordinary. She was, after all, not a marriage guidance counsellor

---

1. *Lessons in Leadership* (Jerusalem: Maggid Books, 2015), 148.

but a speech therapist. Yet so powerful was this one simple ritual that it had massive beneficial side effects, one of which was to transform the relationship between husbands and wives.

I mention this for two reasons, one obvious, the other less so. The obvious reason is that the Sages were puzzled about the major theme of *Parashot Tazria-Metzora*, the skin disease known as *tzaraat*. Why, they wondered, should the Torah focus at such length on such a condition? It is, after all, not a book of medicine, but of law, morality, and spirituality.

The answer they gave was that *tzaraat* was a punishment for *lashon hara*: evil, hateful, or derogatory speech. They cited the case of Miriam who spoke negatively about her brother Moses and was struck by *tzaraat* for seven days (Num. 12). They also pointed to the incident when at the burning bush Moses spoke negatively about the Israelites and his hand was briefly affected by *tzaraat* (Ex. 4:1–7).

The Sages spoke more dramatically about *lashon hara* than any other offence. They said that it is as bad as committing all three cardinal sins: idolatry, incest, and murder. They said that it kills three people: the one who says it, the one he says it about, and the one who listens to it.[2] And in connection with *Parashot Tazria-Metzora*, they said that the punishment fitted the sin. One who speaks *lashon hara* creates dissension within the camp. Therefore his punishment as a *metzora* (a person stricken with *tzaraat*) was to be temporarily banished from the camp.[3]

So far, so clear. Don't gossip (Lev. 19:16). Don't slander. Don't speak badly about people. Judaism has a rigorous and detailed ethics of speech because it believes that "life and death are in the power of the tongue" (Prov. 18:21). Judaism is a religion of the ear more than the eye;[4] of words rather than images. God created the natural world with words and we create or damage the social world with words. We do not say, "Sticks and stones may break my bones but words will never harm me." To the contrary, words can cause emotional injuries that are as painful as physical ones, perhaps more so.

---

2. Maimonides, *Mishneh Torah, Hilkhot Deot* 7:3.
3. Arakhin 16b.
4. See below on *Parashat Ekev*.

So Lena Rustin's rule of praise is the opposite of *lashon hara*. It is *lashon hatov*: good, positive, encouraging speech. According to Maimonides, to speak in praise of people is part of the command to "love your neighbour as yourself."[5] That is straightforward.

But at a deeper level, there is a reason why it is hard to cure people of *lashon hara*, and harder still to cure them of gossip in general. The American sociologist Samuel Heilman wrote an incisive book, *Synagogue Life*, about a Modern Orthodox congregation of which, for some years, he was a member.[6] He devotes an entire lengthy chapter to synagogue gossip. Giving and receiving gossip, he says, is more or less constitutive of being part of the community. Not gossiping defines you as an outsider.

Gossip, he says, is part of "a tight system of obligatory exchange." The person who scorns gossip completely, declining to be either donor or recipient, at the very least "risks stigmatisation" and at the worst "excludes himself from a central activity of collective life and sociability." In short, gossip is the lifeblood of community.

Now, not only Heilman but probably every adult member of the community knew full well that gossip is biblically forbidden and that negative speech, *lashon hara*, is among the gravest of all sins. They also knew the damage caused by someone who gives more gossip than he or she receives. They used the Yiddish word for such a person: a *yenta*. Yet despite this, argued Heilman, the shul was in no small measure a system for the creation and distribution of gossip.

Synagogue Life was published twenty years before Oxford anthropologist Robin Dunbar's famous book, *Grooming, Gossip and the Evolution of Language*.[7] Dunbar's argument is that, in nature, groups are held together by devoting a considerable amount of time to building relationships and alliances. Non-human primates do this by "grooming,"

5. Maimonides, *Mishneh Torah, Hilkhot Deot* 6:3. Elsewhere I have dealt with the problem of the passage in Arakhin 16a that says that one should not speak in praise of others in case this leads others to disagree. For the different views of Rashi and Maimonides on this, see *Covenant and Conversation: Leviticus – The Book of Holiness* (Jerusalem: Maggid Books, 2015), 223–27.
6. Samuel Heilman, *Synagogue Life: A Study in Symbolic Interaction* (Chicago: University of Chicago Press, 1976), 151–92.
7. Robin Dunbar, *Grooming, Gossip and the Evolution of Language* (London: Faber, 1997).

stroking, and cleaning one another's skin (hence the expression, "If you scratch my back, I'll scratch yours"). But this is very time-consuming and puts a limit on the size of the group.

Humans developed language as a more effective form of grooming. You can only stroke one animal or person at a time, but you can talk to several at a time. The specific form of language that bonds a group together, says Dunbar, is gossip – because this is the way members of the group can learn who to trust and who not to. So gossip is not one form of speech among others. According to Dunbar, it is the most primal of all uses of speech. It is why humans developed language in the first place. Heilman's account of synagogue life fits perfectly into this pattern. Gossip creates community, and community is impossible without gossip.

If this is so, it explains why the prohibitions against gossip and *lashon hara* are so often honoured in the breach, not the observance. So common is *lashon hara* that one of the giants of modern Jewry, Rabbi Yisrael Meir HaKohen (the *Ḥafetz Ḥayim*) devoted much of his life to combatting it. Yet it persists, as anyone who has ever been part of a human group knows from personal experience. You can know it is wrong, yet you and others do it anyway.

This is why I found Lena Rustin's work to have such profound spiritual implications. Her work had nothing to do with gossip, but without intending to she had discovered one of the most powerful antidotes to *lashon hara* ever invented. She taught people to develop the habit of speaking well of one another. She taught them to praise, daily, specifically, and sincerely. Anyone who uses Lena's technique for a prolonged period will be cured of *lashon hara*. It is the most effective antidote I know.

What is more, her technique transforms relationships and saves marriages. It heals what *lashon hara* harms. Evil speech destroys relationships. Good speech mends them. This works not only in marriages and families, but also in communities, organisations, and businesses. So, in any relationship that matters to you, deliver praise daily. Seeing and praising the good in people makes them better people, makes you a better person, and strengthens the bond between you. This really is a life-changing idea.

Life-Changing Idea #28

In any relationship that matters to you, deliver praise daily.
Seeing and praising the good in people makes them better people,
makes you a better person, and strengthens the bond between you.

Aḥarei Mot

Cleansing and
Homecoming

In 1968 I had my first encounter with the Lubavitcher Rebbe at 770 Eastern Parkway, Brooklyn, New York. It changed my life. I was a second-year university student, my summer vacation was drawing to a close, and I was due to return to Britain on the Sunday before Rosh HaShana. The day before, the Rebbe held a *fahrbrengen*. This was a huge gathering of thousands of Hasidim at which the Rebbe spoke for several hours, pausing every twenty minutes or so for a *niggun*, a hasidic song which was sung with great gusto by everyone present.

During one of these singing interludes I went up to the Rebbe to say thank you and farewell, but he looked at me with surprise, told me I did not have to return just yet since the Cambridge University term did not begin until several weeks later, and urged me to stay for Rosh HaShana. That was when I discovered that when a rebbe suggests something, you do it. So I came to spend Rosh HaShana with this extraordinary man and heard him blow shofar, an almost otherworldly experience.

One of the local Hasidim invited me for lunch on the first day, and there I found another guest, with a fascinating story to tell. It turned out that he was a successful composer of pop songs – I knew some of his compositions – and had abandoned Judaism several decades earlier. What brought him here, he said, was that he had been driving alone one day in a remote part of the mid-West when it occurred to him that Rosh HaShana must be imminent. At that moment, a tune came into his head, a hasidic *niggun*, which he had been taught as a child. The melody awoke in him a Jewish identity that had lain dormant for years. There and then, he stopped the car, turned around, and headed for 770 Eastern Parkway. It was as if he had suddenly realised that he was lost, and the music from his childhood was calling him home.

He and I, in our different ways, were both examples of a phenomenon that appeared at this time. The phrase used to describe it was an ancient one, but it had hitherto a quite different meaning. It was *baal teshuva*, meaning, a penitent. Classically this meant someone who had committed a specific sin, and now repented of it. In the late 1960s, however, it came to describe an individual who had been, in some sense, distant from Jewish faith or life and had now come back.

This was not an entirely new phenomenon, but hitherto it had been rare. Previously, either people stayed within the fold or they moved away from it – they became assimilated, or in some cases even converted. There was little movement in the opposite direction, with the exception, in the early twentieth century, of unusual individuals like Franz Rosenzweig and Jiri Langer. Something happened around 1967 to change that: Israel's victory in the Six-Day War, together with thoughts of the Holocaust that had surfaced in the anxious weeks before the war, and the general resurgence of ethnic identities at that time. Suddenly it became acceptable to be different and to wear one's Jewish identity openly with pride.

It was around this time that the first *baal teshuva* yeshivas were opened. The work of Chabad which, under the guidance of the Rebbe, had already been active in this territory for many years, began to be re-evaluated and imitated by many other groups. Like my new acquaintance, the songwriter, a generation was coming home. This had not been witnessed on such a scale for many centuries. Indeed, it would be hard to find a precedent in post-biblical times. The fact that it was described using a classic term, *baal teshuva*, concealed its novelty, because the term itself was being given a new sense.

This became evident to me a year or so later. By now I had become a yeshiva student in Israel in Kefar Chabad (a village I described as being five miles and two centuries from Tel Aviv). At the request of his grandson, I paid a visit to Dayan Yehezkel Abramsky, who had earlier been senior judge of the London Bet Din. He asked me what I was studying. "*Teshuva*," I replied. He – a *mitnaged*, strongly opposed to Hasidism – bridled at the answer. "That is the difference between Chabad and me," he said. "I see *teshuva* as something you need when the machine breaks down. They see it as part of the machine itself."

Exactly so. He was using *teshuva* in its classic sense: repenting and atoning for specific sins. It was a form of repair. *Teshuva* in its modern sense was something else entirely. It was coming home to Jewish identity, practice, and faith after estrangement or ignorance. It was a reorientation of the total personality.

In fact, though, this modern sense is the revival of something very old indeed.

In *Parashat Aḥarei Mot*, we are given a detailed description of Aaron's service on Yom Kippur, the Day of Atonement, when he atoned for his sins, those of his "house," and those of all Israel. This became the model for the service of the high priest when the Temple stood. It was an awe-inspiring occasion. On the holiest day of the year, the holiest person in Israel entered the Holy of Holies and performed the rites that restored the relationship between the people Israel and their Father in heaven.

Yet, if we read Tanakh as a whole we find that there are two models of atonement, not one. They see sin differently, they see its rectification differently, and they use a completely different vocabulary. One is priestly, the other prophetic.

The key verse in our *parasha* describing the effect of the high priest's service states: "For on this day, *atonement* shall be made for you to *cleanse* you of all your sins; you shall be *clean* before the Lord" (Lev. 16:30). There are two essential verbs: K-P-R, to atone, and T-H-R, to cleanse, purify.

Within the world of the *kohen*, the priest, a sin is like a stain. The verb K-P-R first appears in the Torah in connection with God's instructions to Noah to make an ark: "Make yourself an ark of cypress wood; make rooms in it and *cover* it with pitch inside and out" (Gen. 6:14). K-P-R means "to cover over." That is one way to rectify a stained garment, by covering the stain with clean fabric. But the stain still exists even if it is not outwardly visible. Hence the importance of the second stage, T-H-R, "to cleanse, purify," meaning to remove the stain altogether.

These two words are not evenly distributed throughout the Torah or through Tanakh as a whole. So, for example, the root K-P-R appears three times in Genesis, three in Deuteronomy, and fifty-nine times in Leviticus. T-H-R appears seven times in Genesis, six in Deuteronomy, and seventy-four times in Leviticus. K-P-R appears twenty-four times in the prophetic literature, and T-H-R twenty-six times, while the key word for the prophets, SH-U-V, to return, appears 480 times.

For the prophets, sin is equivalent to getting lost, straying from the path, being somewhere one should not be. Accordingly, the punishment for sin, measure for measure, is being sentenced to exile, losing home. That is what happened to Adam and Eve, exiled from Eden. It is what happened to Cain, condemned to be a restless wanderer. It is what Moses told the Israelites would happen to them if they disobeyed the covenant. It is what occurred to the people during the Babylonian exile. Hence the key verb used by virtually all the prophets, to *return*:

Return, O Israel, to the Lord your God, for you have fallen because of your sin. (Hos. 14:2)

I wipe away your sins like a cloud, your transgressions like mist; *return* to Me, for I redeem you. (Is. 44:22)

Turn back, rebellious children, declares the Lord… (Jer. 3:14)

Say to them: As I live, declares the Lord God, it is not My desire that the wicked shall die, but that the wicked *turn* from his [evil] ways and live. *Turn back, turn back* from your evil ways, that you may not die, O House of Israel! (Ezek. 33:11)

From the very days of your fathers you have turned away from My laws and have not observed them. *Return* to Me, and I will *return* to you, said the Lord of Hosts… (Mal. 3:7)

Each of the italicised words uses a form of the verb SH-U-V. The prophets did not speak of atonement and purification. They spoke of coming back, coming home. The master-text from which all these prophetic utterances derive is the speech of Moses to the next generation, at the end of his life:

When all these blessings and curses I have set before you come on you, and you take them to heart wherever the Lord your God disperses you among the nations, and when you and your children *return* to the Lord your God and obey Him with all your heart and with all your soul according to everything I command you today, then the Lord your God will *restore* your fortunes and have compassion on you and gather you again from all the nations where He scattered you. (Deut. 30:1–3)

Though it is not evident in translation, the verb SH-U-V appears seven times in this passage (Deut. 30:1–14). According to Nahmanides, this is the source of the mitzva of *teshuva*.

So the new sense of *teshuva* and *baal teshuva* that developed after the Six-Day War was not something unprecedented. It was the recovery of a tradition that is very old indeed, namely the prophetic sense of *repentance as homecoming*. Not "I sinned and I atone" but "I was distant and I seek to return." Nor is it accidental that this happened in the context of the rebirth of the State of Israel and especially the emotions aroused by the Six-Day War. From Moses to Malachi, the prophets connected the return to the land and the return to God. Physical and spiritual homecoming are related.

Hence the life-changing idea: Sometimes we find our life is on the wrong track, not because of a specific sin, but because we have an overall sense of being lost. *Teshuva* means coming home to God.

Life-Changing Idea #29

Sometimes we find our life is on the wrong track, not because of a specific sin but because we have an overall sense of being lost. Teshuva means coming home to God.

Kedoshim

Love Is Not Enough

The opening chapter of *Parashat Kedoshim* contains two of the most powerful of all commands: to love your neighbour and to love the stranger. "Love your neighbour as yourself: I am the Lord" goes the first. "When a stranger comes to live in your land, do not mistreat him" goes the second, and continues, "Treat the stranger the way you treat your native-born. Love him as yourself, for you were strangers in Egypt. I am the Lord your God (Lev. 19:33–34).[1]

The first is often called the "golden rule" and held to be universal to all cultures. This is a mistake. The golden rule is different. In its positive formulation it states, "Act towards others as you would wish them to act towards you," or in its negative formulation, given by Hillel, "What is hateful to you, do not do to your neighbour." These rules are

---

1. Note that some read these two verses as referring specifically to a *ger tzedek*, a convert to Judaism. That, however, is to miss the point of the command, which is: do not allow ethnic differences (that is, between a born Jew and a convert) to influence your emotions. Judaism must be race- and colour-blind.

not about love. They are about justice, or more precisely, what evolutionary psychologists call reciprocal altruism. The Torah does not say, "Be nice or kind to your neighbour, because you would wish him to be nice or kind to you." It says, "*Love* your neighbour." That is something different and far stronger.

The second command is more radical still. Most people in most societies in most ages have feared, hated, and often harmed the stranger. There is a word for this: xenophobia. How often have you heard the opposite word: xenophilia? My guess is, never. People don't usually love strangers. That is why, almost always when the Torah states this command – which it does, according to the Sages, thirty-six times – it adds an explanation: "because you were strangers in Egypt." I know of no other nation that was born as a nation in slavery and exile. We know what it feels like to be a vulnerable minority. That is why love of the stranger is so central to Judaism and so marginal to most other systems of ethics.[2] But here too, the Torah does not use the word "justice." There is a command of justice towards strangers, but that is a different law: "You shall not wrong a stranger or oppress him" (Ex. 22:20). Here the Torah speaks not of justice but of love.

These two commands define Judaism as a religion of love – not just of God ("with all your heart, with all your soul, and with all your might" [Deut. 6:5]), but of humanity also. That was and is a world-changing idea.

But what calls for deep reflection is where these commands appear. They do so in *Parashat Kedoshim* in what, to contemporary eyes, must seem one of the strangest passages in the Torah.

Leviticus 19 brings side by side laws of seemingly quite different kinds. Some belong to the moral life: Don't gossip, don't hate, don't take revenge, don't bear a grudge. Some are about social justice: Leave parts of the harvest for the poor; don't pervert justice; don't withhold wages; don't use false weights and measures. Others have a different feel altogether: Don't crossbreed livestock; don't plant a field with mixed seeds; don't wear a garment of mixed wool and linen; don't eat fruit of

---

2. Had it existed in Europe, there would not have been a thousand years of persecution of the Jews, followed by the birth of racial anti-Semitism, followed by the Holocaust.

the first three years; don't eat blood; don't practise divination; don't lacerate yourself.

At first glance these laws have nothing to do with one another: Some are about conscience, some about politics and economics, and others about purity and taboo. Clearly, though, the Torah is telling us otherwise. They do have something in common. They are all about order, limits, *boundaries*. They are telling us that reality has a certain underlying structure whose integrity must be honoured. If you hate or take revenge you destroy relationships. If you commit injustice, you undermine the trust on which society depends. If you fail to respect the integrity of nature (different seeds, species, and so on), you take the first step down a path that ends in environmental disaster.

There is an order to the universe, part moral, part political, part ecological. When that order is violated, eventually there is chaos. When that order is observed and preserved, we become co-creators of the sacred harmony and integrated diversity that the Torah calls "holy."

Why then is it specifically in this chapter that the two great commands – love of the neighbour and the stranger – appear? The answer is profound and very far from obvious. Because this is where love belongs – in an ordered universe.

Jordan Peterson, the Canadian psychologist, has recently become one of the most prominent public intellectuals of our time. His book *12 Rules for Life* has been a massive best-seller in Britain and America.[3] He has had the courage to be a contrarian, challenging the fashionable fallacies of the contemporary West. Particularly striking in the book is Rule 5: "Do not let your children do anything that makes you dislike them."

His point is more subtle than it sounds. A significant number of parents today, he says, fail to socialise their children. They indulge them. They do not teach them rules. There are, he argues, complex reasons for this. Some of it has to do with lack of attention. Parents are busy and don't have time for the demanding task of teaching discipline. Some of it has to do with Jean-Jacques Rousseau's influential but misleading idea that children

---

3. Jordan Peterson, *12 Rules for Life: An Antidote to Chaos* (London: Allen Lane, 2018).

are naturally good, and are made bad by society and its rules. So the best way to raise happy, creative children is to let them choose for themselves.

Partly, though, he says it is because "modern parents are simply paralysed by the fear that they will no longer be liked or even loved by their children if they chastise them for any reason." They are afraid to damage their relationship by saying "No." They fear the loss of their children's love.

The result is that they leave their children dangerously unprepared for a world that will not indulge their wishes or desire for attention; a world that can be tough, demanding, and sometimes cruel. Without rules, social skills, self-restraints, and a capacity to defer gratification, children grow up without an apprenticeship in reality. His conclusion is powerful:

> Clear rules make for secure children and calm, rational parents. Clear principles of discipline and punishment balance mercy and justice so that social development and psychological maturity can be optimally promoted. Clear rules and proper discipline help the child, and the family, and society, establish, maintain, and expand order. That is all that protects us from chaos.[4]

That is what the opening chapter of *Parashat Kedoshim* is about: clear rules that create and sustain a social order. That is where real love – not the sentimental, self-deceiving substitute – belongs. Without order, love merely adds to the chaos. Misplaced love can lead to parental neglect, producing spoiled children with a sense of entitlement who are destined for an unhappy, unsuccessful, unfulfilled adult life.

Peterson's book, whose subtitle is "An Antidote to Chaos," is not just about children. It is about the mess the West has made since the Beatles sang (in 1967), "All you need is love." As a clinical psychologist, Peterson has seen the emotional cost of a society without a shared moral code. People, he writes, need ordering principles, without which there is chaos. We require "rules, standards, values – alone and together. We require routine and tradition. That's order." Too much order can be bad, but too little can be worse. Life is best lived, he says, on the dividing line

---

4. Ibid., 113–44.

between them. It's there, he says, that "we find the meaning that justifies life and its inevitable suffering." Perhaps if we lived properly, he adds, "we could withstand the knowledge of our own fragility and mortality, without the sense of aggrieved victimhood that produces, first, resentment, then envy, and then the desire for vengeance and destruction."[5]

That is as acute an explanation as I have ever heard for the unique structure of Leviticus 19. Its combination of moral, political, economic, and environmental laws is a supreme statement of a universe of (divinely created) order of which we are the custodians. But the chapter is not just about order. It is about humanising that order through love – the love of neighbour and stranger. And when the Torah says, don't hate, don't take revenge and don't bear a grudge, it is an uncanny anticipation of Peterson's remarks about resentment, envy, and the desire for vengeance and destruction.

Hence the life-changing idea that we have forgotten for far too long: Love is not enough. Relationships need rules.

Life-Changing Idea #30

Clear rules and proper discipline help to establish, maintain, and expand order for more fulfilled children, families, and society. Love is not enough. Relationships need rules.

---

5. Ibid., xxxiv.

Emor

In the Diary

Time management is more than management and larger than time. It is about life itself. God gives us one thing above all: life itself. And He gives it to us all on equal terms. However rich we are, there are still only twenty-four hours in a day, seven days in a week, and a span of years that, however long, is still all too short. Whoever we are, whatever we do, whatever gifts we have, the single most important fact about our life, on which all else depends, is how we spend our time.[1]

"The span of our life is seventy years, or if we are strong, eighty years," says Psalm 90, and despite the massive reduction of premature deaths in the past century, the average life expectancy around the world, according to the most recent United Nations figures (2010–2015), is 71.5 years.[2] So, concludes the Psalm, "Teach us to number our days that we

---

1. For an excellent recent book about the way our behaviour is governed by time, see Daniel Pink, *When: The Scientific Secrets of Perfect Timing* (Edinburgh: Canongate Books Ltd, 2018).
2. https://en.wikipedia.org/wiki/List_of_countries_by_life_expectancy.

may get a heart of wisdom," reminding us that time management is not simply a productivity tool. It is, in fact, a spiritual exercise.

Hence the following life-changing idea, which sounds simple, but isn't. Do not rely exclusively on to-do lists. Use a diary. The most successful people schedule their most important tasks in their diary.[3] They know that if it isn't in there, it won't get done. To-do lists are useful, but not sufficient. They remind us of what we have to do but not when. They fail to distinguish between what is important and what is merely urgent. They clutter the mind with trivia and distract us when we ought to be focusing on the things that matter most in the long run. Only a diary connects *what* with *when*. And what applies to individuals applies to communities and cultures as a whole.

That is what the Jewish calendar is about. It is why chapter 23, in this *parasha*, is so fundamental to the continued vitality of the Jewish people. It sets out a weekly, monthly, and yearly schedule of sacred times. This is continued and extended in *Parashat Behar* to seven- and fifty-year schedules. The Torah forces us to remember what contemporary culture regularly forgets: Our lives must have dedicated times when we focus on the things that give life a meaning. And because we are social animals, the most important times are the ones we share. The Jewish calendar is precisely that: a structure of shared time.

We all need an identity, and every identity comes with a story. So we need a time when we remind ourselves of the story of where we came from and why we are who we are. That happens on Pesaḥ, when we re-enact the founding moment of our people as they began their long walk to freedom.

We need a moral code, an internalised satellite navigation system to guide us through the wilderness of time. That is what we celebrate on Shavuot when we relive the moment when our ancestors stood at Sinai, made their covenant with God, and heard Heaven declare the Ten Commandments.

We need a regular reminder of the brevity of life itself, and hence the need to use time wisely. That is what we do on Rosh HaShana as we stand before God in judgment and pray to be written in the Book of Life.

3. See Kevin Kruse, *15 Secrets Successful People Know about Time Management* (2017).

We need a time when we confront our faults, apologise for the wrong we have done, make amends, resolve to change, and ask for forgiveness. That is the work of Yom Kippur.

We need to remind ourselves that we are on a journey, that we are "strangers and sojourners" on earth, and that where we live is only a temporary dwelling. That is what we experience on Sukkot.

And we need, from time to time, to step back from the ceaseless pressures of work and find the rest in which we can celebrate our blessings, renew our relationships, and recover the full vigour of body and mind. That is Shabbat.

Doubtless, most people – at least, most reflective people – know that these things are important. But knowing is not enough. These are elements of life that become real when we *live* them, not just when we *know* them. That is why they have to be in the diary, not just on a to-do list.

As Alain de Botton points out in his *Religion for Atheists*, we all know that it is important to mend broken relationships. But without Yom Kippur, there are psychological pressures that can make us endlessly delay such mending.[4] If we are the offended party, we may not want to show other people our hurt. It makes us look fragile, vulnerable. And if we are the offending party, it can be hard to admit our guilt, not least because we feel so guilty. As he puts it: "We can be so sorry that we find ourselves incapable of saying sorry." The fact that Yom Kippur exists means that there is a day in the diary on which we have to do the mending – and this is made easier by the knowledge that everyone else is doing so likewise. In his words:

> It is the day itself that is making us sit here and talk about the peculiar incident six months ago when you lied and I blustered and you accused me of insincerity and I made you cry, an incident that neither of us can quite forget but that we can't quite mention either and which has been slowly corroding the trust

---

4. Of course, Yom Kippur atones only for sins between us and God, not for those between us and our fellows. But it is a day when, traditionally, we seek to make amends for the latter also. Indeed most of the sins we confess in the long list, *al ḥet*, are sins between humans and other humans.

and love we once had for one another. It is the day that has given us the opportunity, indeed the responsibility, to stop talking of our usual business and to reopen a case we pretended to have put out of our minds. We are not satisfying ourselves, we are obeying the rules.[5]

Exactly so: We are obeying the rules. We are following the Jewish calendar, which takes many of the most important truths about our lives and, instead of putting them on a to-do list, writes them in the diary.

What happens when you do not have that kind of diary? Contemporary Western secular society is a case study in the consequences. People no longer tell the story of the nation. Hence national identities, especially in Europe, are almost a thing of the past – one reason for the return of the Far Right in countries like Austria, Holland, and France.

People no longer share a moral code, which is why students in universities seek to ban speakers with whose views they disagree. When there is no shared code, there can be no reasoned argument, only the use of force.

As for remembering the brevity of life, Roman Krznaric reminds us that modern society is "geared to distract us from death. Advertising creates a world where everyone is forever young. We shunt the elderly away in care homes, out of sight and mind." Death has become "a topic as taboo as sex was during the Victorian era."[6]

Atonement and forgiveness have been driven out of public life, to be replaced by public shaming, courtesy of the social media. As for Shabbat, almost everywhere in the West the day of rest has been replaced by the sacred day of shopping, and rest itself replaced by the relentless tyranny of smartphones.

Fifty years ago, the most widespread prediction was that by now almost everything would have been automated. The work week would be down to twenty hours, and our biggest problem would be what to do with all our leisure. Instead, most people today find themselves working harder than ever with less and less time to pursue the things

---

5. Alain De Botton, *Religion for Atheists* (New York: Pantheon Books, 2012), 55–56.
6. Roman Krznaric, *Carpe Diem Regained* (London: Unbound, 2017), 22.

that make life meaningful. As Leon Kass recently put it, people "still hope to find meaning in their lives," but they are increasingly confused about "what a worthy life might look like, and about how they might be able to live one."[7]

Hence the life-changing magic of the Jewish calendar. Philosophy seeks timeless truths. Judaism, by contrast, takes truths and translates them into time in the form of sacred, shared moments when we experience the great truths by living them. So, whatever you want to achieve, write it in the diary or it will not happen. And live by the Jewish calendar if you want to experience, not just occasionally think about, the things that give life a meaning.

Life-Changing Idea #31

Do not rely exclusively on to-do lists. Use a diary.
And live by the Jewish calendar to experience the things
that give life a meaning.

---

7. Leon Kass, *Leading a Worthy Life: Finding Meaning in Modern Times* (New York: Encounter Books, 2018), 9.

Behar

We Are What We
Do Not Own

The late Maurice and Vivienne Wohl were one of the most remarkable couples I ever met. They were a study in contrasts. Maurice was quiet, introspective, reflective, and reserved. Vivienne was outgoing and vivacious, a people person in the truest sense. They complemented one another perfectly: two halves of a whole.

What made them special, outwardly, was that they were givers on a monumental scale. In Israel, for example, they donated the 19-acre Rose Garden next to the Knesset and the striking Daniel Libeskind-designed cultural centre at Bar Ilan University. They endowed medical facilities in Tel Aviv and Jerusalem, as well as at King's College and University College, London. They supported Jewish schools in Britain and yeshivas in Israel – and all this hardly touches the surface of their philanthropy.

What was really moving, though, was how they became a couple in the first place, because Vivienne was thirty years younger than Maurice. When they met, Maurice was in his late forties, a dedicated businessman seemingly destined for a life of bachelorhood. Vivienne, not yet twenty, was the daughter of friends of Maurice who had asked whether she could work for him during a vacation.

One day, Maurice offered to take her for lunch. On their way to the restaurant, they passed a beggar in the street. Maurice gave him a coin, and walked on. Vivienne stopped and asked Maurice if he would be kind enough to give her in advance a substantial sum – she named the figure – from this week's wages. Maurice handed over the money. She then walked back and gave it all to the beggar. "Why did you do that?" asked Maurice. "Because what you gave him was not enough to make a change to his life. He needed something more."

When the week came to an end, Maurice said to Vivienne, "I am not going to give you your full wages this week, because you gave away part of the money as a mitzva and I do not want to rob you of it." But it was then that he decided that he must marry her, because, as he told me shortly before he died, "Her heart was bigger than mine."

I tell this story because it illustrates a dimension of *Parashat Behar* we often miss. Leviticus 25 deals with a problem that is as acute today as it was thirty-three centuries ago. It is about the inevitable inequalities that arise in every free market economy. Market economics is good at the creation of wealth but bad at its distribution. Whatever the starting point, inequalities emerge early on between the more and less success-ful, and they become more pronounced over time.[1]

Economic inequality leads to inequality of power, and the result is often the abuse of the weak by the strong. This is a constant refrain of the prophets. Amos speaks of those who "sell the innocent for sil-ver, and the needy for a pair of shoes; who trample on the heads of the poor as on the dust of the ground, and deny justice to the oppressed" (Amos 2:6–7). Isaiah cries, "Woe to those who make unjust laws and issue oppressive decrees…making widows their prey and robbing the fatherless" (Is. 10:1–2). Micah inveighs against people who "covet fields and seize them, houses and take them away; they oppress householder and house, people and their inheritance" (Mic. 2:1–2).

---

1. This is the argument of Thomas Piketty, *Capital in the 21st Century* (Harvard: Harvard University Press, 2014).

This is a problem for almost every society and age. What makes the Torah distinctive is that it refuses a one-dimensional answer to what is a genuinely complex problem. Equality is a value, but so too is freedom. Communism and socialism have been tried, and failed; but the free market generates its discontents also. One principle that can be inferred from Tanakh is that the market was made to serve human beings; human beings were not made to serve the market. The fundamental question is therefore: What best serves humanity under the sovereignty of God?

A careful reading of *Parashat Behar* reveals that the Torah's approach to this question operates at three completely different levels. One is political, a second is psychological, and the third is theological.

The first level is simple. *Parashat Behar* proposes two cycles of redistribution, *Shemitta* and *Yovel*, the seventh and fiftieth year. The intent here is to restore a level playing field through a combination of debt remission, liberation of slaves, and the return of ancestral land to its original owners. This is a way of redressing accumulated inequalities without constant intervention in the economy. That is the political dimension.

The psychological dimension is what the French revolutionaries called fraternity. Ten times the laws in Behar use the word "brother." "Do not wrong your brother" (Lev. 25:14); "If your brother becomes poor" (v. 25); "The nearest redeemer shall come and redeem what his brother has sold" (ibid.) This is sound evolutionary logic. We know from the work of W. D. Hamilton and others on kin selection that the most basic driver of altruism is the family. We make sacrifices most readily for those most closely related to us.

That, in no small measure, is why from the beginning of the Jewish story to today, Jews have thought of themselves as a single family, descendants of Abraham, Isaac and Jacob, Sarah, Rebecca, Rachel and Leah. It is one thing to legislate altruism, through such institutions as the seventh and fiftieth year. It is another to frame a society in such a way as to make people feel bound together in an unbreakable bond of shared responsibility. Hence the narratives of Genesis, focused overwhelmingly on the people of Israel not as a nation but as a family. Law and narrative here go hand in hand. Because the entire Jewish people is a single vastly extended family, we must help when one of our brothers or sisters becomes destitute. This is ethnicity in the service of morality.

Finally, though, and most profoundly, comes the theological dimension. For it is here, in chapter 25, that we hear with unparalleled lucidity what I believe to be the single most fundamental principle of biblical law. Listen carefully to these two passages, the first about land, the second about Hebrew slaves:

> The land shall not be sold in perpetuity, for the land is Mine: you are strangers and sojourners with Me. (v. 23)

> If your brother becomes poor and sells himself to you, you shall not work him as a slave.... For they are My servants whom I brought out of the land of Egypt; they shall not be sold as slaves. You shall not rule over him ruthlessly but shall fear your God. (vv. 39–43)

The Torah is making a radical point. There is no such thing as absolute ownership. There is to be no freehold in the land of Israel because the land belongs ultimately to God. Nor may an Israelite own another Israelite because we all belong to God, and have done so ever since He brought our ancestors out of slavery in Egypt.

It is this principle that alone makes sense of the Torah's narrative of the creation of the universe. The Torah is not a book of science. It is a book of law. That is what the word "Torah" means. It follows that the opening chapter of the Torah is not a scientific account but a legal one. It is not an answer to the question, "How was the universe born?" It is an answer to a different question entirely: "By what right does God command human beings?" The answer is: Because He created the universe. Therefore He owns the universe. Therefore He is entitled to lay down the conditions on which He permits us to inhabit the universe. This is the basis of all biblical law. God rules not by might but by right – the right of a creator vis-à-vis his creation.

Nowhere is this clearer than in *Parashat Behar*, where it becomes the basis of legislation about land ownership and slavery. Jewish law rests on the principle that only God owns anything. What we possess, we do not own but merely hold in trust. That is why the concept of *tzedek/tzedaka* is untranslatable into English, because it means both justice and charity. In English, justice and charity are radically different. We do justice because we must; we give charity because we may. If I give you £1,000 because I owe it to you, that is justice. If I give you the same amount because I owe you nothing but I think you need it, that is charity. An act may be one or the other but not both.

In Judaism, by contrast, what we possess is not ours. It belongs to God. He has merely placed it in our safekeeping. We are looking after it on behalf of God. One of the conditions of that trust is that if we have more than we need, we should share it with those who have less than they need. That is *tzedaka*: justice and charity combined.

That was how Maurice and Vivienne Wohl lived their lives. God had given Maurice success, and he knew that the wealth he had accumulated was not really his at all. God had given it to him to look after, trusting that he would use it wisely to enhance the lives of others. Maurice, though, was honest enough to realise that he was probably better at making money than giving it away, and that if he did not give it away to people and causes that needed it, he was failing in his duty to God and his fellow humans. That is why, when he met Vivienne and saw how sensitively she understood the needs of others and how willing she was to make sacrifices for them, he knew he had to marry her. So, throughout their almost forty years together, they used the blessings God had given them to bring blessings into other people's lives. It was a privilege to know them.

The larger truth of *Parashat Behar* is that you cannot create a just society by political measures alone (debt remission, restoration of ancestral property, and so on). There are psychological and theological dimensions that are also vital.

But at a simple personal level, it contains a genuinely life-changing idea. Think of what you possess not as something you own but as something you hold in trust for the benefit, not only of you and your family, but also of others. In life, ask not, "What can I gain?" but "What can I give?" You will travel more lightly and with greater joy. You will enhance the lives of others. You will feel that your life has been worthwhile. Hardly any of us can give on the scale of a Maurice or Vivienne Wohl, but when it comes to giving, scale does not matter. Be a blessing to others, and you will find that life has been a blessing to you.

Life-Changing Idea #32

In life, ask not, "What can I gain?" but "What can I give?"
Be a blessing to others and you will find that life has been a blessing to you.

Beḥukkotai

In Search of the Why

The most often quoted of all Nietzsche's remarks – indeed one of the most quoted sentences of all in recent times – is his statement that one who has a *why* to live for can bear almost any *how*.[1] If life has a meaning, if our own life has a purpose, if there is a task we have yet to fulfil, then something within us gives us the strength to survive suffering and sorrow. The call of the future helps us get through the pain of the present and the trauma of the past.

Ironically it was Nietzsche himself who saw more clear-sightedly than anyone else that loss of faith in God would result in the death of meaning. This is what he has his madman say as he is announcing the "death of God:"

---

1. The actual quote, from the "Maxims and Arrows" section of *Twilight of the Idols*, is: "If we possess our *why* of life we can put up with almost any *how*" (Nietzsche, *Twilight of the Idols and The Antichrist*, translated by R. J. Hollingdale [London: Penguin, 2003], 33). The irony is that the person who did most to popularise this quote was Viktor Frankl, a survivor of Auschwitz. On Nietzsche's anti-Semitism, see Robert C. Holub, *Nietzsche's Jewish Problem* (Princeton: Princeton University Press, 2016).

What did we do when we unchained the earth from its sun? Whither is it moving now? Whither are we moving now? Away from all suns? Are we not perpetually falling? Backward, sideward, forward, in all directions? Is there any up or down left? Are we not straying as through an infinite nothing? Do we not feel the breath of empty space? Has it not become colder? Is it not more and more night coming on all the time?[2]

Infinite nothing. Empty space. A world without God is, in an ultimate sense, a universe without a *why*. It may have beauty, grandeur, scale, and scope – but not meaning.

Almost precisely the opposite insight occurred, more than two hundred years earlier, to one of the most brilliant mathematicians of the seventeenth century, Blaise Pascal, who wrote, as if in anticipation of Nietzsche, "The eternal silence of these infinite spaces terrifies me." During the night of November 23, 1654, Pascal, then aged thirty-one, had a life-changing religious experience which he described in the following note: "Fire. God of Abraham, God of Isaac, God of Jacob, not of the philosophers and the scholars..." He ended by quoting Psalm 119:16: "I will not forget Thy word. Amen." He sewed this note into his coat, kept it with him always, and dedicated the rest of his life to exploring religious faith.

The God of Abraham, Isaac, and Jacob is the God who speaks, who calls, who listens. The infinite spaces are not silent. Beneath and beyond them is the still, small voice of God, and it is this that gives meaning to history and to our individual lives. As the historian J. H. Plumb wrote: "The concept that within the history of mankind itself a process was at work which would mould his future... seems to have found its first expression among the Jews." For the Jews, said Plumb, "the past became more than a collection of tales." It became "an intimate part of destiny, and an interpretation of the future, more certain, more absolute, more comprehensive, than any divination, either by the stars or oracles could ever be."[3] Jews were the first to find meaning in history. They discovered the *why*. That is

2. Friedrich Nietzsche, *The Gay Science*, translated by Walter Kaufmann (New York: Vintage Books, 1974), 181.
3. J. H. Plumb, *The Death of the Past* (London: Pelican, 1973), 56–57.

why they were able to bear almost any *how*. Judaism is the oldest, deepest expression of humanity as the meaning-seeking and -finding animal.

These are, relatively speaking, modern thoughts. Yet they lie at the heart of *Parashat Beḥukkotai* – if we follow the interpretation of Maimonides. *Parashat Beḥukkotai* begins with the blessings that will ensue if the Israelites are faithful to their mission and covenant with God. Then come the curses that will follow disobedience. They are long, terrifying, and relentless – even if they end, as they do, with a note of consolation: "Yet, despite all this, when they are in the land of their enemies, I will not spurn them, or abhor them so as to destroy them utterly and break My covenant with them; for I am the Lord their God" (Lev. 26:44). How, though, are we to interpret the blessing and the curse?

The keyword of the curses is *keri*. The word appears here seven times – and nowhere else in the entire Tanakh. The basic principle is clear. "If you act towards Me with *keri* – says God – I will act towards you with *keri*." But what the word means is not clear. The various translations include rebelliousness, obstinacy, indifference, hard-heartedness, and reluctance.

Maimonides, however, relates it to the word *mikreh*, meaning "by chance." He interprets the overall message as: If you behave as if history were mere chance, and not divine providence, then, says God, I will leave you to chance. The result will be that Israel – a small nation set in a highly hostile neighbourhood, then and now – will eventually be defeated, devastated, and come close to destruction.

This is a remarkable reading and points towards a distinction that we sometimes forget: between divine punishment on the one hand, and the withdrawal of divine providence on the other – what the Torah calls "the hiding of the face" of God.[4] When God punishes, He punishes the guilty. But when God "hides His face," even the innocent may suffer.

God hides His face from man when man hides his face from God. That is how Maimonides understands the *parasha*, and it is strikingly similar to Nietzsche's claim that "God is dead." When God is eclipsed, all that remains is "infinite nothing" and "empty space." What dies is not God but man, the meaning-seeking animal. In his place, as Nietzsche

---

4. See Deuteronomy 31:18.

knew, comes man the power-seeking animal. From there it is a short step to nihilism and barbarism.

To be a Jew is to have faith that our individual lives and our collective history have meaning. God is there even if we cannot feel Him. He hears us even when we do not hear Him. That is the blessing. It gave our people the courage to survive some of the worst blows ever to befall a people. It is what gives us, as individuals, the strength to come through "the slings and arrows of outrageous fortune."[5] Lose that faith and we lose that strength. We are "left to chance." That is the curse. Chance is not kind but blind. The curse is not a punishment, but a consequence.

Hence the life-changing idea: Search for meaning and you will discover strength. Life is not *mikreh*, mere chance. It is a story of which you are a part, a question to which you are the answer, a call directed to the smartphone of your soul. That is our people's collective destiny, within which each of us has a specific and individual purpose. Find it and your *why* will carry you through almost any *how*. Or as Jordan Peterson puts it:

> Meaning is the Way, the path of life more abundant, the place you live when you are guided by Love and speaking Truth and when nothing you want or could possibly want takes any precedence over precisely that.[6]

Hence his Rule 7: Pursue what is meaningful, not what is expedient.

For everything there is a meaning. It does not always say: This is why such-and-such happened. Sometimes it says: Given that such-and-such happened, this is what you must do. Once we find the *why*, even a curse can be turned into a blessing. Without the *why*, even a blessing can become a curse. So search for the *why* and the rest will follow: strength, fulfilment, peace.

Life-Changing Idea #33

Search for meaning and you will discover strength, fulfilment, and peace.

---

5. From Hamlet's famous soliloquy, "To Be or Not to Be."
6. Peterson, *12 Rules for Life*, 201.

Numbers
במדבר

Bemidbar

The Two Journeys

The books of Exodus and Numbers have some striking similarities. They are both about journeys. They both portray the Israelites as quarrelsome and ungrateful. Both contain stories about the people complaining about food and water. In both the Israelites commit a major sin: in Exodus, the golden calf; in Numbers, the episode of the spies. In both, God threatens to destroy them and begin again with Moses. Both times, Moses' passionate appeal persuades God to forgive the people. It is easy, when reading the book of Numbers, to feel a sense of déjà vu. We have been here before.

But there is a difference. Exodus is about a journey *from*. Numbers is about a journey *to*. Exodus is the story of an escape from slavery. *Exodus* means just that: departure, withdrawal, leaving. By contrast, in the book of Numbers the people have already left Egypt far behind. They have spent a prolonged period in the Sinai desert. They have received the Torah and built the Sanctuary. Now they are ready to move on. This time they are looking forward, not back. They are thinking, not of the danger they are fleeing from, but of the destination they are travelling towards, the Promised Land.

If we had never read the Torah before, we might have assumed that the second half of the journey would be more relaxed, the people more optimistic, the mood more hopeful. After all, the great dangers had passed. After prolonged refusal, finally Pharaoh had let the people go. Miraculously they had been saved at the Red Sea. They had fought and defeated the Amalekites. What else did they have to worry about? They knew that when God was with them, no force could prevail against them.

In fact, though, the opposite is the case. The mood of Numbers is palpably darker than it is in Exodus. The rebellions are more serious. Moses' leadership is more hesitant. We see him giving way, at times, to anger and despair. The Torah, with great realism, is telling us something counterintuitive and of great significance.

The journey *from* is always easier than the journey *to*.

So it is in politics. It may take a revolution to depose a tyrant, but it is easier to do that than to create a genuinely free society with the rule of law and respect for human rights. The Arab Spring, with its high hopes and its legacy of failing states, civil war, and terror, is a compelling example. So is the history of post-Tito Yugoslavia or present-day Russia.

Likewise in the life of individuals. There have been endless stories in the modern world of Jews who were determined to break free of "the ghetto" and what they saw as Jewish provincialism and backwardness. They became great successes in one field after another, only to find themselves – like the Marranos of fifteenth-century Spain – deeply conflicted and doubly alienated, having lost a home in the old world and failed to find full acceptance in the new.

There is a biological reason why this is so. We are genetically predisposed to react strongly to danger. Our deepest instincts are aroused. We move into the fight-or-flight mode, with our senses alert, our attention focused, and our adrenalin levels high. When it comes to fleeing *from*, we often find ourselves accessing strengths we did not know we had.

But fleeing *to* is something else entirely. It means making a home in a place where, literally or metaphorically, we have not been before. We become "strangers in a strange land." We need to learn new skills, shoulder new responsibilities, acquire new strengths. That calls for imagination and willpower. It involves the most unique of all human abilities: envisaging a future that has not yet been and acting to bring it about. Fleeing *to* is a journey into the unknown.

That was the difference between Abraham and his father Terah. The Torah tells us that "Terah took his son Abram … and they went out together from Ur of the Chaldeans to go into the land of Canaan; but when they came to Haran, they settled there" (Gen. 11:31). Terah had sufficient willpower for the journey *from* (Ur of the Chaldeans) but not for the journey *to* (Canaan). It was left to Abraham to reach the destination.

To be a Jew is to know that, in some sense, life is a journey. So it was for Abraham. So it was for Moses. So it is for us, collectively and individually. Hence the importance of knowing at the outset where we are travelling to, and never forgetting, never giving up. Leaving is easy, arriving is hard.

Which is why, when students ask me for advice about their careers, I tell them that the most important thing is to dream. Dream about what you would like to do, to be, to achieve. Dream about the chapter you would like to write in the story of our people. Dream about what difference you would like to make to the world. "In dreams," said W. B. Yeats, "begin responsibilities." I'm not entirely sure what he meant by that, but this I know: In dreams begin destinations. They are where we start thinking about the future. They signal the direction of our journey.

I am amazed by how many people never really dream a future for themselves. They can spend months planning a holiday, but not even a day planning a life. They take it as it comes. They wait, like Charles Dickens' Mr Micawber, for "something to turn up." This is not the best recipe for a life. "Wherever you find the word *vayehi*, 'and it came to pass,'" said the Sages, "it is always the prelude to pain."[1] Letting things happen is passive, not active. It means that you are letting outside factors determine the course of your life. Of course, they will always affect it. However sure we are of what we want to achieve, we are always subject to unexpected occurrences, wrong turns, bad decisions, setbacks, and failures. But if we know where we want to be, eventually we will get back on track.

---

1. Megilla 10b.

Timothy Ferris, compiler of the book *Tribe of Mentors*,[2] asked me an interesting question: "When you feel overwhelmed or unfocused, what do you do?" I told him that just before I became chief rabbi, in 1991, I realised that the sheer pressure of unexpected happenings, especially when you are in public life, can blow anyone off course. When someone asked British Prime Minister Harold Macmillan what he most feared, he replied, "Events, dear boy, events." So it became clear to me that I had to set out my objectives in advance, in such a way as to ensure I would never forget or be distracted from them.

In 1991 we did not yet have smartphones or computerised diaries. I used a pocket notebook called a Filofax. So on the first page of my Filofax I wrote my life goals. This meant that I saw them every time I looked in my diary. I was reminded of them several times daily. I still have them, and they have not changed in all the intervening years. How far I was successful, I do not know. But this I know: I never forgot where I was travelling to. I never lost sight of the destination.

Travelling *from* is easy. I knew I had to overcome my ignorance, Jewish and secular. I knew I had bad habits I had to cure – I am still working on them. But the real challenge is to know where God wants us to travel to. What task were we put in the world, in this time and place, with these gifts, to do? The answer to that constitutes the destination we key in to our satellite navigation system for the journey called life.

The Israelites, in their journey, made a series of mistakes. They focused too much on the present (the food, the water) and too little on the future. When they faced difficulties, they had too much fear and too little faith. They kept looking back to how things were instead of looking forward to how they might be. The result was that almost an entire generation suffered the fate of Abraham's father. They knew how to leave but not how to arrive. They experienced exodus but not entry.

So, in answer to Tim Ferris' question, "What do you do when you feel overwhelmed or unfocused?" I replied with this life-changing

---

2. Timothy Ferris, *Tribe of Mentors: Short Life Advice from the Best in the World* (Boston: Houghton Mifflin Harcourt, 2017).

idea: Remember your destination. This will help you make the single most important distinction in life, which is to distinguish between an opportunity to be seized and a temptation to be resisted.

Life-Changing Idea #34

Remember your destination. This will help you to distinguish between an opportunity to be seized and a temptation to be resisted.

Naso

Lifting Heads

The word *Naso* that gives its name to this *parasha* is a verb of an extraordinary range of meanings, among them: to lift, to carry, and to forgive. Here though, and elsewhere in the wilderness years, it is used, in conjunction with the phrase *et rosh* ("the head") to mean "to count." This is an odd way of speaking, because biblical Hebrew is not short of other verbs meaning to count, among them *limnot*, *lispor*, and *lifkod*. Why then not use one of these verbs? Why not simply say "count" instead of "lift the head"?

The answer takes us into one of the most revolutionary of all Jewish beliefs. If we are each in the image of God, then every one of us has infinite value. We are each unique. Even genetically identical twins share only approximately 50 per cent of their attributes. None of us is substitutable for any other. This may well be the single most important consequence of monotheism. Discovering God, singular and alone, our ancestors discovered the human individual, singular and alone.

This was simply not a value in the ancient world, nor is it one in tyrannical or totalitarian societies today. The ruler might be deemed to have infinite value; so might some of the members of his or her court; but certainly not the masses – as the word "mass" itself implies. Most people were simply regarded as part of a mass: an army, a work force, or a gang of slaves. What mattered was their total number, not their individual lives, their hopes and fears, their loves and dreams.

That is the image we have of Egypt of the Pharaohs. It is how the Sages understood the builders of Babel. They said that if a brick fell from the tower they wept. If a worker fell and died, they paid no attention.[1] Almost a hundred million people died in the twentieth century in Stalin's Russia, Mao's Communist China, and Cambodia under the Khmer Rouge. We say of such regimes that people became "just numbers."[2] That is what the Torah is rejecting as a matter of supreme religious principle. At the very moment when one might be maximally tempted to see people as "just numbers" – namely, when taking a census, as here – the Israelites were commanded to "lift people's heads," to raise their spirits, to make them feel they counted as individuals, not numbers in a mass, ciphers in a crowd.

In the course of my life I have had several deep conversations with Christians, and there is one aspect of Judaism that they find very difficult to understand. The conversation usually turns to the central figure of Christianity, and I am often asked, do I believe that he was the son of God. "I do indeed," I reply, "because we believe that every Jew is a son or daughter of God." What Christianity applies to one figure in its faith, we apply to all. Where Christianity transcendentalises, Judaism democratises. My conversation partners often think I am being evasive, finding a polite way to avoid answering the question. In fact, though, the opposite is true.

The first words God commands Moses to say to Pharaoh were, "My child, My firstborn, Israel" (Ex. 4:22). In Deuteronomy, Moses reminds the Israelites, "You are children of the Lord your God" (Deut. 14:1). "Beloved are Israel," said R. Akiva, "for they are called God's children."[3] One of the key phrases of prayer, *Avinu malkenu*, "Our Father, our King,"

---

1. *Pirkei DeRabbi Eliezer*, 24.
2. As Jews were in Auschwitz.
3. Mishna Avot 3:14.

encapsulates this in two simple words. We are all royalty. We are each children of the King.

To be sure, this is not the only metaphor for our relationship with God. He is also our Sovereign and we are His servants. He is our shepherd and we are His sheep. These evoke more humility than the image of parent-and-child. What is more, when God saw the first human without a partner He said, "It is not good for man to be alone." The Torah is thus signalling one of the defining tensions of all human life: We are *independent* but we are also *interdependent*. Our thoughts and feelings belong to the "I," but much of our existence depends on being part of a "we." Despite its unprecedented estimate of the individual, Judaism is at the same time an irreducibly communal faith. There is no "I" without the "we."

The hasidic master Rabbi Simha Bunim of Przysucha nicely summed up the Jewish approach to the value of a life. He said that we should each have two pockets. In one we should place a piece of paper with the words: "For my sake was the world created."[4] In the other should be the words: "I am but dust and ashes."[5] We are unique. We each have non-negotiable dignity and inalienable rights. But in and of ourselves we are nothing. Our greatness comes not from us but from God. That is the dialectic of life in the conscious presence of our mortality and God's eternity.

The point being made by the Torah, though, is that what matters is not how we see ourselves but how we see, and treat, and behave towards others. The world is not short of self-important people. What it is short of is those who make other people feel important – who "lift their heads."

I will never forget the occasion when Prince Charles, at a banquet given by the Jewish community, spent as much time talking to the young schoolchildren who came to sing in a choir as he did to the great and good among the guests, or when he came to a Jewish primary school and lit Ḥanukka candles with the children, giving each the chance to tell him who they were and what the festival meant to them. That, at least in Britain, is what royalty is and does. Members of the royal family

---

4. Mishna Sanhedrin 4:5.
5. Gen. 18:27.

make other people feel important. That is their work, their service, their role. It is the true meaning of royalty. Watching them, you understand R. Yoḥanan's fine insight that "greatness is humility."[6] You understand also Ben Zoma's axiom: "Who is honoured? One who honours others."[7]

The challenge that emerges from the way the Torah describes taking a census is that we must "lift people's heads." Never let them feel merely a number. Make those you meet feel important, especially the people whom others tend to take for granted: the waiters at a communal meal; the woman who takes your coat in a cloakroom; the *shammas* in the synagogue; the people doing security duty; the caretaker; the most junior member of the office team, and so on. Make eye contact. Smile. Let them know you do not take them for granted. You appreciate them. They matter as individuals.

For this is the life-changing idea: We are as important as we make other people feel.

Life-Changing Idea #35

You are as important as you make other people feel.

---

6. Megilla 31a.
7. Mishna Avot 4:1.

Behaalotekha

Faith and Friendship

In this *parasha* Moses reaches his lowest ebb. Not surprisingly. After all that had happened – the miracles, the exodus, the division of the sea, food from heaven, water from a rock, the revelation at Sinai and the covenant that went with it – the people, yet again, were complaining about the food. And not because they were hungry; merely because they were bored. "If only we had meat to eat! We remember the fish we ate in Egypt for free – and the cucumbers, melons, leeks, onions, and garlic." As for the miraculous "bread from heaven," although it sustained them it had ceased to satisfy them: "Now our appetite is gone; there's nothing to look at but this manna!" (Num. 11:4–6).

Any leader might despair at such a moment. What is striking is the depth of Moses' despair, the candour with which he expresses it, and the blazing honesty of the Torah in telling us this story. This is what he says to God:

> Why have You brought this trouble on Your servant? What have I done to displease You that you put the burden of all these people

on me? Did I conceive all these people? Did I give them birth? Why do You tell me to carry them in my arms, as a nurse carries an infant, to the land You promised on oath to their ancestors? ... If this is how You are going to treat me, please go ahead and kill me – if I have found favour in Your eyes – and do not let me face my own ruin. (vv. 11–15)

Every leader, perhaps every human being, at some time in their life faces failure, defeat, and the looming abyss of despair. What is fascinating is God's response. He does not tell Moses, "Cheer up; pull yourself together; you are bigger than this." Instead He gives him something practical to do:

Gather for Me seventy of the elders of Israel.... I will take some of the spirit that is on you and put it on them; and they shall bear the burden of the people along with you so that you will not bear it all by yourself. (vv. 16–17)

It is as if God were saying to Moses, "Remember what your father-in-law Jethro told you. Do not try to lead alone. Do not try to live alone.[1] Even you, the greatest of the prophets, are still human, and humans are social animals. Enlist others. Choose associates. End your isolation. Have friends."

What is moving about this episode is that, at the moment of Moses' maximum emotional vulnerability, *God Himself speaks to Moses as a friend.* This is fundamental to Judaism as a whole. For us God is not (merely) Creator of the universe, Lord of history, Sovereign, Lawgiver and Redeemer, the God of capital-letter nouns. He is also close,

---

1. To be sure, Rabbi Joseph Soloveitchik wrote a famous and poignant essay, "The Lonely Man of Faith" (published in *Tradition*, 1965, and as a book by Maggid Books, 2018). My first published essay, "Alienation and Faith" (published in *Tradition*, 1973; reprinted in *Tradition in an Untraditional Age* [Vallentine Mitchell, 1990], 219–44), was a critique of this view. It was, I argued, one possible reading of the tradition but not the only one. I still take the view that Rabbi Soloveitchik's account in that essay flowed from the specifics of his life and times. It remains a classic of the genre, but it is not the only way Jewish spirituality has been understood through the ages.

tender, loving: "He heals the broken hearted and binds up their wounds" (Ps. 147:3). He is like a parent: "As a mother comforts her child, so I will comfort you" (Is. 66:13). He is like a shepherd: "Though I walk through the valley of the shadow of death I will fear no evil for You are with me" (Ps. 23:4). He is always there: "God is close to all who call on Him – to all who call on Him in truth" (Ps. 145:18).

In 2006, in the fittingly named Hope Square outside London's Liverpool Street Station, a memorial was erected in memory of the *Kindertransport*, the operation that rescued 10,000 Jewish children from Nazi Germany shortly before the outbreak of war. At the ceremony one of the speakers, a woman by then in her eighties who was one of the saved, spoke movingly about the warmth she felt towards the country that had given refuge to her and her fellow *kinder*. In her speech she said something that left an indelible impression on me. She said, "I discovered that in England a policeman could be a friend." That is what made England so different from Germany. And it is what Jews discovered long ago about God Himself. He is not just a supreme power. He is also a friend. That is what Moses discovered in this *parasha*.

Friends matter. They shape our lives. The Sages believed that good friends tend to make us good, and bad friends bad. The example they gave was the key figures in the Korah rebellion, who were encamped near one another. They concluded, "Woe to the wicked, and woe to his neighbour." In the opposite direction, the tribes of Judah, Issachar, and Zebulun were encamped near Moses and Aaron, and they became distinguished for their expertise in Torah. Hence, "Happy the righteous, and happy his neighbour."[2] Maimonides summarised the idea thus:

> It is natural to be influenced in character and conduct by your friends and associates, and to follow the fashions of your fellow citizens. Therefore one ought to ensure that your friends are virtuous and that you frequent the company of the wise so that you learn from the way they live, and that you keep a distance from bad company.[3]

2. *Tanhuma* (Buber), Numbers 13; Numbers Rabba, *Korah*, 18:5.
3. *Mishneh Torah, Hilkhot Deot*, 6:1.

Or, as the Sages put it more briefly: "Make for yourself a mentor and acquire for yourself a friend."[4] It matters to have friends who have honesty, integrity, generosity of spirit, and loyalty. It helps to make friends with people who embody the virtues to which you aspire.

This ancient idea has been revived recently, albeit in a secular context, by two social scientists, Nicholas Christakis and James Fowler, using data from the Framingham Heart Study. This project, started in 1948, has followed more than 15,000 residents of Framingham, Massachusetts, examining their heart rate, weight, blood levels, and other health indicators, on average every four years. Its purpose was to identify risk factors for heart disease. However, Christakis and Fowler were interested in something else, namely the effects of socialisation. Does it make a difference to your health whether you have friends, and if so, what kind of people they are?

Their discoveries were impressive. Not only does having friends matter; so too does having the right ones. If your friends are active, happy, and have healthy habits, the likelihood is that you will have the same characteristics, and the same is true of the reverse. Another study, in 2000, showed that if at college, you have a roommate who works hard at his or her studies, the probability is that you will work harder. A Princeton study in 2006 showed that if one of your siblings has a child, you are 15 per cent more likely to do so within the next two years. Habits are contagious. They spread through social networks. Even your friends' friends and their friends can still have an influence on your behaviour.[5]

Jordan Peterson, in his *12 Rules for Life*, marshals his own experience and that of his contemporaries, growing up in the small, isolated town of Fairview, Alberta. Those who chose upwardly mobile individuals as friends went on to success. Those who fell into bad company fared badly, sometimes disastrously. Of course, we cannot always choose our friends. I have met young offenders who grew up in abusive families and violent neighbourhoods, with little choice and little hope. They deserve our help, not our condemnation.

---

4. Mishna Avot 1:6.
5. Nicholas Christakis and James Fowler, *Connected: the Surprising Power of Our Social Networks and How They Shape Our Lives* (New York: Little, Brown Spark, 2011).

Peterson's point though is that when we do have the choice, it is important to exercise it well. Sometimes we choose the wrong friends because they boost our self-image. If we have a fault and know we do, we can find reassurance in the fact that the people we associate with have the same fault. This soothes our troubled mind but at the price of making it almost impossible to escape our deficiencies. Hence his Rule 3: Make friends with people who want the best for you.[6]

In the end that is what God did for Moses, and it ended his depression. He told him to gather around him seventy elders who would bear the burden of leadership with him. There was nothing they could do that Moses could not: he did not need their practical or spiritual help. But they did alleviate his isolation. They shared his spirit. They gave him the gift of friendship. We all need it. We are social animals. "It is not good to be alone."[7]

It is part of the intellectual history of the West and the fact that from quite early on, Christianity became more Hellenistic than Hebraic, that people came to think that the main purpose of religion is to convey information (about the origin of the universe, miracles, life after death, and so on). Hence the conflict between religion and science, revelation and reason, faith and demonstration. These are false dichotomies.

Judaism has foundational beliefs, to be sure, but it is fundamentally about something else altogether. For us, *faith is the redemption of solitude*. It is about relationships – between us and God, us and our family, us and our neighbours, us and our people, us and humankind. Judaism is not about the lonely soul. It is about the bonds that bind us to one another and to the Author of all. It is, in the highest sense, about friendship.

Hence the life-changing idea: We tend to become what our friends are. So choose as friends people who are what you aspire to be.

Life-Changing Idea #36

We tend to become what our friends are. So choose friends who are what you aspire to be.

---

6. Peterson, *12 Rules for Life*, 67–83.
7. Gen. 2:18. To be sure, Balaam famously called Israel "a people that dwells alone," but collective singularity is not the same as individual solitude.

Shelaḥ

Seeing What Isn't There

In Philadelphia there lives a gentle, gracious, grey-haired man, by now in his late 90s, whom Elaine and I have had the pleasure of meeting several times and who is one of the most lovely people we have ever known. Many people have reason to be thankful to him, because his work has transformed many lives, rescuing people from depression and other debilitating psychological states.

His name is Aaron T. Beck and he is the founder of one of the most effective forms of psychotherapy yet devised: cognitive behavioural therapy.[1] He discovered it through his work at the depression research clinic he founded in the University of Pennsylvania. He began to detect a pattern among his patients. It had to do with the way they interpreted events. They did so in negative ways that were damaging to their self-respect, and fatalistic. It was as if they had thought themselves

---

1. To be sure, not everyone is convinced of the effectiveness of CBT. Nor is cognitive behavioural therapy necessarily appropriate, for example, for deep trauma. Neither point, however, affects the argument of this essay.

into a condition that one of Beck's most brilliant disciples, Martin Seligman, was later to call "learned helplessness." Essentially they kept telling themselves, "I am a failure. Nothing I try ever succeeds. I am useless.
Things will never change."

They had these thoughts automatically. They were their default
reaction to anything that went wrong in their lives. But Beck found that
if they became conscious of these thoughts, saw how unjustified they
were, and developed different and more realistic thought patterns, they
could, in effect, cure themselves. This also turns out to be a revelatory
way of understanding the key episode of *Parashat Shelaḥ*, namely the
story of the spies.

Recall what happened. Moses sent twelve men to spy out the
land. The men were leaders, princes of their tribes, people of distinction.
Yet ten of them came back with a demoralising report. The land, they
said, is indeed good. It does flow with milk and honey. But the people
are strong. The cities are large and well fortified. Caleb tried to calm the
people. "We can do it." But the ten said that it could not be done. The
people are stronger than we are. They are giants. We are grasshoppers.

And so the terrible event happened. The people lost heart. "If
only," they said, "we had died in Egypt.... Let us choose a leader and
go back" (Num. 14:2–4). God became angry. Moses pleaded for mercy.
God relented, but insisted that none of that generation, with the sole
exceptions of the two dissenting spies, Caleb and Joshua, would live to
enter the land. The people would stay in the wilderness for forty years,
and there they would die. Their children would eventually inherit what
might have been theirs had they only had faith.

Essential to understanding this passage is the fact that the report
of the ten spies was utterly unfounded. Only much later, in the book of
Joshua, when Joshua himself sent spies, did they learn from the woman
who sheltered them, Rahab, what actually happened when the inhabit-
ants of the land heard that the Israelites were coming:

> I know that the Lord has given you the land, and that dread of you
> has fallen on us, and that all the inhabitants of the land melt in
> fear before you.... As soon as we heard it, our hearts melted, and
> there was no courage left in any of us because of you. (Josh. 2:9–11)

The spies were terrified of the Canaanites, and entirely failed to realise that the Canaanites were terrified of them. How could they make such a profound mistake? For this we turn to cognitive behavioural therapy, and to some of the types of distorted thinking identified by Beck's student, David Burns.

One is *all-or-nothing thinking*. Everything is either black or white, good or bad, easy or impossible. That was the spies' verdict on the possibility of conquest. It couldn't be done. There was no room for shading, nuance, complexity. They could have said, "It will be difficult, we will need courage and skill, but with God's help we will prevail." But they did not. Their thinking was a polarised either/or.

Another is *negative filtering*. We discount the positives as being insignificant, and focus almost exclusively on the negatives. The spies began by noting the positives: "The land is good. Look at its fruit" (13:27). Then came the "but": the long string of negatives, drowning out the good news and leaving an overwhelmingly negative impression.

A third is *catastrophising*, expecting disaster to strike, no matter what. That is what the people did when they said, "Why is the Lord bringing us to this land only to let us die by the sword? Our wives and children will be taken as plunder" (14:3).

A fourth is *mind-reading*. We assume we know what other people are thinking, when usually we are completely wrong because we are jumping to conclusions about them based on our own feelings, not theirs. That is what the spies did when they said, "We seemed like grasshoppers in our own eyes, and so we seemed to them" (13:33). They had no way of knowing how they appeared to the people of the land, but they attributed to them, mistakenly, a sentiment based on their own subjective fears.

A fifth is *inability to disconfirm*. You reject any evidence or argument that might contradict your negative thoughts. The spies heard the counter-argument of Caleb but dismissed it. They had decided that any attempt to conquer the land would fail, and they were simply not open to any other interpretation of the facts.

A sixth is *emotional reasoning*: letting your feelings, rather than careful deliberation, dictate your thinking. A key example is the interpretation the spies placed on the fact that the cities were "fortified and very large" (13:28), or "with walls up to the sky" (Deut. 1:28). They did not stop to think that people who need high city walls to protect them are in fact fearful. Had they stopped to think, they might have realised that the Canaanites were not confident, not giants, not invulnerable. But they let their emotions substitute for thought.

A seventh is *blame*. We accuse someone else of being responsible for our predicament instead of accepting responsibility ourselves. This is what the people did in the wake of the spies' report. "They grumbled against Moses and Aaron" (Num. 14:1), as if to say, "It is all your fault. If only you had let us stay in Egypt!" People who blame others have already started down the road of "learned helplessness." They see themselves as powerless to change. They are the passive victims of forces beyond their control.

Applying cognitive behavioural therapy to the story of the spies lets us see how that ancient event might be relevant to us, here, now. It is very easy to fall into these and other forms of cognitive distortion, and the result can be depression and despair – dangerous states of mind that need immediate medical or therapeutic attention.

What I find profoundly moving is the therapy the Torah itself prescribes. I have pointed out elsewhere that the end of the *parasha* – the paragraph dealing with *tzitzit* – is connected to the episode of the spies by two keywords, *ure'item*, "you shall see" (13:18; 15:39), and the verb *latur* (Num. 13:2, 16, 17, 25, 32; 15:39). The key sentence is the one that says about the thread of blue in the *tzitzit*, that "when you see it, you will remember all the commandments of the Lord and do them, and not follow after your own heart and your own eyes" (15:39).

Note the strange order of the parts of the body. Normally we would expect it to be the other way around: as Rashi says in his commentary to the verse, "The eye sees and the heart desires." First we see, then we feel. But in fact the Torah reverses the order, thus anticipating the very point cognitive behavioural therapy makes, which is that often our feelings distort our perception. We see what we fear – and often what we think we see is not there at all. Hence Roosevelt's famous words in his first inaugural address – stunningly relevant to the story of the spies: "The only thing we have to fear is…fear itself – nameless, unreasoning, unjustified terror which paralyses needed efforts to convert retreat into advance."

The blue thread in the *tzitzit*, says the Talmud (Sota 17a), is there to remind us of the sea, the sky, and God's throne of glory. *Tekhelet*, the blue itself, was in the ancient world the mark of royalty. Thus the *tzitzit* is itself a form of cognitive behavioural therapy, saying: "Do not be afraid. God is with you. And do not give way to your emotions, because you are royalty: you are children of the King."

Hence the life-changing idea: Never let negative emotions distort your perceptions. You are not a grasshopper. Those who oppose you are not giants. To see the world as it is, not as you are afraid it might be, let faith banish fear.

Life-Changing Idea #37

Never let negative emotions distort your perceptions. To see the world as it is, not as you are afraid it might be, let faith banish fear.

Korah

The First Populist

he story of Korah has much to teach us about one of the most
disturbing phenomena of our time: the rise of populism in contemporary politics. Korah was a populist, one of the first in recorded history –
and populism has re-emerged in the West, as it did in the 1930s, posing
great danger to the future of freedom.[1]

Populism is the politics of anger.[1] It makes its appearance when
there is widespread discontent with political leaders, when people feel
that heads of institutions are working in their own interest rather than
that of the general public, when there is a widespread loss of trust and
a breakdown of the sense of the common good.

People come to feel that the distribution of rewards is unfair:
a few gain disproportionately and the many stay static or lose. There
is also a feeling that the country they once knew has been taken away

---

1. The best recent treatment is Jan-Werner Muller's *What Is Populism?* (Philadelphia:
University of Pennsylvania Press, 2016). See also the important paper, *Populism: The
Phenomenon*, Bridgewater Associates, March 22, 2017.

from them, whether because of the undermining of traditional values or because of large-scale immigration.

Discontent takes the form of the rejection of current political and cultural elites. Populist politicians claim that they, and they alone, are the true voice of the people. The others, the existing leaders, are sharing out the rewards among themselves, indifferent to the suffering of the masses. Populists stir up resentment against the establishment. They are deliberately divisive and confrontational. They promise strong leadership that will give the people back what has been taken from them.

In 2017, support for populist parties throughout Europe was running at around 35 per cent, the highest level since the late 1930s. Parties of the Far Right gained power in Poland and Hungary, and made a strong showing in Austria, France, and Holland. In Southern Europe, in countries like Spain and Greece, populism tends to be of the Left. Regardless of what form it takes, when populism is on the rise, tyranny is around the corner.[2] Human rights are dispensed with. The public grants the strong leader exceptional powers. So it was in the 1930s with Franco, Hitler, and Mussolini. People are willing to sacrifice their freedom for the promised utopia, and to tolerate great evils against whichever scapegoat the leader chooses to blame for the nation's problems.

The Korah rebellion was a populist movement, and Korah himself an archetypal populist leader. Listen carefully to what he said about Moses and Aaron: "You have gone too far! The whole community is holy, every one of them, and the Lord is among them. Why then do you exalt yourselves above the assembly of the Lord?" (Num. 16:3).

These are classic populist claims. First, implies Korah, the establishment (Moses and Aaron) is corrupt. Moses has been guilty of nepotism in appointing his own brother as high priest. He has kept the leadership roles within his immediate family instead of sharing them out more widely. Second, Korah presents himself as the people's champion. The whole community, he says, is holy. There is nothing special about you, Moses and Aaron. We have all seen God's miracles and heard His voice. We all

---

2. See Timothy Snyder, *On Tyranny: Twenty Lessons from the Twentieth Century* (London: Bodley Head, 2017).

helped build His Sanctuary. Korah is posing as the democrat so that he can become the autocrat.

Next, he and his fellow rebels mount an impressive campaign of *fake news* – anticipating events of our own time. We can infer this indirectly. When Moses says to God, "I have not taken so much as a donkey from them, nor have I wronged any of them" (v. 15), it is clear that he has been accused of just that: exploiting his office for personal gain. When he says, "This is how you will know that the Lord has sent me to do all these things and that it was not my own idea" (v. 28), it is equally clear that he has been accused of representing his own decisions as the will and word of God.

Most blatant is the *post-truth claim* of Dathan and Abiram: "Isn't it enough that you have brought us up out of a land flowing with milk and honey to kill us in the wilderness? And now you want to lord it over us!" (v. 13). This is the most callous speech in the Torah. It combines false nostalgia for Egypt (a "land flowing with milk and honey"!), blaming Moses for the report of the spies, and accusing him of holding on to leadership for his own personal prestige – all three, outrageous lies.

Nahmanides was undoubtedly correct[3] when he says that such a challenge to Moses' leadership would have been impossible at any earlier point. Only in the aftermath of the episode of the spies, when the people realised that they would not see the Promised Land in their lifetime, could discontent be stirred by Korah and his assorted fellow-travellers. They felt they had nothing to lose. Populism is the politics of disappointment, resentment, and fear.

For once in his life, Moses acted autocratically, putting God, as it were, to the test:

> This is how you shall know that the Lord has sent me to do all these works; it has not been of my own accord: If these people die a natural death, or if a natural fate comes on them, then the Lord has not sent me. But if the Lord creates something new, and the ground opens its mouth and swallows them up with all that

---

3. Nahmanides on Num. 16:1.

belongs to them, and they go down alive into Sheol, then you shall know that these men have despised the Lord. (vv. 28–30)

This dramatic effort at conflict resolution by the use of force (in this case, a miracle) failed completely. The ground did indeed open up and swallow Korah and his fellow rebels, but the people, despite their terror, were unimpressed. "On the next day, however, the whole congregation of the Israelites rebelled against Moses and against Aaron, saying, 'You have killed the people of the Lord'" (17:6). Jews have always resisted autocratic leaders.

What is even more striking is the way the Sages framed the conflict. Instead of seeing it as a black-and-white contrast between rebellion and obedience, they insisted on the validity of argument in the public domain. They said that what was wrong with Korah and his fellows was not that they argued with Moses and Aaron, but that they did so "not for the sake of Heaven." The schools of Hillel and Shammai, however, argued for the sake of Heaven, and thus their argument had enduring value.[4] Judaism, as I argued above in the chapter on *Parashat Shemot*, is unique in the fact that virtually all of its canonical texts are anthologies of arguments.

What matters in Judaism is why the argument was undertaken and how it was conducted. An argument not for the sake of Heaven is one that is undertaken for the sake of victory. An argument for the sake of Heaven is undertaken for the sake of truth. When the aim is victory, as it was in the case of Korah, both sides are diminished. Korah died, and Moses' authority was tarnished. But when the aim is truth, both sides gain. To be defeated by the truth is the only defeat that is also a victory. As R. Shimon HaAmsoni said: "Just as I received reward for the exposition, so I will receive reward for the retraction."[5]

In his excellent short book, *What is Populism?*,[6] Jan-Werner Muller argues that the best indicator of populist politics is its delegitimation of other voices. Populists claim that they, and they alone, represent the

---

4. Mishna Avot 5:20.
5. Pesaḥim 22b.
6. See note 1 above.

people. Anyone who disagrees with them is essentially illegitimate. Once in power, they silence dissent. That is why the silencing of unpopular views in university campuses today, in the form of "safe space," "trigger warnings," and "micro-aggressions," is so dangerous. When academic freedom dies, the death of other freedoms follows.

Hence the power of Judaism's defence against populism lies in the form of its insistence on the legitimacy of "argument for the sake of Heaven." Judaism does not silence dissent; to the contrary, it dignifies it. This was institutionalised in the biblical era in the form of the prophets who spoke truth to power. In the rabbinic era it lived in the culture of argument evident on every page of the Mishna, Talmud, and their commentaries. In the contemporary State of Israel, argumentativeness is part of the very texture of its democratic freedom, in the strongest possible contrast to much of the rest of the Middle East.

Hence the life-changing idea: If you seek to learn, grow, pursue truth, and find freedom, seek places that welcome argument and respect dissenting views. Stay far from people, places, and political parties that don't. Though they claim to be friends of the people, they are in fact the enemies of freedom.

Life-Changing Idea #38

If you seek to learn, grow, pursue truth, and find freedom, seek places that welcome argument and respect dissenting views.

Ḥukkat

Kohelet, Tolstoy, and the Defeat of Death

The command of the *para aduma*, the red heifer, with which our *parasha* begins, is known as the hardest of the mitzvot to understand. The opening words, *Zot ḥukkat haTorah*, are taken to mean that this is the supreme example of a *ḥok* in the Torah, that is, a law whose logic is obscure, perhaps unfathomable.

It was a ritual for the purification of those who had been in contact with, or in certain forms of close proximity to, a dead body. A dead body is the primary source of impurity, and the defilement it caused to the living meant that the person affected could not enter the precincts of the Tabernacle or Temple until cleansed, a process that lasted seven days.

A key element of the purification process involved a priest sprinkling the affected person on the third and seventh day with a specially prepared liquid known as "the water of cleansing." First a red heifer had to be found, without a blemish, and which had never been used to perform work – "a yoke had never been placed on it" (Num. 19:2). The heifer was ritually killed and burned outside the camp. Cedar wood, hyssop, and scarlet wool were added to the fire, and the ashes placed in a vessel containing "living," namely fresh, water. It was this that was sprinkled on those who had become impure by contact with death. One of the more paradoxical features of the rite is that though it cleansed the impure, it rendered impure those who were involved with the preparation of the water of cleansing.

Though the ritual has not been practised since the days of the Temple, it nonetheless remains significant, both in itself, and for an understanding of what a *hok*, usually translated as "statute," actually is. Other instances include the prohibition against eating meat and milk together, wearing clothes of mixed wool and linen (*shaatnez*), and sowing a field with two kinds of grain (*kilayim*). Several very different explanations have been offered in an effort to understand the concept of *hok*.

The most famous is that a *hok* is a law whose logic we cannot understand. It makes sense to God, but it makes no sense to us. We cannot aspire to the kind of cosmic wisdom that would allow us to see its point and purpose. Or perhaps, as Rabbenu Saadia Gaon put it, it is a command issued for no other reason than to reward us for obeying it.

The Sages recognised that whereas gentiles might understand Jewish laws based on social justice (*mishpatim*) or historical memory (*edot*), commands such as the prohibition of eating meat and milk together seemed irrational and superstitious. The *hukkim* were laws of which "Satan and the nations of the world made fun."[1]

One of the earliest and most famous explanations of this kind was the one given by R. Yohanan ben Zakkai to his students: "By your life, the dead body does not defile and the waters of the red heifer do not purify. Rather, God says: I have ordained a decree, I have issued a statute, and you have no permission to transgress my decree."[2] On the surface, at any rate, R. Yohanan is saying that the command has no intrinsic logic. It is simply the expression of the divine will. God has ruled that certain things defile, and certain procedures purify, and that is how things are.

Maimonides had a quite different view of *hukkim*. He believed that no divine command was irrational. To suppose otherwise was to think

---

1. Rashi on Num. 19:2.
2. Numbers Rabba 19:8.

of God as inferior to human beings. The ḥukkim only appear to be inexplicable. That is because we have forgotten the original context in which they were ordained. Each of them was a rejection of, and education against, some idolatrous practice. For the most part, however, such practices have died out, which is why we now find the commands hard to understand.

A third view, adopted by Nahmanides in the thirteenth century and further articulated by Rabbi Samson Raphael Hirsch in the nineteenth, is that the ḥukkim were laws designed to teach the integrity of nature. Nature has its own laws, domains, and boundaries; to cross them is to dishonour the divinely created order, and to threaten nature itself. So we do not combine animal (wool) and vegetable (linen) textiles, or mix animal life (milk) and animal death (meat). As for the red heifer, Hirsch says that the ritual is to cleanse humans from depression brought about by reminders of human mortality.

My own view is that ḥukkim are commands deliberately intended to bypass the rational brain, the pre-frontal cortex, and for an extremely important reason. We are not fully rational animals, and we are capable of making momentous mistakes if we think we are. We have a limbic system, an emotional brain. And we also have an extremely powerful set of reactions to potential danger, located in the amygdala, that lead us to freeze, fight, or flee.

In general, the non-rational parts of the brain are faster acting and more powerful than the rational ones. Emotions move us to act; rational reflections can sometimes leave us in the condition of Hamlet, with "the native hue of resolution sicklied o'er by the pale cast of thought."[3] Freud taught us that beneath the surface of apparently orderly lives were swiftly running currents of unconscious fears and drives. Daniel Kahneman and the late Amos Tversky created the field of behavioural economics by showing that people did not behave in the ways economic rationality said they would. They were irrational, in predictable ways. Split-brain patients often come up with elaborate explanations for why they feel as they do, which turn out to be ingenious but false. They rationalise something they feel but cannot explain.

One of the greatest but also the most dangerous movements in the history of civilisation was the eighteenth-century Enlightenment,

---

3. William Shakespeare, *Hamlet*, Act 3, scene 1.

with its "dream of reason." It gave rise to magnificent achievements, most obviously in science, but it neglected the power and persistence of the irrational, which exploded with full force in the next century, in the form of nationalism, racism, and Marxism, a classic case of the "return of the repressed." The eventual cost of these three movements in the twentieth century was two world wars, the Holocaust, Stalinist Russia, and Communist China, and more than a hundred million lives.

A moral system, to be adequate to the human condition, must recognise the nature of the human condition. We are not perfectly rational beings, and if we tried to be, we would be found to be lacking in certain essential human qualities. We could not love or be moved to compassion. We would find it difficult to understand the nature of loyalty. We would not understand other people's fears or hopes, or anxieties or distress. We would lack "emotional intelligence."

That is one reason why, for example, the Torah does something no other law code does in anything like the same degree: it interweaves narrative and law. Laws tend to engage the rational mind, but narrative speaks to emotion. We read the story of the Israelites in Egypt and we are moved. We feel for the oppressed. We weep for the Israelite children put to death. We sense the Israelites' exaltation as they emerge safe from the divided Red Sea and break into song. The laws that follow – based for the most part on creating a just and equitable society – are not mere laws. They are the culmination of the story and the resolution of the emotions it aroused.

One of the most tragic outcomes of human intervention in nature has been environmental destruction on a massive scale. Almost without exception, the first humans to arrive in a new region hunted many species of animal life to extinction as well as over-cultivating the land to exhaustion. The *ḥukkim* about milk and meat, wool and linen, mixed grains, and the like, as well as the command of *shemitta*, to leave the land fallow one year in seven, are powerful ways of teaching that there are limits to our exploitation of nature; that different forms of life have their own integrity; and most importantly, that nature is not ours to do with as we wish. Even today, when most people know about climate change, it is difficult to convince them to make the necessary sacrifices to avoid making it worse. That is where a *ḥok*, a statute, "Thus have I decreed,"

makes all the difference. It bypasses the rational brain and all the ratio-
nalisations we make for carrying on as before.

The most profound fear most of us have is of death. As La Roche-
foucauld said, "Neither the sun nor death can be looked on with a steady
eye." Few have explored death and the tragic shadow it casts over life
more profoundly than the author of Ecclesiastes:

> I said to myself, the fate of the fool awaits me also; why then
> should I be wiser? ... How can it be that the wise man dies like the
> fool? I hated life; this work that is done beneath the sun is evil to
> me. Nothing but fleeting breath, courting the wind. (Eccl. 2:15–17)

> The fate of man is the fate of cattle; the same fate awaits them
> both, the death of one is like the death of the other, their spirits
> are the same, and the pre-eminence of man over beast is nothing,
> for it is all shallow breath. All end in the same place; all emerge
> from dust and all go back to dust. (3:19–20)

The knowledge that he will die robs the author of Ecclesiastes of any
sense of the meaningfulness of life. We have no idea what will happen
after our death to what we have created in our life. Death makes mockery
of virtue: the hero may die young while the coward lives to old age. And
bereavement is tragic in a different way. To lose those we love is to have
the fabric of our life torn, perhaps irreparably. Death defiles in the simplest,
starkest sense: mortality opens an abyss between us and God's eternity.

Hence the rite of the heifer. The animal itself is the starkest symbol of pure, animal life, untamed, undomesticated. The red, like the
scarlet of the wool, is the colour of blood, itself the essence of life. The
cedar, tallest of trees, represents vegetative life. The hyssop symbolises
purity. All these were reduced to ash in the fire, a powerful drama of
mortality. The ash itself was then dissolved in water, symbolising continuity, the flow of life, and the potential of rebirth. The body dies but
the spirit flows on. A generation dies, but another is born. Lives may
end, but life does not. Those who live after us continue what we began,
and we live on in them. Life is a never-ending stream, and a trace of us
is carried onward to the future.

Perhaps those who experienced the rite interpreted it differently, or perhaps did not interpret it at all. That is what a ritual is and does: it is open to many interpretations because it is about doing, not thinking. The root from which the word *ḥok* comes is Ḥ-K-K, meaning "to engrave." Writing is on the surface; engraving cuts much deeper than the surface. Rituals go deep below the surface of the mind. But whoever participated in the ritual knew that it removed the taint of death and allowed one to enter the sacred presence of the God of life.

One person in modern times who experienced what is expressed in Ecclesiastes was Tolstoy, who told the story in his essay *A Confession*. By the time he wrote it, in his early fifties, he had already published two of the greatest novels ever written, *War and Peace* and *Anna Karenina*. His literary legacy was secure. His greatness was universally recognised. He was married. He had children. He had a large estate. His health was good. Yet he was overcome with a sense of the meaninglessness of life in the face of the knowledge that we will all die. He quoted Ecclesiastes at length. He contemplated suicide. The question that haunted him was: "Is there any meaning in my life that will not be annihilated by the inevitability of death which awaits me?"[4]

He searched for an answer in science, but all it told him was that "in the infinity of space and the infinity of time, infinitely small particles mutate with infinite complexity." Science deals in causes and effects, not purpose and meaning. In the end, he concluded that only religious faith rescues life from meaninglessness. "Rational knowledge, as presented by the learned and wise, negates the meaning of life."[5] What is needed is something other than rational knowledge. "Faith is the force of life. If a man lives, then he must believe in something.… If he does understand the illusion of the finite, he is bound to believe in the infinite. Without faith it is impossible to live."[6]

That is why, to defeat the defilement of contact with death, there must be a ritual that bypasses rational knowledge. Hence the rite of the red heifer, in which death is dissolved in the waters of life, and those

4. Leo Tolstoy, *A Confession*, Part V.
5. Ibid., Part VIII.
6. Ibid., Part IX.

on whom it is sprinkled are made pure again so that they can enter the precincts of the *Shekhina,* the Divine Presence, and in their mortality come close to eternity.

We no longer have the red heifer and the seven-day purification ritual, but we do have the *shiva,* the seven days of mourning during which we are comforted by others and thereby reconnected with life. Our grief is gradually dissolved by the contact with friends and family who come to wish us well, as the ashes of the heifer were dissolved in the "living water," and we emerge, still bereaved, but in some measure cleansed, purified, able again to face life.

Hence the life-changing idea: We can emerge from the shadow of death if we allow ourselves to bypass our rational brain and be healed by the God of life. To do so, however, we often need the help of others. It took a priest to sprinkle the waters of cleansing. In a different sense, it takes comforters to lift our grief during our period of mourning. But faith leads us back into life.

Life-Changing Idea #39

We can emerge from the shadow of death if we allow ourselves to be healed by the God of life. To do so, however, we often need the help of others.

Balak

A People That Dwells Alone

This is an extraordinary moment in Jewish history, for good and not-so-good reasons. For the first time in almost 4,000 years we have simultaneously sovereignty and independence in the Land and State of Israel, and freedom and equality in the Diaspora. There have been times – all too brief – when Jews had one or the other, but never before, both at the same time. That is the good news.

The less-good news, though, is that anti-Semitism has returned within living memory of the Holocaust. The State of Israel remains isolated in the international political arena. It is still surrounded by enemies. And it is the only nation among the 193 making up the United Nations whose very right to exist is constantly challenged and always under threat.

Given all this, it seems the right time to re-examine words appearing in this *parasha*, uttered by the pagan prophet Balaam, that have come to seem to many, the most powerful summation of Jewish history and destiny:

> From the peaks of rocks I see them,
> From the heights I gaze upon them.
> This is a people who dwell alone,
> Not reckoning themselves one of the nations. (Num. 23:9)

For two leading Israeli diplomats in the twentieth century – Yaacov Herzog and Naphtali Lau-Lavie – this verse epitomised their sense of Jewish peoplehood after the Holocaust and the establishment of the State of Israel. Herzog, son of a chief rabbi of Israel and brother of Chaim who became Israel's president, was director-general of the prime minister's office from 1965 to his death in 1972. Naphtali Lavie, a survivor of Auschwitz who became Israel's consul-general in New York, lived to see his brother, Rabbi Yisrael Meir Lau, become Israel's chief rabbi. Herzog's collected essays were published under the title, drawn from Balaam's words, *A People That Dwells Alone*. Lavie's were entitled *Balaam's Prophecy* – again a reference to this verse.[1]

For both, the verse expressed the uniqueness of the Jewish people – its isolation on the one hand, its defiance and resilience on the other. Though it has faced opposition and persecution from some of the greatest superpowers the world has ever known, it has outlived them all.

Given, though, the return of anti-Semitism, it is worth reflecting on one particular interpretation of the verse, given by the dean of Volozhyn Yeshiva, Rabbi Naftali Zvi Yehudah Berlin (Netziv, Russia, 1816–1893). Netziv interpreted the verse as follows: For every other nation, when its people went into exile and assimilated into the dominant culture, they found acceptance and respect. With Jews, the opposite was the case. In exile, when they remained true to their faith and

---

1. Yaacov Herzog, *A People That Dwells Alone* (London: Weidenfeld and Nicolson, 1975). Naphtali Lau-Lavie, *Balaam's Prophecy* (Jerusalem: The Toby Press, 2015). In the introduction, Amichai Yehuda Lau-Lavie quotes this verse. In Hebrew, however, the work was entitled *Am KeLavi*, a reference to the later words of Balaam, "The people rise like a lion; they rouse themselves like a young lion" (Num. 23:24) – a play on the Hebrew name Lavie, meaning "lion."

way of life, they found themselves able to live at peace with their gentile neighbours. When they tried to assimilate, they found themselves despised and reviled.

The sentence, says Netziv, should therefore be read thus: "If it is a people content to be alone, faithful to its distinctive identity, then it will be able to dwell in peace. But if Jews seek to be like the nations, the nations will not consider them worthy of respect."[2]

This is a highly significant statement, given the time and place in which it was made, namely Russia in the last quarter of the nineteenth century. At that time, many Russian Jews had assimilated, some converting to Christianity. But anti-Semitism did not diminish. It grew, exploding into violence in the pogroms that happened in more than a hundred towns in 1881. These were followed by the notorious anti-Semitic May Laws of 1882. Realising that they were in danger if they stayed, between three and five million Jews fled to the West.

It was at this time that Leon Pinsker, a Jewish physician who had believed that the spread of humanism and enlightenment would put an end to anti-Semitism, experienced a major change of heart and wrote one of the early texts of secular Zionism, *Auto-Emancipation* (1882). In words strikingly similar to those of Netziv, he said, "In seeking to fuse with other peoples, [Jews] deliberately renounced to some extent their own nationality. Yet nowhere did they succeed in obtaining from their fellow citizens recognition as natives of equal status." They tried to be like everyone else, but this only left them more isolated.

Something similar happened in Western Europe also. Far from ending hostility to Jews, enlightenment and emancipation merely caused it to mutate, from religious Judaeophobia to racial anti-Semitism. No one spoke of this more poignantly than Theodor Herzl in *The Jewish State* (1896):

We have honestly endeavoured everywhere to merge ourselves in the social life of surrounding communities and to preserve the faith of our fathers. We are not permitted to do so. In vain are we loyal patriots, our loyalty in some places running to extremes; in

2. *Haamek Davar* on Num. 23:9.

vain do we make the same sacrifices of life and property as our fellow citizens; in vain do we strive to increase the fame of our native land in science and art, or her wealth by trade and commerce. In countries where we have lived for centuries we are still cried down as strangers.... If we could only be left in peace.... But I think we shall not be left in peace.

The more we succeeded in being like everyone else, implied Herzl, the more we were disliked by everyone else. Consciously or otherwise, these nineteenth-century voices were echoing a sentiment first articulated twenty-six centuries ago by the prophet Ezekiel, speaking in the name of God to the would-be assimilationists among the Jewish exiles in Babylon: "You say, 'We want to be like the nations, like the peoples of the world, who serve wood and stone.' But what you have in mind will never happen" (Ezek. 20:32).

Anti-Semitism is one of the most complex phenomena in the history of hate, and it is not my intention here to simplify it. But there is something of lasting significance in this convergence of views between Netziv, one of the greatest rabbinic scholars of his day, and the two great secular Zionists, Pinsker and Herzl, though they differed on so much else. Assimilation is no cure for anti-Semitism. If people do not like you for what you are, they will not like you more for pretending to be what you are not.

Jews cannot cure anti-Semitism. Only anti-Semites can do that, together with the society to which they belong. The reason is that Jews are not the *cause* of anti-Semitism. They are the objects of it, but that is something different. The cause of anti-Semitism is a profound malaise in the cultures in which it appears. It happens whenever a society feels that something is badly amiss, when there is a profound cognitive dissonance between the way things are and the way people think they ought to be. People are then faced with two possibilities. They can either ask, "What did we do wrong?" and start to put it right, or they can ask, "Who did this to us?" and search for a scapegoat.

In century after century Jews have been made the scapegoat for events that had nothing to do with them, from medieval plagues to poisoned wells, to inner tensions in Christianity, to Germany's defeat in the First World War, to the underachievement of many Muslim states today. Anti-Semitism is a sickness, and it cannot be cured by Jews. It is also evil, and those who tolerate it when they could have protested are accomplices to evil.

We have nothing to apologise for in our insistence on being different. Judaism began as a protest against empires, symbolised by Babel in Genesis and ancient Egypt in Exodus. These were the first great empires, and they achieved the freedom of the few at the cost of the enslavement of the many.

Jews have always been the irritant of empires because of our insistence on the dignity of the individual and his or her liberty. Anti-Semitism is either the last gasp of a declining culture or the first warning sign of a new totalitarianism. God commanded our ancestors to be different, not because they were better than others – "It is not because of your righteousness that the Lord your God is giving you this good land" (Deut. 9:6) – but because by being different we teach the world the dignity of difference. Empires seek to impose unity on a plural world. Jews know that unity exists in heaven; God creates diversity on earth.

There is one fundamental difference between anti-Semitism today and its precursors in the past. Today we have a State of Israel. We need no longer fear what Jews discovered after the Evian Conference in 1938, when the nations of the world closed their doors and Jews knew that they had not one square inch on earth they could call home in the Robert Frost sense, namely the place where "when you have to go there, they have to let you in."[3] Today we have a home – and every assault on Jews and Israel today only serves to make Jews and Israel stronger. That is why anti-Semitism is not only evil but also self-destructive. Hate destroys the hater. Nothing has ever been gained by making Jews, or anyone else, the scapegoat for your sins.

None of this is to diminish the seriousness with which we must join with others to fight anti-Semitism and every other religious or racial hate. But let the words of Netziv stay with us. We should never abandon our distinctiveness. It is what makes us who we are. Nor is there any contradiction between this and the universalism of the prophets. To

---

3. Robert Frost, "The Death of the Hired Man," https://www.poetryfoundation.org/poems/44261/the-death-of-the-hired-man.

the contrary – and this is the life-changing idea: In our uniqueness lies our universality. By being what only we are, we contribute to humanity what only we can give.

Life-Changing Idea #40

In our uniqueness lies our universality. By being what only we are, we contribute to humanity what only we can give.

Pinḥas

The Lost Masterpiece

A true story that took place in 1995: It concerns the legacy of an unusual man with an unusual name, Mr Ernest Onians, a farmer in East Anglia whose main business was as a supplier of pigswill. Known as an eccentric, his hobby was collecting paintings. He used to go around local auctions and whenever a painting came on sale, especially if it was old, he would make a bid for it. Eventually he collected more than five hundred canvases. There were too many to hang them all on the walls of his relatively modest home, Baylham Mill in Suffolk. So he simply piled them up, keeping some in his chicken sheds.

His children did not share his passion. They knew he was odd. He used to dress scruffily. Afraid of being burgled, he rigged up his own home-made alarm system, using klaxons powered by old car batteries, and always slept with a loaded shotgun under his bed. When he died, his children asked Sotheby's, the London auction house, to sell the paintings. Before any major sale of artworks, Sotheby's publishes a catalogue so that interested buyers can see in advance what will be on offer.

A great art expert, Sir Denis Mahon (1910–2011), was looking through the catalogue one day when his eye was caught by one painting in particular. The photograph in the catalogue, no larger than a postage stamp, showed a rabble of rampaging people setting fire to a large building and making off with loot. Onians had bought it at a country house sale in the 1940s for a mere £12. The catalogue listed the painting as *The Sack of Carthage*, painted by a relatively little-known artist of the seventeenth century, Pietro Testa. It estimated that it would fetch £15,000.

Mahon was struck by one incongruous detail. One of the looters was making off with a seven-branched candelabrum. What, Mahon wondered, was a menora doing in Carthage? Clearly the painting was not depicting that event. Instead it was a portrait of the destruction of the Second Temple by the Romans. But if what he was looking at was not *The Sack of Carthage*, then the artist was probably not Pietro Testa.

Mahon remembered that the great seventeenth-century artist Nicholas Poussin had painted two portraits of the destruction of the Second Temple. One was hanging in the art museum in Vienna. The other, painted in 1626 for Cardinal Barberini, had disappeared from public view sometime in the eighteenth century. No one knew what had happened to it. With a shock Mahon realised that he was looking at the missing Poussin.

At the auction, he bid for the picture. When a figure of the eminence of Sir Dennis bid for a painting the other potential buyers knew that he must know something they did not, so they too put in bids. Eventually Sir Dennis bought the painting for £155, 000. A few years later he sold it for its true worth, £4.5 million, to Lord Rothschild who donated it to the Israel Museum in Jerusalem where it hangs today in the memory of Sir Isaiah Berlin.

I know this story only because, at Lord Rothschild's request, I together with the then director of the National Gallery, Neil MacGregor, gave a lecture on the painting while it was shown briefly in London before being taken to its new and permanent home. I tell the story because it is so graphic an example of the fact that we can lose a priceless legacy simply because, not loving it, we do not come to appreciate its true value. From this we can infer a corollary: we inherit what we truly love.

This surely is the moral of the story of the daughters of Zelophehad in this *parasha*. Recall the story: Zelophehad, of the tribe of Manasseh, had died in the wilderness before the allocation of the land.

He left five daughters but no sons. The daughters came before Moses, arguing that it would be unjust for his family to be denied their share in the land simply because he had daughters but not sons. Moses brought their case before God, who told him: "What Zelophehad's daughters are saying is right. You must certainly give them property as an inheritance among their father's relatives and give their father's inheritance to them" (Num. 27:7). And so it came to pass.

The Sages spoke of Zelophehad's daughters in the highest praise. They were, they said, very wise and chose the right time to present their request. They knew how to interpret Scripture, and they were perfectly virtuous.[1] Even more consequentially, their love of the land of Israel was in striking contrast to that of the men. The spies had come back with a negative report about the land, and the people had said, "Let us appoint a [new] leader and return to Egypt" (Num. 14:4). But Zelophehad's daughters wanted to have a share in the land, which they were duly granted.[2]

This led to the famous comment of Rabbi Ephraim Luntschitz of Prague (1550–1619) on the episode of the spies. Focusing on God's words, "Send for yourself men to spy out the land of Canaan" (Num. 14:2), Luntschitz argued that God was not commanding Moses but permitting him to send men. God was saying, "From My perspective, seeing the future, it would have been better to send women, because they love and cherish the land and would never come to speak negatively about it. However, since you are convinced that these men are worthy and do indeed value the land, I give you permission to go ahead and send them."[3]

The result was catastrophic. Ten of the men came back with a negative report. The people were demoralised, and the result was that they lost the chance to enter the land in their lifetime. They lost their chance to enjoy their inheritance in the land promised to their ancestors. The daughters of Zelophehad, by contrast, did inherit the land – because they loved it. What we love, we inherit. What we fail to love, we lose.

I cannot help but think that in some strange way the stories of the daughters of Zelophehad and the auction of the missing Poussin

---

1. Bava Batra 110b.
2. *Sifrei* Numbers 133.
3. *Kli Yakar* on Num. 13:2.

illustrate the state of Jewish identity today. For many of my contemporaries, Judaism was like the story of Ernest Onians' penchant for paintings. Judaism was something their parents had but not something that was meaningful to them. Like Onians' children they were willing to let go of it, unaware that it was a legacy of immense value. When we don't fully appreciate the value of something, we can lose a treasure without ever knowing it is a treasure.

Judaism, of course, is not a painting. It's an identity. And you can't sell an identity. But you can lose it. And many Jews are losing theirs. Our ancestors have given us the gift of a past. We owe them the gift of a future faithful to that past. At least we should not relinquish it simply because we don't know how valuable it is.

The life-changing idea here is surely simple yet profound: If we truly wish to hand on our legacy to our children, we must teach them to love it. The most important element of any education is not learning facts or skills but learning what to love. What we love, we inherit. What we fail to love, we lose.

Life-Changing Idea #41

If we truly wish to hand on our legacy to our children, we must teach them to love it.

Matot

Subject/Object

Our *parasha* opens with an account of the laws of vows and oaths: "When a man makes a vow to the Lord or takes an oath to obligate himself by a pledge, he must not break his word but must do everything he said" (Num. 30:3).

The Torah commands us to take vows and oaths with utmost seriousness. The Israelites were nearing the land where they were summoned to construct a society unlike any other. It was to be a free society based on a covenant between the people and God. The rule of law was to be secured not by the use of force but by people honouring their moral commitments, their voluntary undertaking to God that what He commanded, they would do.

A covenantal society is one in which words are holy, sacrosanct. This is the principle at the heart of Judaism as a code of collective freedom, a constitution of liberty. Ironically it was one of the great critics of Judaism, Friedrich Nietzsche, who had the insight to see that the capacity to bind ourselves by words is the basis of both morality and human freedom. This is what he says in his book, *On the Genealogy of Morality*:

To breed an animal with the prerogative to make promises – is that not precisely the paradoxical task which nature has set herself with regard to humankind? Is it not the real problem of humankind?[1]

Homo sapiens is distinguished from other animals by its use of language. That is well known. What Nietzsche saw, however, is that we use language in many different ways. We use it to describe, communicate, categorise, and explain. Language in this sense is a kind of picture of reality, a translation of what is into a set of signs, symbols, and images.

But we can also use language in a quite different way – not to describe what is, but to commit ourselves to some form of behaviour in the future. So for instance when a groom says to his bride under the *ḥuppa*, "Behold you are betrothed to me…" he is not describing a marriage. He is getting married. He is undertaking a set of obligations to the woman he has chosen as his wife. Philosophers call this a "performative utterance."

Nietzsche saw how fundamental this is to the human condition:

In order to have that degree of control over the future, man must first learn to distinguish between what happens by accident and what by design…and before he can do this, man himself will really have to become reliable, regular, necessary, even in his own self-image, so that he, as someone making a promise, is answerable for his own future![2]

When we bind ourselves by words, we are using language not to describe but to create – to create an orderly future out of the chaos of human instincts and desires. What makes humans unique is not just the use of language. Other animals use forms of language. Dolphins do. So do primates. Even bees convey information to other bees through complex dances.

---

1. Friedrich Nietzsche, *On the Genealogy of Morality*, trans. Carol Diethe (New York: Cambridge University Press, 2007), 35–36.
2. Ibid., 36.

What is unique to humans is that we use language to bind our own future behaviour so that we can form bonds of mutuality and trust with other human beings. One such bond is the promise. Another is marriage. A third – unique to Judaism – is society understood as a covenant, a set of mutually binding promises between the Jewish people and God.

It is this use of language, not to describe something already in existence but to create something that didn't exist before, that links us to God. God used words to bring the natural universe into being: "And God said ... and there was." *We* use words to bring a social universe into being. What the Torah is telling us is that words create because words are holy; that is to say, they bind. When words bind, they generate trust. Trust is to society what predictability is to nature: the basis of order as opposed to chaos.

Social institutions in a free society depend on trust, and trust means that we keep our word. We do what we say we are going to do. If we make a vow, an oath, a promise, a verbal undertaking, then we hold ourselves bound by it. This means that we will actually fulfil our commitment unless we can establish that, due to circumstances unforeseeable at the time, we are simply unable to do so.

However, there is a fundamental difference between a vow and an oath. A vow, *neder*, affects the status of an object (*heftza*). It dedicates it in such a way as to render it inaccessible to me for my personal use. I may vow not to eat something. That something is now, for me, forbidden food. However, an oath, *shevua*, affects the person (*gavra*) not the object. What is now forbidden is not the food but my act of eating it. Both acts bind but in different ways.

This distinction led Rav Soloveitchik into a fascinating philosophical reflection on the existential difference between oaths and vows.[3] The difference between *gavra* and *heftza*, he suggests, is the difference between subject and object. "When I say that I am writing a letter, I am the *gavra*, the subject of the action, while the letter is the *heftza*." A *gavra* acts, a *heftza* is acted on. A *gavra* influences, a *heftza* is influenced. A *gavra* is active, a *heftza* passive. A doctor cures, a patient is cured. A

3. Rabbi Avishai C. David, *Darosh Darash Yosef: Discourses of Rav Yosef Dov Halevi Soloveitchik on the Weekly Parasha* (Jerusalem: Urim, 2011), 369–75.

judge passes sentence, a prisoner is sentenced. These are two different modes of being. Sometimes we are one, sometimes the other.

By way of illustration, Soloveitchik cites the example of Moses at Mount Sinai and the difference between the first and second set of tablets. There is a commentary in the *Yalkut Shimoni*[4] that suggests that Moses did not break the first set of tablets deliberately. Rather, as he descended the mountain at God's command and saw the people dancing around the golden calf, the letters flew off the tablets which then became so heavy that he could no longer bear their weight. They fell from his hands and broke.

However, God subsequently told Moses to carve two tablets and bring them up the mountain, which Moses duly did, despite the fact that they were not yet inscribed. How, asked the Rav, could the first tablets without their inscription be too heavy for Moses to carry, while he was able to carry the second set, also uninscribed?

The answer the Rav gave was that on the first occasion Moses was a *ḥeftza*. He did not choose to descend the mountain. He was ordered to do so, against his inclination, by God. On the second he was a *gavra*. It was his passionate pleading that had caused the people to be forgiven and he was eager to obtain the second tablets as a sign that the covenant was still in force. When we act out of our own inclination and desire, we have energy, and strength that we lack if forced into a situation not of our choosing.

Perhaps the most vivid example of *ḥeftza* and *gavra* in biblical narrative is the case of Joseph. In every scene in his early life we see him as the *ḥeftza* . He rarely acts; he is almost always acted on. His father loves him more than his other sons. He gives him a richly embroidered cloak. His brothers hate him, think of killing him, and eventually sell him as a slave. Potiphar's wife attempts to seduce him and when she fails, accuses him of rape. The other significant episodes either happen to him – the dreams – or are explicitly attributed to God: his success in running Potiphar's household, and later, the prison and his ability to interpret the dreams of others. Throughout this time Joseph is the object, not the subject, of verbs. His life is determined by what other people do to him.

---

4. *Remez* 393.

All this changes when, having interpreted Pharaoh's dreams, he proposes a solution to the crisis the dreams portend. From that moment onward he is the most active character in the Torah, organising the Egyptian economy, using the famine to restructure Egyptian society, putting his brothers to a test to see whether they have reformed, sending for his father and the rest of the family, and settling them in the land of Goshen. The *ḥeftza* has become a *gavra*, the object has become a subject, Joseph-the-passive has become Joseph-the-active, even hyperactive.

Rav Soloveitchik quotes the statement in the Gemara that an oath is administered to each of us before we are born, saying, "Be righteous and not wicked."[5] The fact that this is an oath not a vow is essential. It means: Be a *gavra* not a *ḥeftza*, be a free and responsible choosing subject, not the passive object of other people's acts. "If a human being is to act as an emissary of God, then they must be a *gavra*, constantly moving upward."[6]

The difference between a vow and an oath thus becomes a metaphor for two different kinds of life, one defined by others and one self-created. That is the distinction Rav Soloveitchik drew with great force in his essay, *Halakhic Man*. One kind of person, he says, is "receptive, passive…wholly under the influence of other people and their views." The other is "not passive but active. His personality is not characterised by receptivity but by spontaneity. He does not simply abandon himself to the rule of the species but blazes his own individual trail."[7] This latter, he says, is the man of God.

Things happen to us and they affect us, sometimes very deeply. To that extent we are a *ḥeftza*. We are the object of events, and of other people's deeds. But the challenge of faith is to become a *gavra*, to be our best self, undeflected and undefeated by what others do or say. It is not easy; it is never less than challenging. But this is the life-changing idea: Faith is the call to be not an object but a subject, not passive but active, to influence more than to be influenced by our environment. We are called on to be more than others make us.

---

5. Nidda 30b.
6. David, *Darosh Darash Yosef,* 374.
7. Rabbi Joseph Soloveitchik, *Halakhic Man* (Philadelphia: Jewish Publication Society of America, 1983), 127–28.

Life-Changing Idea #42

Faith is the call to be not an object but a subject, not passive but active, to influence more than to be influenced by our environment.

Masei

Miles to Go Before I Sleep

Ê *tre ailleurs*, "To be elsewhere – the great vice of this race, its great and secret virtue, the great vocation of this people." So wrote the French poet and essayist Charles Peguy (1873–1914), a philo-Semite in an age of anti-Semitism. He continued: "Any crossing for them means the crossing of the desert. The most comfortable houses, the best built from stones as big as the temple pillars, the most real of real estate, the most overwhelming of apartment houses will never mean more to them than a tent in the desert."[1]

What he meant was that history and destiny had combined to make Jews aware of the temporariness of any dwelling outside the Holy Land. To be a Jew is to be on a journey. That is how the Jewish story began when Abraham first heard the words *"Lekh lekha,"* with their call to leave where he was and travel "to the land I will show you" (Gen. 12:1). That is how it began again in the days of Moses, when the family had become a people. And that is the point almost endlessly

---

1. Charles Peguy, *Basic Verities* (New York: Pantheon, 1943), 141.

repeated in *Parashat Masei*: "They set out from X and camped at Y. They set out from Y and camped at Z" – forty-two stages in a journey of forty years (Num. 33). We are the people who travel. We are the people who do not stand still. We are the people for whom time itself is a journey through the wilderness in search of the Promised Land.

In one sense this is a theme familiar from the world of myth. In many cultures, stories are told about the journey of the hero. Otto Rank, one of Freud's most brilliant colleagues, wrote about it. So did Joseph Campbell, a Jungian, in his book, *The Hero with a Thousand Faces*.[2] Nonetheless, the Jewish story is different in significant ways:

1. The journey – set out in the books of Exodus and Numbers – is undertaken by everyone, the entire people: men, women, and children. It is as if, in Judaism, we are all heroes, or at least all summoned to a heroic challenge.

2. It takes longer than a single generation. Perhaps, had the spies not demoralised the nation with their report, it might have taken only a short while. But there is a deeper and more universal truth here. The move from slavery to the responsibilities of freedom takes time. People do not change overnight. Therefore evolution succeeds; revolution fails. The Jewish journey began before we were born and it is our responsibility to hand it on to those who will continue it after us.

3. In myth, the hero usually encounters a major trial: an adversary, a dragon, a dark force. He (it is usually a he) may even die and be resurrected. As Campbell puts it: "A hero ventures forth from the world of common day into a region of supernatural wonder: fabulous forces are there encountered and a decisive victory is won: the hero comes back from this mysterious adventure with the power to bestow boons on his fellow man."[3] The Jewish story is different. The adversary the Israelites encounter is themselves: their fears, their weaknesses, their constant urge to return and regress.

---

2. Joseph Campbell, *The Hero with a Thousand Faces* (Novato, CA: New World Library, 2008).
3. Ibid., 23.

It seems to me, here as so often elsewhere, that the Torah is not myth but anti-myth, a deliberate insistence on removing the magical elements from the story and focusing relentlessly on the human drama of courage versus fear, hope versus despair, and the call, not to some larger-than-life hero but to all-of-us-together, given strength by our ties to our people's past and the bonds between us in the present. The Torah is not some fabled escape from reality but reality itself, seen as a journey we must all undertake, each with our own strengths and contributions to our people and to humanity.

We are all on a journey. And we must all rest from time to time. That dialectic between *setting out* and *encamping*, walking and standing still, is part of the rhythm of Jewish life. There is a time for *Nitzavim*, standing, and a time for *Vayelekh*, moving on. Rav Kook spoke of the two symbols in Balaam's blessing, "How goodly are your tents, Jacob, and your dwelling places, Israel" (Num. 24:5). Tents are for people on a journey. Dwelling places are for people who have found home.

Psalm 1 uses two symbols of the righteous individual. On the one hand he or she is on the way, while the wicked begin by walking, then transition to standing and sitting. On the other hand, the righteous is compared to a tree, planted by streams of water, that gives fruit in due season and whose leaves do not wither. We walk, but we also stand still. We are on a journey but we are also rooted like a tree.

In life, there are journeys and encampments. Without the encampments, we suffer burnout. Without the journey, we do not grow. And life is growth. There is no way to avoid challenge and change. The late Rabbi Aharon Lichtenstein once gave a beautiful talk[4] on Robert Frost's poem, "Stopping by Woods on a Snowy Evening," with its closing verse:

> The woods are lovely dark and deep.
> But I have promises to keep,
> And miles to go before I sleep,
> And miles to go before I sleep.

---

4. http://etzion.org.il/en/woods-are-lovely-dark-and-deep-reading-poem-robert-frost.

He analyses the poem in terms of Kierkegaard's distinction between the aesthetic and ethical dimensions of life. The poet is enchanted by the aesthetic beauty of the scene, the soft silence of the falling snow, the dark dignity of the tall trees. He would love to stay here in this timeless moment, this eternity-in-an-hour. But he knows that life has an ethical dimension also, and this demands action, not just contemplation. He has promises to keep; he has duties towards the world. So he must walk on despite his fatigue. He has miles to go before he sleeps: he has work to do while the breath of life is within him.

The poet has stopped briefly to enjoy the dark wood and falling snow. He has encamped. But now, like the Israelites in *Parashat Masei*, he must set out again. For us as Jews, as for Kierkegaard the theologian, and Robert Frost the poet, ethics takes priority over aesthetics. Yes, there are moments when we should, indeed must, pause to see the beauty of the world, but then we must move on, for we have promises to keep, including the promises to ourselves and to God.

Hence the life-changing idea: Life is a journey, not a destination. We should never stand still. Instead we should constantly set ourselves new challenges that take us out of our comfort zone. Life is growth.

Life-Changing Idea #43

Life is a journey, not a destination. We should constantly set ourselves new challenges that take us out of our comfort zone. Life is growth.

Deuteronomy
דברים

Devarim

The Effective Critic

The first verse of Deuteronomy, the fifth and culminating book of the Torah, sounds prosaic. "These are the words that Moses spoke to all Israel beyond the Jordan – in the wilderness, on the plain opposite Suph, between Paran and Tophel, Laban, Hazeroth, and Di-zahab." There is no hint of drama in these words. But the Sages of the Talmud found one, and it is life-changing.

What is odd in the verse is the last place-name: Di-zahab (*DiZahav* in Hebrew). What and where is this place? It hasn't been mentioned before, nor is it mentioned again anywhere else in Tanakh. But the name is tantalising. It seems to mean, "Enough gold." Gold is certainly something we have heard about before. It was the metal of which the calf was made while Moses was on the mountain receiving the Torah from God. This was one of the great sins of the wilderness years. Might the enigmatic mention of a place called "Enough gold" have something to do with it?

From these clues and cues, the Sages inferred a remarkable drama. This is what they said:

Moses spoke audaciously (*hitiah devarim*) towards Heaven....
The school of R. Yannai learned this from the words *DiZahav*.
What do these words mean? They said in the school of R. Yannai:
Thus spoke Moses before the Holy One, blessed be He: "Sovereign of the Universe, the silver and gold (*zahav*) which You
showered on Israel until they said 'Enough (*dai*)' was what caused
them to make the calf."... R. Ḥiyya bar Abba said: It is like the
case of a man who had a son. He bathed him and anointed him
and gave him plenty to eat and drink and hung a purse around
his neck and set him down at the door of a house of ill-repute.
How could he help sinning?[1]

Moses, in this dramatic re-reading, is portrayed as counsel for the defence
of the Jewish people. Yes, he admits to God, the people did indeed commit a sin. But it was You who provided them with the opportunity and
the temptation. If the Israelites had not had gold in the wilderness, they
could not have made a golden calf. Besides which, who needs gold in
a wilderness? There was only one reason the Israelites had gold with
them: because they were following Your instructions. You said: "Tell
the people that every man is to ask his neighbour and every woman is
to ask her neighbour for objects of silver and gold" (Ex. 11:2). Therefore,
do not blame them. Please, instead, forgive them.

This is a wonderful passage in its own right. It represents what the
Sages called *ḥutzpa kelapei Shemaya*, "audacity towards Heaven."[2] (We
tend to think of *ḥutzpa* as a Yiddish word, but it is in fact Aramaic and
comes to us from the Babylonian Talmud.) The question, though, is:
Why did the Sages choose this passage to make the point?

After all, the episode of the Golden Calf is set out in full in Exodus 32–34. The Torah tells us explicitly how daring Moses was in prayer.
First, when God tells him what the people have done, Moses immediately responds by saying, "Lord, why should Your anger burn against
Your people?... Why should the Egyptians say, 'It was with evil intent
that He brought them out, to kill them in the mountains and to wipe

1. Berakhot 32a.
2. Sanhedrin 105a.

them off the face of the earth'?" (Ex. 32:11–12). This is audacious. Moses tells God that, regardless of what the people have done, it will be His reputation that will suffer if it becomes known that He did not lead the Israelites to freedom, but instead killed them in the desert.

Then, descending the mountain and seeing what the people have done, he does his single most daring act. He smashes the tablets, engraved by God Himself. The audacity continues. Moses goes back up the mountain and says to God, "These people have indeed committed a great sin. They have made themselves an idol of gold. But now, please forgive their sin – but if not, then blot me out of the book You have written" (Ex. 32:31–32). This is unprecedented language. *This* should be the passage to which the Sages attached an account of Moses' boldness in defence of his people. Why then attach it here, to an obscure place-name in the first verse of Deuteronomy, where it is radically out of keeping with the plain sense of the verse?[3]

I believe the answer is this. Throughout Deuteronomy Moses is relentless in his criticism of the people: "From the day you left Egypt until you arrived here, you have been rebellious against the Lord.... You have been rebellious against the Lord ever since I have known you." (Deut. 9:7, 24). His critique extends to the future: "If you have been rebellious against the Lord while I am still alive and with you, how much more will you rebel after I die!" (Deut. 31:27). Even the curses in Deuteronomy, delivered by Moses himself,[4] are bleaker than those in Leviticus 26 and lack any note of consolation.

Criticism is easy to deliver but hard to bear. It is all too easy for people to close their ears, or even turn the criticism around ("He's blaming us, but he should be blaming himself. After all, he was in charge"). What does it take for criticism to be heeded? The people have to know, beyond a shadow of a doubt, that the leader is always ready to defend them. They have to know that he cares for them, wants the best for them,

---

3. Note, for example, that Rashi gives almost the opposite interpretation.
4. According to the Talmud, Megilla 31b, Moses delivered the curses in Leviticus but the words themselves came from God; the curses in Deuteronomy were formulated by Moses himself. Obviously, the fact that they are in the Torah means that God ratified them.

and is prepared to take personal risks for their sake. Only when people know for certain that you want their good, do they listen to you when you criticise them.

That is what led the Sages to give the interpretation they did to the place-name Di-zahab in the first verse of Deuteronomy. Why was Moses able to be as critical as he was in the last month of his life? Because the people he was talking to knew that he had defended them and their parents in his prayers for divine forgiveness, that he had taken the risk of challenging God, that he had declined God's offer to abandon the Israelites and begin again with him – in short, that his whole life as a leader was dedicated to doing what was the best for the people. When you know that about someone, you listen to them even when they criticise you.

One of my all-time heroes is the great hasidic rabbi Levi Yitzhak of Berditchev (1740–1809). Many stories are told of how he interceded with Heaven on behalf of the Jewish people. My favourite, doubtless apocryphal, story is this: Levi Yitzhak once saw a Jew smoking in the street on Shabbat. He said, "My friend, surely you have forgotten that it is Shabbat today." "No," said the other, "I know what day it is." "Then surely you have forgotten that smoking is forbidden on Shabbat." "No, I know it is forbidden." "Then surely you must have been thinking about something else when you lit the cigarette." "No," the other replied, "I knew what I was doing." At this, Levi Yitzhak turned his eyes upward to heaven and said, "Sovereign of the Universe, who is like Your people Israel? I give this man every chance, and still he cannot tell a lie!"

The great leaders of Israel were the great defenders of Israel, people who saw the good within the not-yet-good. That is why they were listened to when they urged people to change and grow. That is how the Sages saw Moses. This was the man who had the audacity to win forgiveness for the people who had made the golden calf.

It is easy to criticise, hard to defend. But the midrash about Moses tells us a life-changing idea: If you seek to change someone, make sure that you are willing to help them when they need your help, defend them when they need your defence, and see the good in them, not just the bad. Anyone can complain, but we have to earn the right to criticise.

Life-Changing Idea #44

If you seek to change someone, make sure that you are willing to help them when they need your help, defend them when they need your defence, and see the good in them, not just the bad.

Va'ethanan

Making Love Last

Over the past few months I've been having conversations with leading thinkers, intellectuals, innovators, and philanthropists for a BBC series on moral challenges of the twenty-first century. Among those I spoke to was David Brooks, one of the most insightful moralists of our time. His conversation is always scintillating, but one remark of his was particularly beautiful. It is a key that helps us unlock the entire project outlined by Moses in Deuteronomy, the fifth and final book of the Torah.

We had been talking about covenants and commitments. I suggested that many people in the West today are commitment-averse, reluctant to bind themselves unconditionally and open-endedly to something or someone. The market mindset that predominates today encourages us to try this, sample that, experiment, and keep our options open for the latest version or the better deal. Pledges of loyalty are few and far between.

Brooks agreed and noted that nowadays freedom is usually understood as freedom *from*, meaning the absence of restraint. We don't like to be tied down. But the real freedom worth having, in his view, is freedom *to*, meaning the ability to do something that's difficult and requires effort and expertise.[1] So, for example, if you want to have the freedom to play the piano, you have to chain yourself to it and practise every day.

Freedom in this sense does not mean the absence of restraint, but rather, choosing the right restraint. That involves commitment, which involves a choice to forgo certain choices. Then he said: "My favourite definition of commitment is falling in love with something and then building a structure of behaviour around it for the moment when love falters."

That struck me as a beautiful way into one of the fundamental features of the book of Deuteronomy specifically, and Judaism generally. The book of Deuteronomy is more than simply Moses' speeches in the last months of his life, his *tzavaa* or ethical will to the future generations. It is more, also, than *Mishneh Torah*,[2] a recapitulation of the rest of the Torah, a restatement of the laws and history of the people since their time in Egypt.

It is a fundamental theological statement of what Judaism is about. It is an attempt to integrate law and narrative into a single coherent vision of what it would be like to create a society of law-governed liberty under the sovereignty of God: a society of justice, compassion, respect for human dignity, and the sanctity of human life. And it is built around an act of mutual commitment, by God to a people and by the people to God.

The commitment itself is an act of love. At the heart of it are the famous words from the *Shema* in this *parasha*: "You shall love the Lord your God with all your heart, with all your soul, and with all your might" (Deut. 6:5). The Torah is the foundational narrative of the fraught, sometimes tempestuous, marriage between God and an often obstinate people. It is a story of love.

---

1. This is similar to, though not identical with, Isaiah Berlin's distinction between negative and positive freedom, in his famous essay, "Two Concepts of Liberty," reprinted in Isaiah Berlin, *Liberty*, ed. Henry Hardy (Oxford: Oxford University Press, 2002), 166–217.
2. This was the original rabbinical name for the book. The name Deuteronomy, from the Latin meaning "second law," was an attempt to capture the sense of the book as a restatement of the laws.

We can see how central love is to the book of Deuteronomy by noting how often the root A-H-V, "to love," appears in each of the five books of the Torah. It occurs fifteen times in Genesis, but none of these is about the relationship between God and a human being. They are about the feelings of husbands for wives or parents for children. This is how often the verb appears in the other four books: Exodus – twice; Leviticus – twice; Numbers – it does not appear at all; Deuteronomy – twenty-three times.

Again and again we hear of love, in both directions, of the Israelites for God and of God for the Israelites. It is the latter that are particularly striking. Here are some examples:

> The Lord did not set His affection on you and choose you because you were more numerous than other peoples, for you were the fewest of all peoples. But it was because the Lord loved you… (Deut. 7:7–8)

> To the Lord your God belong the heavens, even the highest heavens, the earth, and everything in it. Yet the Lord set His affection on your ancestors and loved them, and He chose you, their descendants, above all the nations – as it is today. (Deut. 10:14–15)

> The Lord your God would not listen to Balaam but turned the curse into a blessing for you, because the Lord your God loves you. (Deut. 23:5)

The real question is how this vision is connected to the legal, halakhic content of much of Deuteronomy. On the one hand we have this passionate declaration of love by God for a people; on the other, we have a detailed code of law covering most aspects of life for individuals and the nation as a whole once it enters the land. Law and love are not two things that go obviously together. What has the one to do with the other?

That is what David Brooks' remark suggests: Commitment is falling in love with something and then building a structure of behaviour around it to sustain that love over time. Law, the mitzvot, halakha, is that structure of behaviour. Love is a passion, an emotion, a heightened state, a peak experience. But an emotional state cannot be guaranteed forever. We wed in poetry, but we stay married in prose.

Which is why we need laws, rituals, habits of deed. Rituals are the framework that keeps love alive. I once knew a wonderfully happy married couple. The husband, with great devotion, brought his wife breakfast in bed every morning. I am not entirely sure she needed or even wanted breakfast in bed every morning, but she graciously accepted it because she knew it was the homage he wished to pay her, and it did indeed keep their love alive. After decades of marriage, they still seemed to be on their honeymoon.

Without intending any precise comparison, that is what the vast multiplicity of rituals in Judaism, many of them spelled out in the book of Deuteronomy, actually achieved. They sustained the love between God and a people. You hear the cadences of that love throughout the generations. It is there in the book of Psalms: "You, God, are my God, earnestly I seek You; I thirst for You, my whole being longs for You, in a dry and parched land where there is no water" (Ps. 63:1). It is there in Isaiah: "Though the mountains be shaken and the hills be removed, yet My unfailing love for you will not be shaken nor My covenant of peace be removed" (Is. 54:10). It is there in the siddur, in the blessing before the *Shema*: "You have loved us with great love / with everlasting love." It is there, passionately, in the song *Yedid Nefesh*, composed in the sixteenth century by Safed kabbalist Elazar Azikri. It remains there in the songs composed year after year in present-day Israel. Whether they speak of God's love for us or ours for Him, the love remains strong after thirty-three centuries. That is a long time for love to last, and we believe it will do so forever.

Could it have done so without the rituals, the 613 commands, that fill our days with reminders of God's presence? I think not. Whenever Jews abandoned the life of the commands, within a few generations they lost their identity. Without the rituals, eventually love dies. With them, the glowing embers remain, and still have the power to burst into flame. Not every day in a long and happy marriage feels like a wedding, but even love grown old will still be strong, if the choreography of fond devotion, the ritual courtesies and kindnesses, are sustained.

In the vast literature of halakha we find the "how" and "what" of Jewish life, but not always the "why." The special place of Deuteronomy in Judaism as a whole is that here, more clearly than almost anywhere else, we find the "why." Jewish law is the structure of behaviour built around the love between God and His people, so that the love remains long after the first feelings of passion have grown old.

Hence the life-changing idea: If you seek to make love undying, build around it a structure of rituals – small acts of kindness, little gestures of self-sacrifice for the sake of the beloved – and you will be rewarded with a quiet joy, an inner light, that will last a lifetime.

Life-Changing Idea #45

To make love undying, build around it a structure of rituals.

Ekev

Listen, Really Listen

Some twenty or so years ago, with help from the Ashdown Foundation, I initiated a conference at the Hebrew University, Jerusalem, on the future of Jewish peoplehood. I feared the deepening divisions between secular and ultra-orthodox in Israel, between the various denominations in the Diaspora, and between Israel and the Diaspora themselves.

It was a glittering array of Jewry's brightest minds: academics from sixteen different countries representing all the shadings of Jewish identity. There were professors from Harvard, Yale, and Princeton as well as most of Israel's universities. It was a scintillating success and, at the same time, a total failure.

Halfway through the second day, I turned to my wife Elaine and said, "The speaking is brilliant. The listening is non-existent." Eventually I could bear it no longer. "Let's leave," I said to her. I could not handle yet more skilled presentations from minds that were *parti pris*, lucid, coherent, but totally closed to ideas that lay outside the radius of their preconceptions. Far from being a set of solutions to the divisions within Jewry, the conference perfectly epitomised the problem.

We decided to travel south to Arad, to meet for the first time the great (and very secular) novelist Amos Oz. I mentioned this to a friend. He winced. "What," he asked, "do you hope to achieve? Do you really want to convert him?" "No," I replied, "I want to do something much more important. I want to listen to him."

And so it was. For two hours we sat in Amos' book-lined basement study at the edge of the desert, and listened. Out of that meeting came, I believe, a genuine friendship. He stayed secular. I stayed religious. But something magical, transformative, happened nonetheless. We listened to one another.

I cannot speak for Amos, but I can for myself. I felt the presence of a deep mind, a feeling of intellect, a master of language – Amos was one of the few people I knew incapable of uttering a boring sentence – and one who wrestled in his own way with what it means to be a Jew. Thereafter I had a public dialogue with him, and another with his daughter Fania Oz-Salzberger. But it began with an act of sustained, focused listening.

Shema is one of the key words of the book of Deuteronomy, where it appears no less than ninety-two times. It is, in fact, one of the key words of Judaism as a whole. It is central to the two passages that form the first two paragraphs of the prayer we call the *Shema*,[1] one in the previous *parasha*, the other in this *parasha*.

What is more: It is untranslatable. It means many things: to hear, to listen, to pay attention, to understand, to internalise, and to respond. It is the closest biblical Hebrew comes to a verb that means "to obey."

In general, when you encounter a word in any language that is untranslatable into your own, you are close to the beating pulse of that culture. To understand an untranslatable word, you have to be prepared to move out of your comfort zone and enter a mindset that is significantly different from yours.

---

1. Technically, reciting the *Shema* is not an act of prayer at all. It is a fundamentally different type of action: it is an act of *Talmud Torah*, of learning Torah (see Menaḥot 99b). In prayer, we speak to God. In study we listen to God.

At the most basic level, *Shema* represents that aspect of Judaism that was most radical in its day: that God cannot be seen. He can only be heard. Time and again Moses warns against making or worshipping any physical representation of the divine. As he tells the people: It is a theme that runs through the Bible. Moses insistently reminds the people that at Mount Sinai, "The Lord spoke to you out of the fire. You heard the sound of words but saw no form; there was only a voice" (Deut. 4:12). Even when Moses mentions seeing, he is really talking about listening. A classic example occurs in the opening verses of the next *parasha* – *Re'eh*:

> See (*re'eh*), I am setting before you today a blessing and a curse – the blessing if you listen (*tishme'u*) to the commands of the Lord your God that I am giving you today; the curse if you do not listen (*lo tishme'u*) to the commands of the Lord your God. (Deut. 11:26–28)

This affects our most basic metaphors of knowing. To this day, in English, virtually all our words for understanding or intellect are governed by the metaphor of sight. We speak of insight, hindsight, foresight, vision, and imagination. We speak of people being perceptive, of making an observation, of adopting a perspective. We say, "It appears that." When we understand something, we say, "I see."[2] This entire linguistic constellation is the legacy of the philosophers of ancient Greece, the supreme example in all history of a visual culture.

Judaism, by contrast, is a culture of the ear more than the eye. As Rabbi David Cohen, the disciple of Rav Kook known as "the Nazirite," pointed out in his book, *Kol HaNevua*, the Babylonian Talmud consistently uses the metaphor of hearing. So when a proof is brought, it says *Ta shema*, "Come and hear." When it speaks of inference it says, *Shema mina*, "Hear from this." When someone disagrees with an argument, it says *Lo shemiya leih*, "He could not hear it." When it draws a conclusion it says, *Mashma*, "From this it can be heard." Maimonides calls the oral tradition, *Mipi hashemua*, "From the mouth of that which was heard."

---

2. See George Lakoff and Mark Johnson, *Metaphors We Live By* (Chicago: University of Chicago Press, 1980).

In Western culture understanding is a form of seeing. In Judaism it is a form of listening.[3]

What Moses is telling us throughout Deuteronomy is that God does not seek blind obedience. The fact that there is no word for "obedience" in biblical Hebrew, in a religion of 613 commands, is stunning in itself (modern Hebrew had to borrow a verb, *letzayet*, from Aramaic). He wants us to *listen*, not just with our ears but with the deepest resources of our minds. If God had simply sought obedience, He would have created robots, not human beings with a will of their own. Indeed if He had simply sought obedience, He would have been content with the company of angels, who constantly sing God's praises and always do His will.

God, in making human beings "in His image," was creating otherness. And the bridge between self and other is conversation: speaking and listening. When we speak, we tell others who and what we are. But when we listen, we allow others to tell us who they are. This is the supremely revelatory moment. And if we can't listen to other people, then we certainly can't listen to God, whose otherness is not relative but absolute.

Hence the urgency behind Moses' double emphasis in this *parasha*, the opening line of the second paragraph of the *Shema*: "If you indeed heed (*shamo'a tishme'u*) My commands with which I charge you today, to love the Lord your God and worship Him with all your heart and with all your soul" (Deut. 11:13). A more forceful translation might be: "If you listen – and I mean really listen."

One can almost imagine the Israelites saying to Moses, "OK. Enough already. We hear you," and Moses replying, "No you don't. You simply don't understand what is happening here. The Creator of the entire universe is taking a personal interest in your welfare and destiny: you, the smallest of all nations and by no means the most righteous. Have you any idea of what that means?" Perhaps we still don't.

Listening to another human being, let alone God, is an act of opening ourselves up to a mind radically other than our own. This takes courage. To listen is to make myself vulnerable. My deepest certainties may be shaken by entering into the mind of one who thinks quite

---

3. For more on the contrast between visual and hearing cultures, see *Parashat Vayeḥi*.

differently about the world. But it is essential to our humanity. It is the antidote to narcissism: the belief that we are the centre of the universe. It is also the antidote to the fundamentalist mindset characterised by the late Professor Bernard Lewis as, "I'm right; you're wrong; go to hell."[4]

Listening is a profoundly spiritual act. It can also be painful. It is comfortable not to have to listen, not to be challenged, not to be moved outside our comfort zone. Nowadays, courtesy of Google filters, Facebook friends, and the precise targeting of individuals made possible by the social media, it is easy to live in an echo-chamber in which we only get to hear the voices of those who share our views. But, as I said in a TED lecture in 2017, "It's the people not like us who make us grow."

Hence the life-changing idea: Listening is the greatest gift we can give to another human being. To be listened to, to be heard, is to know that someone else takes me seriously. That is a redemptive act.

Twenty years ago I sat in a lecture hall in a university in Jerusalem and listened to a series of great minds not listening to one another. I concluded that the divisions in the Jewish world were not about to heal, and would never heal until we understood the deep spiritual truth in Moses' challenge: "If you listen – and I mean, really listen."

Life-Changing Idea #46

Listening is the greatest gift we can give to another human being.

---

4. Bernard Lewis, "I'm Right; You're Wrong; Go to Hell," *The Atlantic*, May 2003.

Re'eh

The Choice

In May 1944, at the age of sixteen, Edith Eger, together with her mother, father, and sister Magda, along with twelve thousand other Jews from her town, Kosice, in Hungary, were first interned and then taken to Auschwitz.[1] Her parents were killed immediately. When she asked an inmate of the concentration camp when she would see her mother again, the woman pointed to the smoke rising from a chimney in the distance, and said, "She is burning there. Talk about her in the past tense." Somehow Edith survived not only the horrors of Auschwitz but also the death march that killed almost all her companions. When she was eventually discovered by American GIs, lying beneath a pile of corpses, she had typhoid fever, pneumonia, pleurisy, and a broken back.

She married a fellow patient at the hospital where she was recovering. Eventually she moved with her family to the United States, where she became a psychologist. But the trauma of Auschwitz remained, until,

---

1. This opening section is taken from my book *Morality: Restoring the Common Good in Divided Times* (London: Hodder & Stoughton, 2020).

at the age of fifty-three, she returned there to confront her demons. Much later, at the age of ninety, vigorous and life-affirming, she wrote her autobiography, *The Choice*, which appeared in 2017 and became a bestseller.[2] She is living testimony to the powerful assertion of Viktor Frankl, another survivor of Auschwitz, who said that in the death camps they took away every freedom except one: the freedom to decide how to respond. As Edith Eger's mother said to her as they were being transported to Auschwitz: "Just remember, no one can take away from you what you've put in your mind."

Suffering, Eger says in her book, is universal, but victimhood is optional.[3] "There is a difference," she says, "between victimisation and victimhood." All of us are likely to be victimised at some stage. We will suffer abuse, injury, ill fortune, or failure. We live exposed to forces beyond our control. Victimisation comes from the outside. But victimhood comes from the inside. "No one can make you a victim but you." We develop a particular kind of mindset, "a way of thinking and being that is rigid, blaming, pessimistic, stuck in the past, unforgiving, punitive, and without healthy limits or boundaries." We become "our own jailors."

Eger is emphatic in not blaming the victims – among them her own parents. As she says, victimisation comes from the outside, often in the form of forces we cannot control. But healing comes when we refuse the self-definition of victim. It was that refusal that kept her alive and that she tries to help her patients discover within themselves. Hence the title of her book. There is always a choice. Often we cannot choose what happens to us, but we can always choose how to react. We are never defined by events. To allow ourselves to be so defined is to hand sovereignty over our own lives to others. Eger, in contrast, asked how her own sufferings could enable her to help other sufferers. She uses her own strength to inspire strength in them, helping them on their walk through their particular valley of the shadow of death.

Choice is one of the fundamental themes of the book of Deuteronomy, set out at the beginning of our *parasha*:

2. Edith Eger, *The Choice* (London: Rider, 2018).
3. Ibid., 9.

See, I am setting before you today a blessing and a curse: the blessing, when you heed the commandments of the Lord your God
that I am giving you today; and the curse, if you do not heed the
commandments of the Lord your God, but stray from the way I
am commanding you today… (Deut. 11:26–28)

This idea is repeated, yet more emphatically, near the end of the book:

This day I call the heavens and the earth as witnesses against
you that I have set before you life and death, the blessing and
the curse. Now choose life, so that you and your children may
live. (Deut. 30:19)

The choice, implies Moses, is yours, individually and collectively. We
cannot choose what happens to us, but we can choose how we respond
to what happens to us. That choice, between acting well and acting badly,
doing good or committing evil, is always there. Other people may harm
us, but there is always some residue of freedom, something deep within
the soul, giving us the resilience to survive.

I remember my first meeting with the Lubavitcher Rebbe in the
summer of 1968. He asked me what I was doing to strengthen Jewish life
at my university. I began my answer with a painfully English circumlo-
cution: "In the situation in which I find myself…" He interrupted me in
the middle of the sentence, something I guess he did not do often. He
said, "You do not *find* yourself in a situation. You *put* yourself in a situation. And if you put yourself in one situation, you can put yourself in
another." You always have a choice – that was what he was saying. We
are not mere prisoners of circumstance.

This may seem obvious, but it is really not. Many in the ancient
world believed that we are the playthings of the gods, without any control over our destiny. The Greeks believed in blind fate. Following Paul,
most Christians came to believe that we are tainted by original sin, incapable of doing good by our own devices. Calvinists believed in predes-
tination. Others from the eighteenth century onwards believed in the
inexorability of history, unconscious drives, blind evolution, genetic
determinism, or the inevitable consequences of the struggle for power.

None of these worldviews emphasised choice. Instead they spoke, at best, of stoic endurance, acceptance, or submission.

The Jewish idea that we are equally capable of good and evil, and that the choice is ours, is known in Christianity as the Pelagian heresy. The Pelagian heresy – named after a British fourth-century monk – is the belief that human beings can by themselves choose between good and evil. This belief, fundamental to Judaism, is heretical in Christianity because it negates the Paulian doctrine of "original sin," namely that we are all tainted by the sin of the first humans in the Garden of Eden and cannot do good without divine grace. Interestingly, this fundamental dividing line between Judaism and Christianity is about humanity, rather than about God.

In an important recent book, *The Theology of Liberalism*,[4] Eric Nelson, professor of government at Harvard University, argues that the founders of liberalism in the seventeenth century all embraced the Pelagian heresy. Without a belief in freedom of choice, the free society could not have been born.[5] Judaism is that rare phenomenon of a faith that has persistently insisted on the human ability and responsibility to choose.

More than most, Jews were victims, at the hands of the Egyptians, the Assyrians, the Babylonians, the Persians, the Greeks, the Romans, the medieval empires of Christianity and Islam, the Third Reich, and the Soviet Union. It is a horrendous history of suffering. Yet Jews did not allow themselves to be defined by their oppressors. They were looked down on as slaves, aliens, barbarians, children of Satan, infidels, subhuman, vermin, lice. Yet for the most part, they kept their humanity and sense of freedom intact. Victimisation was what happened to them. It was not the essence of who they were.

Homo sapiens is unique in its ability to use the future tense. In any given situation we can look back or we can look forward. We can ask, "Why did this happen?" – that involves looking back for some cause in the past. Or we can ask, "What then shall I do?" – this involves looking

---

4. Eric Nelson, *The Theology of Liberalism* (Cambridge, MA: The Belknap Press, 2019).

5. This is my interpretation, not necessarily Nelson's. He is more interested in the concept of distributive justice.

forward, trying to work out some future destination given that this is our starting point.

There is a massive difference between the two. I can't change the past, but I can change the future. Looking back, I see myself as an object acted on by forces largely beyond my control. Looking forward, I see myself as a subject, a choosing moral agent, deciding which path to take from here to where I eventually want to be. Both are legitimate ways of thinking, but one leads to powerlessness and resentment. The other leads to challenge, courage, strength of will, and self-control.

That is what Edith Eger, survivor of Auschwitz, tells us in her book. "The most important truth I know," she says, is "that the biggest prison is in your own mind, and in your pocket you already hold the key: the willingness to take absolute responsibility for your life."[6] "You can't change what happened, you can't change what you did or what was done to you. But you can choose how you live now."[7]

"See, I am setting before you today a blessing and a curse." That was Moses' insistent message in the last month of his life. There is always a choice. We can always choose to be free.

Hence the life-changing idea: We are bigger than what happens to us. There is always a choice as to how to respond to what happens to us, and by exercising the strength to choose, we can rise above fate.

Life-Changing Idea #47

We are not defined by what happens to us. There is always a choice, and by exercising the strength to choose, we can rise above fate.

---

6. Eger, *The Choice*, 358.
7. Ibid., 360.

Shofetim

To Lead Is to Serve

Parashat Shofetim talks about monarchy: "When you enter the land that the Lord your God is giving you, and have taken possession of it and settled in it, and you say, 'I will set a king over me, like all the surrounding nations,' set over you a king whom the Lord your God chooses" (Deut. 17:14–15). So it should be relatively easy to answer the question: From a Jewish perspective, is having a king a good thing or a bad thing? It turns out, however, to be almost unanswerable.

On the one hand, the *parasha* does say, "Set over you a king." This is a positive command. Maimonides counts it among the 613. On the other hand, of no other command anywhere does it say that that it is to be acted on when the people say that they want to be "like all the surrounding nations." The Torah doesn't tell us to be like everyone else. The word *kadosh*, "holy," means, roughly, to be set apart, singular, distinctive, unique. Jews are supposed to have the courage to be different, to be *in* but not entirely *of* the surrounding world.

Matters are made no clearer when we turn to the famous episode in which the Israelites did actually ask for a king, in the days of Samuel

269

(I Sam. 8). Samuel is upset. He thinks the people are rejecting him. Not so, says God, the people are rejecting Me (I Sam. 8:7). Yet God does not command Samuel to resist the request. To the contrary, He says, in effect, tell them what monarchy will cost, what the people stand to lose. Then, if they still want a king, give them a king.

So the ambivalence remains. If having a king is a good thing, why does God say that it means that the people are rejecting Him? If it is a bad thing, why does God tell Samuel to give the people what they want even if it is not what God would wish them to want?

Nor does the historical record resolve the issue. There were many bad kings in Jewish history. Of many, perhaps most, Tanakh says, "He did evil in the eyes of God." But then there were also good kings: David who united the nation, Solomon who built the Temple, Hezekiah and Josiah who led religious revivals. It would be easy to say that, on the whole, monarchy was a bad thing because there were more bad kings than good ones. But one could equally argue that without David and Solomon, Jewish history would never have risen to the heights.

Even within individual lives, the picture is fraught with ambivalence. David was a military hero, a political genius, and a religious poet without equal in history. But this is also the man who committed a grievous sin with another man's wife. With Solomon the record is even more chequered. He was the man whose name was synonymous with wisdom, author of Song of Songs, Proverbs, and Ecclesiastes. At the same time he was the king who broke all three of the Torah's caveats about monarchy, mentioned in this *parasha*, namely he should not have too many wives, or too many horses, or too much money (Deut. 17:16–17). Solomon – as the Talmud says[1] – thought he could break all the rules and stay uncorrupted. Despite all his wisdom, he was wrong.

Even stepping back and seeing matters on the basis of abstract principle, we have as close as Judaism comes to a contradiction. On the one hand, "We have no king but You," as we say in *Avinu Malkeinu*.[2] On the other hand, the closing sentence of the book of Judges (21:25) reads:

1. Sanhedrin 21b.
2. The source is R. Akiva in Taanit 25b.

"In those days, there was no king in Israel. Everyone did what was right in his own eyes." In short: without monarchy, anarchy.

So, in answer to the question, is having a king a good thing or a bad one, the answer is an unequivocal yes-and-no. And as we would expect, the great commentators run the entire spectrum of interpretation. For Maimonides, having a king was a good thing and a positive command. For Ibn Ezra it was a permission, not an obligation. For Abrabanel it was a concession to human weakness. For Rabbenu Bahya it was its own punishment. Why then is the Torah so ambivalent about this central element of its political programme?

The simplest answer was given by the outsider who saw most clearly that the Hebrew Bible was the world's first tutorial in freedom: Lord Acton. He is the man who wrote:

> Thus the example of the Hebrew nation laid down the parallel lines on which all freedom has been won...the principle that all political authorities must be tested and reformed according to a code which was not made by man.[3]

But he is also the originator of the classic statement: "All power tends to corrupt, and absolute power corrupts absolutely."

Almost without exception, history has been about what Hobbes described as "a general inclination of all mankind: a perpetual and restless desire of power after power, that ceaseth only in death."[4] Power is dangerous. It corrupts. It also diminishes. If I have power over you, then I stand as a limit to your freedom. I can force you to do what you don't want to do. Or as the Athenians said to the Melians: The strong do what they want, and the weak suffer what they must.

The Torah is a sustained exploration of the question: To what extent can a society be organised *not* on the basis of power? Individuals are different. Michelangelo, Shakespeare, and Rembrandt needed no power to achieve creative genius. But can a society? We all have desires. Those desires conflict. Conflict eventually leads to violence. The result

---

3. Lord Acton, *Essays on the History of Liberty* (Indianapolis, IN: Liberty Classics, 1985), 8.
4. Thomas Hobbes, *The Leviathan*, Book 1, ch. 11.

is the world before the Flood, when God regretted that He had made man on earth. Hence there is a need for a central power to ensure the rule of law and the defence of the realm.

Judaism is not an argument for powerlessness. The briefest glance at two thousand years of Jewish history in the Diaspora tells us that there is nothing dignified in powerlessness, and after the Holocaust it is unthinkable. Daily we should thank God, and all His helpers down here on earth, for the existence of the State of Israel and the restoration to the Jewish people of the power of self-defence, itself a necessary condition of the collective right to life.

Instead, Judaism is an argument for the limitation, secularisation, and transformation of power.

Limitation: Israel's kings were the only rulers in the ancient world without the power to legislate.[5] For us, the laws that matter come from God, not from human beings. To be sure, in Jewish law, kings may issue temporary regulations for the better ordering of society, but so may rabbis, courts, or local councils (the *shiva tuvei ha'ir*).

Secularisation: In Judaism, kings were not high priests and high priests were not kings. Jews were the first people to create a "separation of powers," a doctrine normally attributed to Montesquieu in the eighteenth century. When some of the Hasmonean rulers sought to combine the two offices, the Talmud records the objection of the Sages: "Let the royal crown be sufficient for you; leave the priestly crown to the descendants of Aaron."[6]

Transformation: Fundamental to Judaism is the idea of servant leadership. There is a wonderful statement of it in our *parasha*. The king must have his own Torah scroll, "and he shall read from it all the days of his life ... not considering himself superior to his kinsfolk, or straying from the commandments to the right or to the left" (Deut. 17:19–20). Humility is the essence of royalty, because to lead is to serve.

Failure to remember this caused what, in retrospect, can be seen as the single most disastrous political decision in Jewish history. After the

---

5. See, e.g., Michael Walzer, *In God's Shadow: Politics in the Hebrew Bible* (New Haven: Yale University Press, 2012).
6. Kiddushin 66a.

death of Solomon, the people came to Rehoboam, his son, asking him to lighten the load that Solomon's projects had imposed on the people. The king asked his father's advisers what he should do. They told him to accede to their request: "If today you will be a *servant* to these people and *serve* them and give them a favourable answer, they will always be your *servants*" (I Kings 12:7). Note the threefold appearance of the word "serve" in this verse. Rehoboam ignored their advice. The kingdom split and the nation never fully recovered.

The radical nature of this transformation can be seen by recalling the two great architectural symbols of the world's first empires: the Mesopotamians built ziggurats, the Egyptians built pyramids. Both are monumental statements in stone of a hierarchical society, broad at the base, narrow at the top. The people are there to support the leader. The great Jewish symbol, the Menora, inverts the triangle. It is broad at the top, narrow at the base. The leader is there to support the people.

In contemporary terms, Jim Collins in his book *From Good to Great*[7] tells us on the basis of extensive research that the great organisations are those with what he calls "Level 5 leaders," people who are personally modest but fiercely ambitious for the team. They seek, not their own success, but the success of those they lead.

This is counterintuitive. We think of leaders as people hungry for power. Many are. But power corrupts. That is why most political careers end in failure. Even Solomon's wisdom could not save him from temptation.

Hence the life-changing idea: To lead is to serve. The greater your success, the harder you have to work to remember that you are there to serve others; they are not there to serve you.

Life-Changing Idea #48

To lead is to serve. The greater your success, the harder you have to work to remember that you are there to serve others; they are not there to serve you.

---

7. James Collins, *From Good to Great* (New York: Harper Business, 2001).

Ki Tetzeh

Social Capital and Fallen Donkeys

Many years ago, Elaine and I were being driven to the Catskills, a long-time favourite summer getaway for Jews in New York, and our driver told us the following story: One Friday afternoon, he was making his way to join his family in the Catskills for Shabbat when he saw a man wearing a yarmulke, bending over his car at the side of the road. One of the tires was flat, and he was about to change the wheel.

Our driver told us that he pulled over to the roadside, went over to the man, helped him change the wheel, and wished him "Good Shabbos." The man thanked him, took his yarmulke off and put it in his pocket. Our driver must have given him a quizzical look, because the man turned and explained: "Oh, I'm not Jewish. It's just that I know that if I'm wearing one of these" – he gestured to the yarmulke – "someone Jewish will stop and come to help me."

I mention this story because of its obvious relevance to the command in *Parashat Ki Tetzeh*: "Do not see your kinsman's donkey or his ox fallen on the road and ignore it. Help him lift it up" (Deut. 22:4). On the face of it, this is one tiny detail in a *parasha* full of commands. But its real significance lies in telling us what a covenant society should look like. It is a place where people are good neighbours, and are willing to help even a stranger in distress. Its citizens care about the welfare of others. When they see someone in need of help, they don't walk by.

The Sages debated the precise logic of the command. Some held that it is motivated by concern for the welfare of the animal involved, the ox or the donkey, and that accordingly *tzaar baalei ḥayim*, prevention of suffering to animals, is a biblical command.[1] Others, notably Maimonides, held that it had to do with the welfare of the animal's owner, who might be so distressed that he came to stay with the animal at a risk to his own safety[2] – the keyword here being "on the road." The roadside in ancient times was a place of danger.

Equally the Sages discussed the precise relationship between this command and the similar but different one in Exodus (23:5): "If you see your *enemy*'s donkey fallen under its load, do not pass by. Help him load it." They said that, all other things being equal, if there is a choice between helping an enemy and helping a friend, helping an enemy takes precedence since it may "overcome the inclination," that is, it may help end the animosity and turn an enemy into a friend.[3] This, the ethic of "help your enemy," is a principle that works, unlike the ethic of "love your enemy," which has never worked and has led to some truly tragic histories of hate.

In general, as Maimonides states, one should do for someone you find in distress what you would do for yourself in a similar situation. Better still, one should put aside all considerations of honour and go "beyond the limit of the law." Even a prince, he says, should help the lowliest commoner, even if the circumstances do not accord with the dignity of his office or his personal standing.[4]

---

1. See Bava Metzia 31a.
2. *Mishneh Torah, Hilkhot Rotze'aḥ* 13:2, 14.
3. Bava Metzia 32b; see also *Tosafot*, Pesaḥim 113b.
4. *Hilkhot Rotze'aḥ* 13:4.

All of this is part of what sociologists nowadays call social capital: The wealth that has nothing to do with money and everything to do with the level of trust within a society – the knowledge that you are surrounded by people who have your welfare at heart, who will return your lost property (see the lines immediately prior to the fallen donkey: Deut. 22:1–3), who will raise the alarm if someone is breaking into your house or car, who will keep an eye on the safety of your children, and who generally contribute to a "good neighbourhood," itself an essential component of a good society.

The man who has done more than anyone else to chart the fate of social capital in modern times is Harvard sociologist Robert Putnam. In a famous article, "Bowling Alone," and the subsequent book of the same title,[5] he drew attention to the sharp loss of social capital in modern times. It was symbolised by the fact that more people than ever were going ten-pin bowling, but fewer than ever were joining bowling teams. Hence "bowling alone," which seemed to epitomise the individualism of contemporary society and its corollary: loneliness.

Ten years later, in an equally fascinating study, *American Grace*,[6] he argued that in fact social capital was alive and well in the United States, but in specific locations, namely religious communities: places of worship that still bring people together in shared belonging and mutual responsibility.

His extensive research, carried out throughout the United States between 2004 and 2006, showed that frequent church- or synagogue-goers are more likely to give money to charity, regardless of whether the charity is religious or secular. They are also more likely to do voluntary work for a charity, give money to a homeless person, give excess change back to a shop assistant, donate blood, help a neighbour with housework, spend time with someone who is feeling depressed, allow another driver to cut in front of them, offer a seat to a stranger, or help someone find a job. Religious Americans are measurably more likely than their secular

---

5. Robert Putnam, *Bowling Alone: The Collapse and Revival of American Community* (New York: Simon & Schuster, 2000).
6. Robert Putnam, David E. Campbell, and Shaylyn Romney Garrett, *American Grace: How Religion Divides and Unites Us* (New York: Simon & Schuster, 2010).

counterparts to give of their time and money to others, not only within but also beyond their own communities.

Regular attendance at a house of worship turns out to be the best predictor of altruism and empathy: better than education, age, income, gender or race. Religion creates community, community creates altruism, and altruism turns us away from self and towards the common good. Putnam goes so far as to speculate that an atheist who went regularly to church (perhaps because of a spouse) would be more likely to volunteer in a soup kitchen than a believer who prays alone. There is something about the tenor of relationships within a religious community that makes it an ongoing tutorial in citizenship and good neighbourliness.

At the same time one has to make sure that "religiosity" does not get in the way. One of the cruellest of all social science experiments was the "Good Samaritan" test organised, in the early 1970s, by two Princeton social psychologists, John Darley and Daniel Batson.[7] The well-known parable tells the story of how a priest and a Levite failed to stop and help a traveller by the roadside who had been attacked and robbed, while a Samaritan did so. Wanting to get to the reality behind the story, the psychologists recruited students from Princeton Theological Seminary and told them they were to prepare a talk about being a minister. Half were given no more instructions than that. The other half were told to construct the talk around the Good Samaritan parable.

They were then told to go and deliver the talk in a nearby building where an audience was waiting. Some were told that they were late, others that if they left now they would be on time, and a third group that there was no need to hurry. Unbeknown to the students, the researchers had positioned, directly on the students' route, an actor playing the part of a victim slumped in a doorway, moaning and coughing – replicating the situation in the Good Samaritan parable.

You can probably guess the rest: Preparing a talk on the Good Samaritan had no influence whatever on whether the student actually stopped to help the victim. What made the difference was whether the

---

7. J. M. Darley and C. D. Batson, "From Jerusalem to Jericho: A Study of Situational and Dispositional Variables in Helping Behavior," *Journal of Personality and Social Psychology* 27, no. 1 (1973): 100–108.

student had been told he was late, or that there was no hurry. On several occasions, a student about to deliver a talk on the Good Samaritan, "literally stepped over the victim as he hurried on his way."

The point is not that some fail to practise what they preach.[8] The researchers themselves simply concluded that the parable should not be taken to suggest that Samaritans are better human beings than priests or Levites, but rather, it all depends on time and conflicting duties. The rushed seminary students may well have wanted to stop and help, but were reluctant to keep a whole crowd waiting. They may have felt that their duty to the many overrode their duty to the one.

The Princeton experiment does, though, help us understand the precise phrasing of the command in our *parasha*: "Do not see…and ignore." Essentially it is telling us to slow down when you see someone in need. Whatever the time pressure, don't walk by.

Think of a moment when you needed help and a friend or stranger came to your assistance. Can you remember such occasions? Of course. They linger in the mind forever, and whenever you think of them, you feel a warm glow, as if to say, the world is not such a bad place after all. That is the life-changing idea: Never be in too much of a rush to stop and come to the aid of someone in need of help. Rarely if ever will you better invest your time. It may take a moment but its effect may last a lifetime. Or as William Wordsworth put it: "The best portion of a good man's life: his little, nameless, unremembered acts of kindness and of love."[9]

Life-Changing Idea #49

Never be in too much of a rush to stop and come to the aid of someone in need of help.

---

8. Tosefta Yevamot 8:7; Yevamot 63b.
9. Wordsworth, "Lines Written a Few Miles above Tintern Abbey."

Ki Tavo

The God of History

The setting: Jerusalem some twenty centuries ago. The occasion: bringing first fruits to the Temple. Here is the scene as the Mishna describes it:

> Throughout Israel, villagers would gather in the nearest of twenty-four regional centres. There, overnight, they would sleep in the open air. The next morning, the leader would summon the people with words from the book of Jeremiah (31:5): "Arise and let us go up to Zion, to the House of the Lord our God."

> Those who lived near Jerusalem would bring fresh figs and grapes. Those who lived far away would bring dried figs and raisins. An ox would walk ahead of them, its horns covered with gold and its head decorated with an olive wreath. Someone would play a flute. When they came close to Jerusalem they would send a messenger ahead to announce their arrival and they would start to adorn their first fruits. Governors and officials of the city would come

out to greet them and the artisans would stop their work and call out, "Our brothers from such-and-such a place: Come in peace!"

The flute would continue playing until the procession reached the Temple Mount. There, they would each place their basket of fruit on their shoulder – the Mishna says that even King Agrippa would do so – and carry it to the Temple forecourt. There the Levites would sing (Ps. 30:2), "I will praise You, God, for You have raised me up and not let my enemies rejoice over me." (Mishna Bikkurim 3:2–6)

The scene, as groups converged on the Temple from all parts of Israel, must have been vivid and unforgettable. However, the most important part of the ceremony lay in what happened next. With the baskets still on their shoulders the arrivals would say, "I declare today to the Lord your God that I have come to the land that the Lord swore to our ancestors to give us." Each would then hold their basket by the rim, the priest would place his hand under it and ceremoniously wave it, and the bringer of the fruit would say the following passage, whose text is set out in this *parasha*:

My ancestor was a wandering Aramean. He went down into Egypt and lived there as a stranger, few in number, and there became a great nation, strong and numerous. The Egyptians mistreated us and made us suffer, subjecting us to harsh labour. We cried out to the Lord, God of our ancestors. The Lord heard our voice and saw our suffering, our toil and our oppression. The Lord brought us out of Egypt with a mighty hand and an outstretched arm, with terrifying power and signs and wonders. He brought us into this place and gave us this land, a land flowing with milk and honey. And now I am bringing the first fruit of the soil that You, O Lord, have given me. (Deut. 26:5–10)

This passage is familiar to us because we expound part of it, the first four verses, in the Haggada on Seder night. But this was no mere ritual. As Yosef Hayim Yerushalmi explained in his *Zakhor: Jewish History and*

Memory, it constituted one of the most revolutionary of all Judaism's contributions to world civilisation.[1]

What was original was not the celebration of first fruits. Many cultures have such ceremonies. What was unique about the ritual in our *parasha*, and the biblical worldview from which it derives, is that our ancestors saw God in history rather than nature. Normally what people would celebrate by bringing first fruits would be nature itself: the seasons, the soil, the rain, the fertility of the ground, and what Dylan Thomas called "the force that through the green fuse drives the flower."[2] The biblical first-fruits ceremony is quite different. It is not about nature but about the shape of history, the birth of Israel as a nation, and the redemptive power of God who liberated our ancestors from slavery.

This is what was new about this worldview:

1. Jews were, as Yerushalmi points out, the first to see God in history.
2. They were the first to see history itself as an extended narrative with an overarching theme. That vision was sustained for the whole of the biblical era, as the events of a thousand years were interpreted by the prophets and recorded by the biblical historians.
3. The theme of biblical history is redemption. It begins with suffering, has an extended middle section about the interactive drama between God and the people, and ends with homecoming and blessing.
4. The narrative is to be internalised: This is the transition from history to memory, and this is what the first-fruits declaration was about. Those who stood in the Temple saying those words were declaring: This is my story. In bringing these fruits from this land, I and my family are part of it.
5. Most importantly: The story was the basis of identity. Indeed, that is the difference between history and memory. History is an answer to the question, "What happened?" Memory is an answer to the question, "Who am I?" In Alzheimer's Disease, when

---

1. Yosef Hayim Yerushalmi, *Zakhor: Jewish History and Memory* (Seattle, WA: University of Washington Press, 1982).
2. Dylan Thomas, "The Force That Through the Green Fuse Drives the Flower," 1933.

you lose your memory, you lose your identity. The same is true of a nation as a whole.[3] When we tell the story of our people's past, we renew our identity. We have a context in which we can understand who we are in the present and what we must do to hand down our identity to the future.

It is difficult to grasp how significant this was and is. Western modernity has been marked by two quite different attempts to escape from identity. The first, in the eighteenth century, was the European Enlightenment. This focused on two universalisms: science and philosophy. Science aims at discovering laws that are universally true. Philosophy aims at disclosing universal structures of thought.

Identity is about groups, about "Us" and "Them." But groups conflict. Therefore the Enlightenment sought a world without identities, in which we are all just human beings. But people can't live without identities, and identity is never universal. It is always and essentially particular. What makes us the unique person we are is what makes us different from people in general. Therefore, no intellectual discipline that aims at universality will ever fully grasp the meaning and significance of identity.

This was the Enlightenment's blind spot. Identity came roaring back in the nineteenth century, based on one of three factors: nation, race, or class. In the twentieth century, nationalism led to two world wars. Racism led to the Holocaust. Marxist class warfare led eventually to Stalin, the Gulag, and the KGB.

Since the 1960s, the West has been embarked on a second attempt to escape from identity, in favour not of the universal but the individual, in the belief that identity is something each of us freely creates for him- or herself. But identity is never created this way. It is always about membership in a group. Identity, like language, is essentially social.[4]

---

3. The historian David Andress has just published a book, *Cultural Dementia*, subtitled *How the West Has Lost Its History and Risks Losing Everything Else* (London: Head of Zeus, 2018), applying a similar insight to the contemporary West.

4. In his new book, *21 Lessons for the 21st Century* (London: Jonathan Cape, 2018), Yuval Harari argues passionately against stories, meanings, and identities and opts instead for consciousness as the basis of our humanity, and meditation as a way of living with meaninglessness. He takes a position diametrically opposed to everything argued

Just as happened after the Enlightenment, identity has come roaring back to the West, this time in the form of identity politics (based on gender, ethnicity, or sexual orientation). This will, if allowed to flourish, lead to yet more historical disasters. It is a major threat to the future of liberal democracy.

What was happening in Jerusalem when people brought their first fruits was of immense consequence. It meant that that they regularly told the story of who they were and why. No nation has ever given greater significance to retelling its collective story than Judaism, which is why Jewish identity is the strongest the world has ever known, the only one to have survived for twenty centuries with none of the normal bases of identity: political power, shared territory, or a shared language of everyday speech.

Clearly, not all identities are the same. Characteristic of Jewish identities and others inspired by the Hebrew Bible are what Dan McAdams calls "the redemptive self."[5] People with this kind of identity, he says, "shape their lives into a narrative about how a gifted hero encounters the suffering of others as a child, develops strong moral convictions as an adolescent, and moves steadily upward and onward in the adult years, confident that negative experiences will ultimately be redeemed." More than other kinds of life story, the redemptive self embodies the "belief that bad things can be overcome and affirms the narrator's commitment to building a better world."

What made the biblical story unique was its focus on redemption. In partnership with God, we can change the world. This story is our heritage as Jews and our contribution to the moral horizons of humankind. Hence the life-changing idea: Our lives are shaped by the story we tell about ourselves, so make sure the story you tell is one that speaks to your highest aspirations, and tell it regularly.

---

for in this essay. In the modern age, Jews – whether as philosophers, Marxists, postmodernists, or Buddhists – have often been leaders of the opposition to identity. The late Shlomo Carlebach put it best: "If someone says, 'I'm a Catholic,' I know that's a Catholic. If someone says, 'I'm a Protestant,' I know that's a Protestant. If someone says, 'I'm just a human being,' I know that's a Jew."

5. Dan McAdams, *The Redemptive Self: Stories Americans Live By* (Oxford: Oxford University Press, 2006).

Life-Changing Idea #50

Make sure the story you tell is one that speaks to your highest aspirations, and tell it regularly.

Nitzavim

The World Is Waiting for You

Something remarkable happens in this *parasha*, almost without our noticing it, that changed the very terms of Jewish existence, and has life-changing implications for all of us. Moses renewed the covenant. This may not sound dramatic, but it was.

Thus far, in the history of humanity as told by the Torah, God had made three covenants. The first, in Genesis 9, was with Noah, and through him, with all humanity. I call this the covenant of human solidarity. According to the Sages it contains seven commands, the *sheva mitzvot benei Noaḥ*, most famous of which is the sanctity of human life: "He who sheds the blood of man, by man shall his blood be shed, for in the image of God did God make man" (Gen. 9:6).

The second, the "Covenant between the Pieces" in Genesis 15, and its sign, circumcision in Genesis 17, was with Abraham and his descendants:

> When Abram was ninety-nine years old, the Lord appeared to him and said, "I am God Almighty. Walk before Me and have integrity, and I will grant My covenant between Me and you…. I will establish My covenant between Me and you and your descendants after you throughout the generations as an eternal covenant." (vv. 1–7)

That made Abraham the father of a new faith that would not be the faith of all humanity but would strive to be a blessing to all humanity: "Through you all the families of the earth will be blessed."

The third was with the Israelites in the days of Moses, when the people stood at Mount Sinai, heard the Ten Commandments, and accepted the terms of their destiny as "a kingdom of priests and a holy nation" (Ex. 19:6).

Who, though, initiated these three covenants? God. It was not Noah, or Abraham, or Moses, or the Israelites who sought a covenant with God. It was God who sought a covenant with humanity.

There is, though, a discernible change as we trace the trajectory of these three events. From Noah God asked no specific response. There was nothing Noah had to do to show that he accepted the terms of covenant. He now knew that there are seven rules governing acceptable human behaviour, but God asked for no positive covenant-ratifying gesture. Throughout the process Noah was passive.

From Abraham, God did ask for a response – a painful one.

> This is My covenant which you shall keep between Me and you and your descendants after you: Every male among you shall be circumcised. You must circumcise the flesh of your foreskin. This shall be the sign of the covenant between Me and you. (Gen. 17:10–11)

The Hebrew word for circumcision is *mila*, but to this day we call it *brit mila* or even, simply, *brit* – which is, of course, the Hebrew word for covenant. God asks, at least of Jewish males, something very demanding: an initiation ceremony.

From the Israelites at Sinai God asked for much more. He asked them in effect to recognise Him as their sole sovereign and legislator.

The Sinai covenant came not with seven commands as for Noah, or an eighth as for Abraham, but with 613 of them. The Israelites were to incorporate God-consciousness into every aspect of their lives.

So, as the covenants proceed, God asks more and more of His partners, or to put it slightly differently, He entrusts them with ever greater responsibilities.

Something else happened at Sinai that had not happened before. God tells Moses to announce the nature of the covenant before making it, to see whether the people agree. They do so no less than three times: "Then the people answered as one, saying, 'All that the Lord has spoken we will do'" (Ex. 19:7); "The people all responded with a single voice, 'We will do everything the Lord has spoken'" (Ex. 24:3); "The people said, 'All that the Lord has spoken we will do and heed'" (Ex. 24:7).

This is the first time in history that we encounter the phenomenon enshrined in the American Declaration of Independence, namely "the consent of the governed." God only spoke the Ten Commandments after the people had signalled that they had given their consent to be bound by His word. God does not impose His rule by force.[1] At Sinai, covenant-making became mutual. Both sides had to agree.

So the human role in covenant-making grows greater over time. But *Parashat Nitzavim* takes this one stage further. Moses, seemingly of his own initiative, renewed the covenant:

> All of you are standing today before the Lord your God – your leaders, your tribes, your elders and officials, all the men of Israel, your children, your wives, the strangers in your camp, from woodcutter to water-drawer – to enter into the covenant of the Lord your God and its oath, which the Lord your God is making with you today, to establish you today as His people, that He may

---

1. Of course, the Babylonian Talmud argues that at Sinai God did impose the covenant by force, namely by "suspending the mountain" over the people's heads. But the Talmud then immediately notes that "this constitutes a fundamental challenge to the authority of the Torah" and concludes that the people finally accepted the Torah voluntarily "in the days of Ahasuerus" (Shabbat 88a). The only question, therefore, is: *When* was there free consent?

be your God, as He promised you and swore to your ancestors, Abraham, Isaac, and Jacob. (Deut. 29:9–12)

This was the first time that the covenant was renewed, but not the last. It happened again at the end of Joshua's life (Josh. 24), and later in the days of Jehoiada (II Kings 11:17), Hezekiah (II Chr. 29), and Josiah (I Kings 23: 1–3; II Chr. 34:29–33). After the Babylonian exile, Ezra and Nehemiah convened a national gathering to renew the covenant (Neh. 8). But it happened first in this *parasha*.

It happened because Moses knew it had to happen. The terms of Jewish history were about to shift from divine initiative to human initiative. This is what Moses was preparing the Israelites for in the last month of his life. It is as if he had said: Until now God has led – in a pillar of cloud and fire – and you have followed. Now God is handing over the reins of history to you. From here on, you must lead. If your hearts are with Him, He will be with you. But you are now no longer children; you are adults. An adult still has parents, as a child does, but his or her relationship with them is different. An adult knows the burden of responsibility. An adult does not wait for someone else to take the first step.

That is the epic significance of *Parashat Nitzavim*, the *parasha* that stands almost at the end of the Torah and that we read almost at the end of the year. It is about getting ready for a new beginning: in which we act for God instead of waiting for God to act for us.

Translate this into human terms and you will see how life-changing it can be. Many years ago, at the beginning of my rabbinical career, I kept waiting for a word of encouragement from a senior rabbinical figure. I was working hard, trying innovative approaches, seeking new ways of getting people engaged in Jewish life and learning. You need support at such moments, because taking risks and suffering the inevitable criticism is emotionally draining. The encouragement never came. The silence hurt. It ate, like acid, into my heart.

Then in a lightning-flash of insight, I thought: What if I turn the entire scenario around. What if, instead of waiting for Rabbi X to encourage me, I encouraged him? What if I did for him what I was hoping he would do for me? That was a life-changing moment. It gave me a strength I never had before.

I began to formulate it as an ethic. Don't wait to be praised: Praise others. Don't wait to be respected: Respect others. Don't stand on the sidelines, criticising others. Do something yourself to make things better. Don't wait for the world to change: Begin the process yourself, and then win others to the cause. There is a statement attributed to Gandhi (actually he never said it,[2] but in a parallel universe he might have done): "Be the change you seek in the world." Take the initiative.

That was what Moses was doing in the last month of his life, in that long series of public addresses that make up the book of Deuteronomy, culminating in the great covenant-renewal ceremony in this *parasha*. Deuteronomy marks the end of the Jewish people's childhood. From there on, Judaism became God's call to human responsibility. For us, faith is not waiting for God. Faith is the realisation that God is waiting for us.

Hence the life-changing idea: Whenever you find yourself distressed because someone hasn't done for you what you think they should have done, turn the thought around, and then do it for them.

Don't wait for the world to get better. Take the initiative yourself. The world is waiting for you.

Life-Changing Idea #51

Don't wait for the world to get better. Take the initiative yourself. The world is waiting for you.

---

2. See Brian Morton, "Falser Words Were Never Spoken," *New York Times*, August 29, 2011. The closest he came was, "If we could change ourselves, the tendencies in the world would also change. As a man changes his own nature, so does the attitude of the world change towards him.... We need not wait to see what others do."

Vayelekh

The Second Mountain

What do you do when you have achieved it all, when you have risen to whatever career heights fate or providence has in store for you? What do you do as age lengthens its shadow, the sun sinks, and the body is no longer as resilient, or the mind as sharp, as it once was?

That has become a major problem as life expectancy has increased in most parts of the world. There has been nothing quite like it in history. In America, in 1900, average life expectancy was around 41 years, in Europe 42.5. Today in Britain, for men it is 79, for women 83. Much of that has to do with a huge reduction in infant mortality. Nonetheless, the sheer pace in the rise in longevity – every decade since 1900, life expectancy has risen by about three years – remains remarkable. What will keep you young in spirit even if the body does not always keep pace?

The biblical case study is Moses, of whom we are told that even at the end of his life, "his eye was undimmed and his natural energy unabated" (Deut. 34:7). At the opening of *Parashat Vayelekh* he says, "I am now a hundred and twenty years old. I can no longer come and go, and the Lord has told me, 'You shall not cross this Jordan'" (31:2). Rashi points out that the "I can no longer" does not mean that he lacked the strength. It means that he no longer had permission. The moment had come when he had to hand over the role of leader to his successor and disciple, Joshua. He himself stayed full of vigour, as the passion of his speeches in the book of Deuteronomy, delivered in the last month of his life, testifies.

To understand what Moses epitomises at the end of his life, two closely related concepts are helpful. The first is developmental psychologist Erik Erikson's idea of generativity, the seventh of his eight life stages. Relatively late in life, he argues, many people's perspective changes. They begin thinking about legacy, about what will outlive them. Their focus often shifts from self to others. They may devote more time to family, or community, or care or voluntary work. Some mentor young people who are following in their career path. They make commitments to others. They ask themselves: How can I contribute to the world? What trace will I leave on those who will live on after me? What, in the world, is better because of me?

The second and related idea is David Brooks' concept of the second mountain.[1] Speaking to people over seventy, he found that early in their lives they had identified the mountain they were going to climb. They had specific aspirations about family and career. They had a vision of the self they wanted to become. By age seventy, some had achieved it and were happy. Others had achieved it only to find it not entirely satisfying. Yet others had been knocked off the mountain by misfortune.

At a certain age, though, many identified a second mountain they wanted to climb. This mountain was not about achieving but about giving. It was less about external accomplishment (success, fame) than about internal accomplishment. It was spiritual, moral; it was about devoting yourself to a cause or giving back to the community. It is often, he says, a yearning for righteousness, an inner voice that says, "I want to do something really good with my life." This second peak, associated with later life, may well prove more significant to our sense of self-worth than the ego-driven ascent of the first mountain.

---

1. See David Brooks, *The Second Mountain* (New York: Random House, 2019).

The case of Moses sets all this in dramatic perspective. What do you do if you have already achieved what no human being has ever done before or will ever do in the future? Moses had spoken to God face to face. He had become His faithful servant. He had led his people from slavery to freedom, put up with their complaints, endured their rebellions, and prayed for – and achieved – their forgiveness in the eyes of God. He had been the agent through which God had performed His miracles and delivered His word. What else is left to do after such a life?

His closest friends and allies, his sister Miriam and brother Aaron, had already died. He knew that the decree had been sealed that he would not cross the Jordan and lead the people on the last stage of their journey. He would not set foot in the Promised Land. Unlike Aaron, whose children inherited his priesthood to eternity, Moses had to live with the fact that neither of his sons, Gershom and Eliezer, would become his successor. That role would go to his assistant and faithful servant Joshua. These were, surely, huge disappointments to set alongside the momentous achievements.

So, as Moses faced his own life's end, what was there left to do? The book of Deuteronomy contains and constitutes the answer. As it says in its opening chapter: "In the fortieth year, on the first day of the eleventh month, Moses spoke to the Israelites.... On the east bank of the Jordan, in the land of Moab, Moses began expounding this law..." (1:3–5). No longer the liberator and miracle-worker, Moses became <i>Rabbenu</i>, "our teacher," the man who taught Torah to the next generation.

The way he does so in Deuteronomy is stunning. No longer, as before, does he simply articulate the law. He explains the theology behind the law. He speaks about the love of God for Israel and the love Israel should show to God.[2] He speaks with equal power about the past and the future, reviewing the wilderness years and anticipating the challenges ahead.

Above all, coming at the subject from every conceivable direction, he warns the young people who will enter and inherit the land, that the real challenge will not be failure but success; not slavery but freedom; not the bread of affliction but the temptations of affluence. Remember,

2. See above on <i>Parashat Va'ethanan.</i>

he says again and again; listen to the voice of God; rejoice in what He has given you. These are the key verbs of the book, and they remain the most powerful immune-system ever developed against the decadence and decline that has affected every civilisation since the dawn of time.

That last month in Moses' life, which culminates in this *parasha* as he finally hands over the reins of leadership to Joshua, is one of the supreme instances in Tanakh of generativity: speaking not to your contemporaries but to those who will live on after you. It was Moses' second mountain.

And perhaps the very things that seemed, at first sight, to have been disappointments, turned out in the end to have played their part in shaping this last chapter in that great life. The fact that he knew he would not accompany the people into the land, and that he would not be succeeded by his sons, meant that he had to turn into a teacher of the next generation. He had to pass on to them his insights into the future. He had to make the people his disciples – and we have all been his disciples ever since.

All of this suggests a powerful and potentially life-changing message for all of us. Whatever our life has been thus far, there is another chapter to be written, focused on being a blessing to others, sharing whatever gifts we have with those who have less, handing on our values across the generations, using our experience to help others come through difficult times of their own, doing something that has little to do with personal ambition and much to do with wanting to leave some legacy of kindness that made life better for at least someone on earth.

Hence the life-changing idea: Whatever your achievements, there is always a second mountain to climb, and it may turn out to be your greatest legacy to the future.

Life-Changing Idea #52

Whatever your achievements, there is always a second mountain to climb, and it may turn out to be your greatest legacy to the future.

Haazinu

Emotional Intelligence

In March 2015 I had a public conversation at Yale with the university's President Peter Salovey. The occasion was quite an emotional one. It celebrated the sixtieth anniversary of the Marshall Scholarships, created by the British parliament as a way of expressing thanks to the United States for the Marshall Plan, that helped Western Europe rebuild its economies after the Second World War. The scholarships fund outstanding young Americans to study at any university in the United Kingdom. So the gathering that evening was about the links between Britain and the United States, and the role of universities in cultivating that generosity of spirit, epitomised by the Marshall Plan, that understands the need to build peace, not just wage war.

But it had another emotional resonance. Yale is one the world's great universities. Yet there was a time, between the 1920s and 1960s, when it had a reputation for being guarded about, even quietly hostile to, the presence of Jews among its students and staff.[1] Happily that has not been the case since 1960 when its president, A. Whitney Griswold, issued a directive that religion should play no role in the admissions process. Today it is warmly welcoming to people of all faiths and ethnicities. Noting that fact, the president pointed out that not only was Yale that afternoon hosting a rabbi, but he too – Salovey – was Jewish and the descendant of a great rabbinic dynasty. Salovey is an Anglicisation of the name Soloveitchik.

Thinking back to that occasion, I wondered whether there was a more than merely family connection between the university president and his great distant relative, Rabbi Joseph Soloveitchik, the man known to generations of his students at Yeshiva University as simply, "The Rav." Was there an intellectual and spiritual link also, however oblique?

There is, and it is significant. Peter Salovey's great contribution to the thought of our time is the concept he formulated together with John Mayer in a landmark 1989 article,[2] namely emotional intelligence – popularised in 1995 by Daniel Goleman's best-selling book of the same title.

For many decades, intelligence as measured by IQ (intelligence quotient) tests was viewed as the best indicator of ability and used, for example, to determine promotion in military rank. These tests focused on a specific set of cognitive and reasoning skills as the primary measure of intelligence. It took another brilliant Jewish psychologist of our time, Howard Gardner (of Harvard), to break this paradigm and argue for the idea of multiple intelligences.[3] Solving puzzles is not the only skill that matters.

What Salovey and Mayer did was to show that our ability to understand and respond to not only our own emotions but also those of others is an essential element of success in many fields, indeed of human interaction in general. There are fundamental elements of our humanity that have to do with the way we feel, not just the way we

1. Dan A. Oren, *Joining the Club: A History of Jews and Yale* (New Haven: Yale University Press, 1988).
2. P. Salovey and J. D. Mayer, "Emotional Intelligence," *Imagination, Cognition and Personality*, 9, no. 3 (1989): 185–211.
3. Howard Gardner, *Frames of Mind: The Theory of Multiple Intelligences* (New York: Basic Books, 1983).

think. Even more importantly, we need to understand how *other people* feel – the gift of empathy – if we are to form a meaningful bond with them. That is what the Torah is referring to when it says, "Do not oppress a stranger because *you know what it feels like* to be a stranger" (Ex. 23:9).

Emotions matter. They guide our choices. They move us to action. Intellect alone cannot do this. It has been a failing of intellectuals throughout history to believe that all we need to do is to think straight and we will act well. It isn't so. Without a capacity for sympathy and empathy, we become more like a computer than a human being, and that is fraught with danger.

It was precisely this point – the need for emotional intelligence – about which Rabbi Soloveitchik spoke in one of his most moving addresses, "A Tribute to the Rebbetzin of Talne."[4] People, he said, are mistaken when they think there is only one *mesora*, one Jewish tradition handed on through the generations. In fact, he said, there are two: one handed down by fathers, the other by mothers. He quoted the famous verse from Proverbs 1:8, "Listen, my son, to the instruction of your father (*musar avikha*), and do not forsake the teaching of your mother (*torat imekha*)." These are two distinct but interwoven strands of the religious personality.

From a father, he said, we learn how to read a text, comprehend, analyse, conceptualise, classify, infer, and apply. We also learn how to act: what to do and what not to do. The father-tradition is "an intellectual-moral one." Turning to "the teaching of your mother," Soloveitchik became personal, speaking of what he learned from his own mother. From her, he said:

> I learned that Judaism expresses itself not only in formal compliance with the law but also in a living experience. She taught me that there is a flavour, a scent and warmth to *mitzvot*. I learned from her the most important thing in life – to feel the presence of the Almighty and the gentle pressure of His hand resting upon my frail shoulders. Without her teachings, which quite often were

---

4. Joseph B. Soloveitchik, "A Tribute to the Rebbetzin of Talne," *Tradition*, 17:2 (1978): 73–83.

transmitted to me in silence, I would have grown up a soulless being, dry and insensitive.[5]

In other words: *Torat imekha* is about emotional intelligence. I have long felt that alongside Rabbi Soloveitchik's great essay, *Halakhic Man,* there was another one he might have written called *Aggadic Woman.* Halakha is an intellectual-moral enterprise. But Aggada, the non-halakhic dimension of rabbinic Judaism, is directed to the broader aspects of what it is to be a Jew. It is written in narrative rather than law. It invites us to enter the minds and hearts of our spiritual forebears, their experiences and dilemmas, their achievements and their pain. It is the emotional dimension of the life of faith.

Speaking personally, I am disinclined to think of this in terms of a male-female dichotomy.[6] We are all called on to develop both sensibilities. But they are radically different. Halakha is part of *Torat Kohanim,* Judaism's priestly voice. In the Torah, its key verbs are *lehavdil,* to distinguish/analyse/categorise, and *lehorot,* to instruct/ guide/issue a ruling. But in Judaism there is also a prophetic voice. The key words for the prophet are *tzedek umishpat,* righteousness and justice, and *ḥesed veraḥamim,* kindness and compassion. These are about I-Thou relationships, between humans, and between us and God.

The priest thinks in terms of universal rules that are eternally valid. The prophet is attuned to the particularities of a given situation and the relationships between those involved. The prophet has emotional intelligence. He or she (there were, of course, women prophets: Sarah, Miriam, Deborah, Hannah, Abigail, Huldah, and Esther) reads the mood of the moment and how it relates to longstanding relationships. The prophet hears the silent cry of the oppressed, and the incipient anger of Heaven. Without the law of the priest, Judaism

---

5. Ibid., 77.
6. There are, to be sure, serious thinkers who have made just this claim, about the superior emotional intelligence of women. See Steven Pinker, *The Blank Slate* (New York: Allen Lane, 2002); Simon Baron Cohen, *The Essential Difference* (New York: Penguin, 2004). See also Carol Gilligan's classic, *In a Different Voice* (Harvard University Press, 1982).

would have no structure or continuity. But without the emotional intelligence of the prophet, it would become, as Rav Soloveitchik said, soulless, dry and insensitive.

Which brings us to *Parashat Haazinu*. In this *parasha*, Moses does the unexpected but necessary thing. He teaches the Israelites a song. He moves from prose to poetry, from speech to music, from law to literature, from plain speech to vivid metaphor:

> Listen, heavens, and I will speak;
> And let the earth hear the words of my mouth.
> May my teaching fall like rain,
> My speech flow down like dew;
> Like gentle rain on tender plants,
> Like showers on the grass. (Deut. 32:1–2)

Why? Because at the very end of his life, the greatest of all the prophets turned to emotional intelligence, knowing that unless he did so, his teachings might enter the minds of the Israelites but not their hearts, their passions, their emotive DNA. It is feelings that move us to act, give us the energy to aspire, and fuel our ability to hand on our commitments to those who come after us.

Without the prophetic passion of an Amos, a Hosea, an Isaiah, a Jeremiah, without the music of the Psalms, and the songs of the Levites in the Temple, Judaism would have been a plant without water or sunlight; it would have withered and died. Intellect alone does not inspire in us the passion to change the world. To do that you have to take thought and turn it into song. That is *Parashat Haazinu*, Moses' great hymn to God's love for His people and his role in ensuring, as Martin Luther King put it, that "the arc of the moral universe is long but it bends towards justice." In *Parashat Haazinu*, the man of intellect and moral courage becomes the figure of emotional intelligence, allowing himself to be, in Judah Halevi's lovely image, the harp for God's song.

This is a life-changing idea: If you want to change lives, speak to people's feelings, not just to their minds. Enter their fears and calm them. Understand their anxieties and allay them. Kindle their hopes and instruct them. Raise their sights and enlarge them. Humans are more than algorithms. We are emotion-driven beings.

Speak from the heart to the heart, and mind and deed will follow.

Life-Changing Idea #53

If you want to change lives, speak to people's feelings, not just to their minds.

Vezot Haberakha

Unfinished Symphony

Each year, as we near the end of the Mosaic books and Moses' life, I find myself asking: Did it really have to end that way, with Moses denied the chance to even set foot on the land to which he led the people for forty tempestuous years? In the heavenly court, could justice not have yielded to mercy for the few days it would have taken Moses to cross the Jordan and see his task fulfilled? And for what was Moses being punished? One moment's anger when he spoke intemperately to the Israelites when they were complaining about the lack of water? Can a leader not be forgiven for one lapse in forty years? In the words of the Sages: Is this the Torah and this its reward?[1]

The scene in which Moses climbs Mount Nebo to see in the distance the land he would never enter is one of the most poignant in all Tanakh. There is a vast midrashic literature that turns Moses' request, "Let me cross over to see the good land beyond the Jordan" (Deut. 3:25), into high drama, with Moses mounting argument after argument in his

---

1. Berakhot 61b.

defence only to be met by unbending refusal from Heaven: "Enough from you; do not speak to Me of this matter again" (v. 26). Why?

This is the man who, eighteen times in Tanakh, is called "God's servant." No one else is so described except Joshua, twice. His own obituary in the Torah reads: "Never again did there arise in Israel a prophet like Moses" (34:10). Why was he treated so seemingly harshly by God among whose attributes are forgiveness and compassion?

Clearly the Torah is telling us something fundamental. What, though, is it? There are many explanations, but I believe the most profound and simplest takes us back to the beginning of beginnings: "In the beginning God created heaven and earth." There is heaven and there is earth, and they are not the same.

In the history of civilisation, one question has proved hardest of all. In the words of Psalm 8: "What is man that you are mindful of him?" What is it to be human? We are an infinitesimal speck in an almost infinite universe of a hundred billion galaxies each with a hundred billion stars. We know that our lives are like a bare microsecond set against the almost-eternity of the cosmos. We are terrifyingly small. Yet we are also astonishingly great. We dominate the planet. We have ever-increasing control over nature. We are the only life form thus far known capable of asking the question, "Why?"

Hence the two temptations that have faced Homo sapiens since the beginning: to think of ourselves as smaller than we actually are, or greater than we actually are. How are we to understand the relationship between our mortality and fallibility and the almost-infinities of space and time?

Civilisations have regularly blurred the line between the human and the divine. In myth, the gods behave like humans, arguing, fighting and contending for power, while some humans – the heroes – are seen as semi-divine. The Egyptians believed that pharaohs joined the gods after death; some were seen as gods even during their lifetime. The Romans declared Julius Caesar a god after his death. Other religions have believed that God has taken human form.

It has proved exceptionally difficult to avoid worshipping the human founder of a faith. In the modern age, the blurring of boundaries has been democratised. Nietzsche argued that we would have to become like gods to vindicate our dethroning of God Himself. The anthropologist Edmund Leach began his Reith Lectures with the words, "Men have become like gods. Isn't it about time that we understood our divinity?" As Jews we believe that this is too high an estimate of our, or anyone's, humanity.

In the opposite direction humans have been seen, in myth and more recently in science, as next-to-nothing. In King Lear, Shakespeare has Gloucester say, "As flies to wanton boys are we to the gods. They kill us for their sport." We are the easily discarded playthings of the gods, powerless in the face of forces beyond our control. As I pointed out in the essay on *Parashat Toledot*, some contemporary scientists have produced secular equivalents of this view. They say: There is nothing qualitatively to distinguish between Homo sapiens and other animals. There is no soul. There is no self. There is no free will.

Voltaire spoke of humans as "insects devouring one another on a little atom of mud." Stephen Hawking said that "the human race is just a chemical scum on a moderate size planet, orbiting round a very average star in the outer suburb of one among a billion galaxies." Philosopher John Gray wrote that "human life has no more meaning than that of slime mould." In *Homo Deus*, Yuval Harari states that "looking back, humanity will turn out to be just a ripple within the cosmic data flow."

Judaism is humanity's protest against both ideas. We are not gods. And we are not chemical scum. We are dust of the earth, but there is within us the breath of God. What is essential is never to blur the boundary between heaven and earth. The Torah speaks only obliquely about this. It tells us that there was a time, prior to the Flood, when "the sons of God saw that the daughters of man were lovely, and they married whomever they chose" (Gen. 6:2). It also tells us that, after the Flood, humans gathered in a plain in Shinar and said, "Come, let us build ourselves a city and a tower that reaches heaven, and make a name for ourselves" (Gen. 11:4). Regardless of what these stories mean, what they speak of is a blurring of the line between heaven and earth – "sons of God" behaving like humans and humans aspiring to live among the gods.

When God is God, humans can be human. First, separate, then relate. That is the Jewish way.

For us as Jews, humanity at its highest is still human. We are mortal. We are creatures of flesh and blood. We are born, we grow, we learn, we mature, we make our way in the world. If we are lucky we find love. If we are blessed, we have children. But we also age. The body grows old even if the spirit stays young. We know that this gift of life does not last forever because in this physical universe, nothing lasts forever, not even planets or stars.

For each of us, therefore, there is a river we will not cross, a promised land we will not enter, and a destination we will not reach. Even the greatest life is an unfinished symphony. Moses' death on the far side of the Jordan is a consolation for all of us. None of us should feel guilty or frustrated or angry or defeated that there are things we hoped to achieve but did not. That is what it is to be human.

Nor should we be haunted by our mistakes. That, I believe, is why the Torah tells us that Moses sinned. Did it really have to include the episode of the water, the stick, the rock, and Moses' anger? It happened, but did the Torah have to tell us it happened? It passes over thirty-eight of the forty years in the wilderness in silence. It does not report every incident, only those that have a lesson for posterity. Why not, then, pass over this too in silence, sparing Moses' good name? What other religious literature has ever been so candid about the failings of even the greatest of its heroes?

Because that is what it is to be human. Even the greatest human beings made mistakes, failed as often as they succeeded, and had moments of black despair. What made them great was not that they were perfect but that they kept going. They learned from every error, refused to give up hope, and eventually acquired the great gift that only failure can grant, namely humility. They understood that life is about falling a hundred times and getting up again. It is about never losing your ideals even when you know how hard it is to change the world. It's about getting up every morning and walking one more day towards the Promised Land even though you know you may never get there, but knowing also that you helped others get there.

Maimonides writes in his law code that "every human being can become righteous like Moses our teacher or wicked like Jeroboam."[2] That is an astonishing sentence. There only ever was one Moses. The Torah

---

2. *Mishneh Torah, Hilkhot Teshuva* 5:2.

says so. Yet what Maimonides is saying is clear. Prophetically, there was only one Moses. But morally, the choice lies before us every time we make a decision that will affect the lives of others. That Moses was mortal, that the greatest leader who ever lived did not see his mission completed, that even he was capable of making a mistake, is the most profound gift God could give each of us.

Hence the three great life-changing ideas with which the Torah ends. We are mortal; therefore make every day count. We are fallible; therefore learn to grow from each mistake. We will not complete the journey; therefore inspire others to continue what we began.

Life-Changing Ideas #54–56

- *We are mortal; therefore make every day count.*
- *We are fallible; therefore learn to grow from each mistake.*
- *We will not complete the journey; therefore inspire others to continue what we began.*

The fonts used in this book are from the Arno family

Maggid Books
The best of contemporary Jewish thought from
Koren Publishers Jerusalem Ltd.